Metonymy and Language

Metonymy and Language offers a radically new theory of language and communication in which metonymy and metonymic processing play a central role. It shows how the cognitive skill of recognizing relatedness between signs and parts of signs is indispensable in language use at all levels. It shows how theory across a whole range of linguistic phenomena can be reframed in terms of metonymic processing. This is developed into a General Theory of Metonymy. It is argued that metonymic competence explains language's great flexibility and fitness for purpose. It is shown that metonymic behaviour is often pursued for its own sake in recreational activities such as quizzes, puzzles and play. *Metonymy and Language* provides an invaluable survey of existing knowledge in the rapidly growing field of metonymy studies, while taking the concept of metonymy further than any scholar has to date. The monograph is based on rigorous primary research, using original data, and is the first to apply cognitive metonymy theory to the fields of text analysis, language learning and translation. It is argued that research with metonymy at its centre can provide a powerful tool for reframing and solving problems in diverse fields of human activity across the arts and sciences.

Charles Denroche lectures in Linguistics and Applied Language Studies at the University of Westminster, London. He studied at the universities of Oxford, Florence, Düsseldorf, London and Westminster. He has worked as a language teacher, translator and lexicographer.

Routledge Studies in Linguistics

1 **Polari—The Lost Language of Gay Men**
Paul Baker

2 **The Linguistic Analysis of Jokes**
Graeme Ritchie

3 **The Irish Language in Ireland**
From Goídel to Globalisation
Diarmait Mac Giolla Chríost

4 **Conceptualizing Metaphors**
On Charles Peirce's Marginalia
Ivan Mladenov

5 **The Linguistics of Laughter**
A Corpus-assisted Study of Laughter-talk
Alan Partington

6 **The Communication of Leadership**
The Design of Leadership Style
Jonathan Charteris-Black

7 **Semantics and Pragmatics of False Friends**
Pedro J. Chamizo-Domínguez

8 **Style and Ideology in Translation**
Latin American Writing in English
Jeremy Munday

9 **Lesbian Discourses**
Images of a Community
Veronika Koller

10 **Structure in Language**
A Dynamic Perspective
Thomas Berg

11 **Metaphor and Reconciliation**
The Discourse Dynamics of Empathy in Post-Conflict Conversations
Lynne J. Cameron

12 **Relational Semantics and the Anatomy of Abstraction**
Tamar Sovran

13 **Language Contact and the Origins of the Germanic Languages**
Peter Schrijver

14 **Metonymy and Language**
A New Theory of Linguistic Processing
Charles Denroche

Metonymy and Language

A New Theory of Linguistic Processing

Charles Denroche

Routledge
Taylor & Francis Group
LONDON AND NEW YORK

First published 2015 by Routledge

2 Park Square, Milton Park, Abingdon, Oxon OX14 4RN
711 Third Avenue, New York, NY 10017, USA

Routledge is an imprint of the Taylor & Francis Group, an informa business

First issued in paperback 2016

Library of Congress Cataloging-in-Publication Data
Denroche, Charles, 1956–
Metonymy and language : a new theory of linguistic processing / By Charles Denroche.
p. cm. — (Routledge studies in linguistics; 14)
Includes bibliographical references and index.
1. Metonyms. 2. Metaphor. 3. Figures of speech.
4. Communications. 5. Computational linguistics. I. Title.
P301.5.M49D46 2015
401′.43—dc23
2014032570

ISBN: 978-1-138-81062-4 (hbk)
ISBN: 978-1-138-24531-0 (pbk)

Typeset in Times New Roman
by Apex CoVantage, LLC

To SEW

Contents

Figures

Tables

Typographical Conventions

The following conventions are used in this book for linguistic analysis:

italics	=	lexical item
'single inverted commas'	=	technical or coined term
"double inverted commas"	=	linguistic data
SMALL CAPS	=	semantic features and conceptual metaphors
SMALL CAPS (italics)	=	systematic metaphors

Acknowledgments

I am indebted to David Block, Graham Low and Steven Wootton for their invaluable assistance in developing the ideas in this book and helping to bring it into print. Also to my informants and to Margo Irvin and Katie Laurentiev at Routledge Research, New York.

The author and publishers also wish to thank the copyright holders for permission to reproduce the quotations, illustrations and other material appearing in this book, in particular:

Collins Dictionaries, www.collinsdictionary.com.

Billy Marsh Associates, as agents of the estates of Morecambe & Wise, excerpts from recordings broadcast on *Variety Fanfare*.

Graham Rawle, *Lost Consonants*, reproduced with permission from the artist.

Miles Cole, *The Entertainers* illustration, Copyright © 2010, reproduced with permission from the artist.

Time Out, 'Ten Things You Need to Know about James Gooding' in *London Time Out*, August 20–September 3, 2003, page 14. Copyright © 2003. Original article written by Paul Burston, August 20, 2003, and supplied with permission from *Time Out*.

Stella Cottrell, *The Exam Skills Handbook: Achieving Peak Performance, 2007*, Palgrave Macmillan, reproduced with permission of Palgrave Macmillan.

Terrence Higgins Trust, '2008 Annual Report and Newsletter', with permission from Terrence Higgins Trust.

Faber and Faber Ltd and Farrar, Straus and Giroux, LLC, extracts from 'Water' and 'Toads Revisited' by Philip Larkin. Copyright the Estate of Philip Larkin, by permission.

Metro Newspapers, 'Baggies in a Hurry to Make Double Swoop' and 'Heelys Boy Hit by Car Fights for Life', in *London Metro*, 13 August 2002 and 31 January 2007 respectively. Copyright, Associated Newspapers Limited and its subsidiaries, by permission.

New Scientist, 'Brighter Future for the Humble Soyabean', in *New Scientist*, 14 April 1983, page 73. Copyright © 1983. With permission from Reed Business Information Ltd, England. All rights reserved. Distributed by Tribune Content Agency.

News Syndication, 'Saw Close!' in *The Sun*, 26 July 2001. Copyright, News UK, by permission.

KBH On-Train Media, '2.5 million fans at every gig', from Traincards promotional material, 2010, with permission from KBH On-Train Media.

Dirk Geeraerts (Ed.), *Cognitive Linguistics: Basic Readings,* Berlin: Mouton de Gruyter, 2006, pp. 1–27, with permission from de Gruyter, www.degruyter.com/.

Hans Peter Krings, 'Translation Problems and Translation Strategies of Advanced German Learners of French (L2)', in J. House and S. Blum-Kulka (eds.) *Interlingual and Intercultural Communication,* Gunter Narr, 1986, page 269, reproduced with permission of Gunter Narr Verlag.

Roger Bell, *Translating and Translation: Theory and Practice*, Longman, 1991, Figure 2.2, page 59, with permission from Longman.

1 Introduction

This book is about metonymy. By 'metonymy' I mean the recognition of part-whole relatedness between things, words and concepts. The book derives from an overwhelming impression, gained over many years, both that metonymy plays a fundamental role in conceptualization and communication and that its role has not been fully recognized. This impression has come from everyday observations of naturally-occurring language but also from my experience as a language professional in the fields of language teaching, translation and lexicography. The book presents a General Theory of Metonymy, a theory which extends the notion of metonymy beyond the sphere in which it is normally considered to a more general application. In so doing, I demonstrate a commonality among a whole range of semiotic and linguistic phenomena which are normally seen as distinct.

This is not an exercise simply of renaming; it is more ambitious than that. It reveals that what at first appear to be diverse phenomena rely on a common basic and universal cognitive operation: the ability to recognize relatedness. Things, words and concepts are related if they have an element in common, if a part-whole relationship exists between them. The part may be a physical part or an attribute. It is the manipulation of these 'parts' which allows us to realize the full meaning-making potential of the lexicon and the fullest expression of our conceptual system. It is argued in this study that morphology, syntax, lexis and phraseology, as they are conventionally represented, account only for basic meaning making in language, and that it is metonymy—or better, 'metonymic processing'—which gives us the flexibility and subtleties on and above those systems, on which we constantly rely in our social dealings with others.

The starting point of the book was the observation that conventional metonymic expressions in English, such as *pay with plastic*, *the small screen*, *go for a bite*, *a roof over your head*, *bums on seats*, are common; it progressed by recognizing that metonymy does not just provide an alternative way of referring to things, but plays a role in giving nuance—*swingeing cuts* and *efficiency savings* refer to the same thing but highlight different aspects; it went on to the observation that metonymy operates at many different levels, from the sub-word level to the level of discourse, genre and intertext. Further, metonymy is not only prevalent but often salient in everyday communication, many interactions revolving around a metonymic component to the extent that the metonymic associations become what the interaction is 'about' rather than just a means to an end, the carrier of the message.

In order to confirm this hunch, I set myself the task of noting down examples of interactions in which metonymy played a central role to which I was party over a period of two days. Among them was a range of exchanges, some involving language, some not. Some interactions involved individual words or phrases, such as: discussing what *Sasha* was short for and why *Cantab* stands for Cambridge not Canterbury (the relation between short and long forms); solving 'quick' crosswords (the clues ask for synonyms); discussing the origin of the expressions *to be buff, buff up, to be in the buff* (the etymology takes us via a series of shifts back to *buffalo*); identifying someone at a party through a salient characteristic, eg *the woman wearing red boots*; observing an advertisement on the London underground with invented names for stations based on foods, eg *Oxtail Circus/Oxford Circus, Highbury & Biscuit Tin/Highbury and Islington,* the invented names and the real names being related in form; the use of salient personal characteristics of appearance when hailing someone, eg *Hey Fatso!, You, Michael Palin!* Other interactions involved metonymy as an organizing principle at the level of the whole discourse, for example being asked what my favourite scene was in a film (part for whole) and a TV reporter interviewing individuals in the crowd waiting for the New Year fireworks on the banks of the Thames (individual testimonies used to convey a general sense of what it was like to be there). Others were not verbal but involved similarities of other kinds: playing a card game where the aim is to end up with sets of related cards, either adjacent numbers in the same suit or the same number in different suits (cards in each set share characteristics); playing Sudoku (grids and lines of numbers are compared for similarities and differences); sorting out a spare room by ordering things by category (putting like with like); being told, when buying on Amazon, that "customers who bought this book also bought . . ." (similarities in past choices suggesting future preferences); remarking on the similarity between people you encounter and figures in the public eye (so-called 'lookalikes'). These are all activities in which the recognition of part-whole relationships plays a central role.

The methodology used in this book can broadly be described as 'reflective' or 'speculative'; some would characterize it as 'armchair linguistics'. This contrasts with what is typical for social-science research in that it does not contain rigorously collected and analyzed data or sections/chapters devoted to methods of data collection and analysis. The argument in this book is progressed in stages, the conclusion of one stage becoming the premise for the next. The purpose is to 'reconfigure' theory, that is, to make new connections across existing theoretical frameworks. It would be misleading, however, to suggest that the methodology is solely in the nature of a theoretical investigation, as the argument is supported throughout by a substantial quantity of original data, either actively collected through small-scale studies, tasks and interviews or gained opportunistically from naturally-occurring sources. This sits well with the tradition of scholars from various fields concerning language and communication, among whom I would include: theoretical linguists, such as Jakobson (1971), Saussure (1983) and Chomsky (1965); discourse analysts, such as Levinson (1983) and Coulthard (1985); functional grammarians, such as Halliday (1994); cognitive linguists, such as Lakoff (1987b); applied linguists, such as Widdowson (1983) and Cook (2000); and semioticians, such as Kress (2010). It is also the approach of scholars such as Bourdieu ('field' and 'habitus'), Bernstein ('elaborated code' and 'restricted code') and Giddens ('structuration' and 'modernity'); and, going back further in time, it characterizes the indirect or circumstantial evidence used by Charles Darwin to support his 'big idea' thesis, the theory of evolution through natural selection presented in *On the Origin of Species* (Dawkins 2010).

This book explores the following principal questions:

- **What role does metonymy play in communication?**
- **What role does metonymy play in structuring discourse and text?**
- **What role does metonymy play in language-learner interaction?**
- **What role does metonymy play in translation?**

To investigate these questions in a way different from the one proposed would run the risk both of arriving at misleading conclusions and being untrue to the intentions of the study. Metonymy occurs in a complex environment; it operates at many different levels, at once being the mechanism behind the scenes and the process in the foreground of the interaction. Attempting to isolate metonymy through statistical analysis is unlikely to be successful; it would be like investigating how the definite article is used in expressing gender roles by applying chi-square tests to rigorously sampled data—it is unlikely to be conclusive and could easily throw up 'phantom' results, as is seen in studies such as Cooper (1999) on processing idioms by L2 learners. There is a principle involved here which parallels Grice's maxim of 'quantity', whereby the chosen methodology needs to offer as much information as is needed and no more. For these reasons the empirical data in this volume are from a range of different sources: corpus data, lexicographic data, internet searches, contrastive studies across languages, news-reporting, texts from the press, political speeches, promotional material, packaging, television shows, literary texts, jokes and other forms of humour, semi-structured interviews, experiments with informants, data from translators, post-task interviews and invented examples. In addition to these, I make frequent use of the data I have collected over many years, noted down in numerous field data notebooks.

There are five primary data sets used in this work. They are: translations of common lexical items collected from student bilingual informants in 2008; family sayings and expressions collected from five informants in 2007; bilingual informants speaking monologues in two languages on 'social change over the last decade', recorded in 2006; data on 'speech slips' from my field notebooks, collected over a period of six weeks in 2008; and first drafts and final versions of translations and retrospective interviews carried out by a trainee translator in London in 2009 and a professional translator in Germany in 2010.

This book is about metonymy and its importance in communication. But it does not start with metonymy. Preliminary chapters 'set the scene': Chapter 3 shows how metonymy is located within metaphor and Chapter 2 shows how metaphor is located within the overall picture of linguistic communication, frames of reference which need to be established before a discussion of metonymy can be attempted. An in-depth discussion of metonymy is found first in Chapter 4; the subsequent chapters then develop metonymic theory with regard to communication and its implications for text analysis, language learners and translators. What follows is a brief summary of the chapter contents.

Chapter 2, 'Modelling the Linguistic Mind', presents an original model of the linguistic mind. The purpose is to give an overview of linguistic phenomena essential in processing language and to identify where figurative language fits in. The model consists of six domains, comprising three stores and three skill centres. The stores, the Mental Lexicon, the Mental Phraseicon and the Mental Schema Store, are vast passive storehouses of information on lexis, phraseology and frames. These are acted on by the skill centres, the Grammar Processor, the Metaphor Processor and the Pragmatic Processor, which manipulate morphosyntax, metaphor and pragmatics, respectively. The model separates out phenomena which are confused in the literature and in so doing characterizes metaphor under three distinct headings, 'knowing metaphor', 'using metaphor', and 'doing metaphor'. These involve: information about systematic and conceptual metaphor, stored in the Mental Schema Store, such as GOOD IS UP, LIFE IS A JOURNEY; information about conventional metaphor, eg *couch potato*, *spill the beans*, in the Mental Phraseicon; and the ability to manage novel metaphor in the Metaphor Processor. These findings are situated within contemporary theories of intelligence and cognition. It is made clear that these domains are abilities and stores rather than discrete locations in the brain. The model is extended to the bilingual mind.

Chapter 3, 'The Ability to Metaphorize', investigates what is involved when understanding and generating novel metaphor and identifies three essential features: the involvement of two domains, directionality and selective transfer. I present an original model, the Stack of Counters model, to explain novel metaphor, in which semantic features, visualized as counters, are selectively manipulated. The model can be seen as a generative model, indicating that metaphor need not be considered anomalous and outside a generative description of language, as it is often portrayed, but instead sits comfortably within it. I go further and suggest that metaphor is the best proof we have that word meaning is stored as features, as no other phenomenon makes movements at feature level so evident. The model explains why processing metaphor is both predictable and involves little effort: it is predictable because the information is already in the 'stack' of features; and it is carried out with relative ease because the basic operation involved is the same one every individual carries out thousands of times a day. It also explains why language learners create novel metaphor with little effort in a language they are not particularly proficient in: because they are applying a skill they use repeatedly in their first language. The literature on the discourse functions of metaphor is reviewed in this chapter and the information plotted against two axes: whether metaphor increases or reduces the specificity of the message, and whether metaphor is used more in transaction or interaction. The purpose of this is to show the diversity of the discourse functions of metaphor, to the extent that they often represent diametric opposites, demonstrating that the 'selection stage' is more fundamental than 'choice of domain' in metaphorizing.

Chapter 4, 'The Vital Role of Metonymy in Conceptualization and Communication', moves the narrative of the book to metonymy, demonstrating that metonymic processing is fundamental in many contexts—understanding word categories, when moving between sense and reference, when dealing with differences between competence and performance, in pragmatic inferencing and in the change of word meaning over time, to name some of them. This offers a perspective which reconfigures existing theory and shows a commonality across a spectrum of linguistic phenomena not normally considered together, a General Theory of Metonymy in communication. It is argued that language is by nature metonymic, as signs are partial and language under-refers, and that metonymic processing allows us both to deal with a system which under-refers and to exploit this phenomenon to our advantage. The language user is presented with a choice of strategies for naming entities. Original data from thirteen languages for the items *floating rib*, *rib cage*, *answering machine* and *mobile phone* are used to demonstrate how these choices become conventionalized. A more precise understanding of metonymy is developed in this chapter drawing on the vast and complex literature from cognitive linguistics in this area, focussing particularly on domain theory, the notion of the metonymy-metaphor continuum and metonymy typologies. It is argued that metonymic, literal and metaphoric language all involve the recognition of part-whole relations, the differences between them being the nature of the part-whole relation and the use to which it is put.

Chapter 5, 'Metonymy in Culture and Recreation', argues that metonymy not only offers alternatives when naming but also opportunities for expressing nuance, giving emphasis and creating 'spin'. It is argued that a model of communication which includes metonymy goes some way towards explaining how the language system permits the extraordinary subtleties of expression and nuance we are able to display. I demonstrate how a single lexical item often has three distinct senses, a metonymic, a literal and a metaphoric, each occupying a distinct semantic space and reinforced by local grammar. I call this the 'Triangle of Tropes'. The chapter gathers together evidence from a wide range of everyday texts and commonplace objects, demonstrating the unexpectedly wide range of cultural and recreational phenomena where metonymy and metonymic processing play a part, such as quiz shows, puzzles, games, humour, noticing lookalikes and using nicknames. I also interpret in-family expressions, the role of metonymy in avoiding cooperation and punning/wordplay, which I call 'Formal Metonymy', in terms of Metonymic Processing Theory.

Chapter 6, 'Metonymy and Metaphor in Discourse and Text', investigates figurative text phenomena, that is, where the use of metaphor and metonymy have a role in organizing language at the level of the whole text either through patterning lexis or changing register. Metaphor-in-discourse phenomena include 'metaphor chains', 'metaphor clusters' and 'extended metaphors'; scholars, such as Cameron & Maslen, the Pragglejaz Group (MIP) and Steen et al (MIPVU), have engaged in metaphor-led discourse analysis and metaphor identification across genres. But overall there has been much more attention on local 'emergent' meaning in spoken interaction than on the impact of metaphor on longer stretches of language, and few have recognized the equally important role of metonymy in organizing longer stretches of language. I identify four distinct phenomena: the systematic use of metaphors, such as *COALITIONS ARE MARRIAGES* or *FOOTBALL IS A RELIGION* over long stretches of text, which I label 'Textual Metaphor'; the use of metonymy to change the register in a section of text by narrowing the focus to specific examples, or the use of testimonies and vox pops (Discourse Metonymy); the progressive enrichment of a text through the use of co-referential chains of metonymically-related items (Textual Metonymy); and the use of concentrated clusters of conventional metaphors to create less determinate registers (Discourse Metaphor). I bring together authors from different fields and different eras in this context into a single framework, from Jakobson, Lodge and Lakoff & Johnson to Al-Sharafi, Koller and Semino, while also reinterpreting Halliday & Hasan's work on cohesion in terms of figurative thought and extending Goossens' concept of 'metaphtonymy' to the level of text.

Chapter 7, 'Metonymy and Language Learners', looks at the role played by metonymy in interactions between learners and their interlocutors. Approaches to figurative language have broadened recently to include systematic approaches to learning idioms, phrasal verbs and single words; Littlemore and Low have taken the discussion further with their notions 'metaphoric competence' and 'figurative thinking' in learning. But the notion of Metonymic Competence in learner-speaker interactions has so far remained unexplored. Metonymic processing plays a role in the ability of interlocutors to accommodate to learner talk by 'translating' unfamiliar features of phonology, morphosyntax, semantics and pragmatics into familiar features. It also plays a role in the register interlocutors adopt when speaking to learners, called 'foreigner talk', characterized by a more articulated pronunciation, fewer pronouns, a less complex syntax and more high-frequency lexical items. It also allows learners to acquire new items through scaffolding using existing knowledge and to meet the demands of face-to-face interactions by inventing novel approximations from the resources they have to hand. The figurative language English Language Teaching has tended to focus on has principally been low-frequency conventional metaphor, or 'idioms'. I suggest a more fruitful use of classroom and practice time is a focus on metonymy rather than metaphor, high frequency rather than low frequency items—expressions such as *head for the door*, *bums on seats*, *small screen*, *pay with plastic* rather than *light at the end of the tunnel* and *spill the beans*—and novel rather than conventional metonymy. This opens up a hugely rich resource for learners to draw upon and use 'on the fly'. Learning itself is characterized in terms of metonymic processing. I end the chapter by arguing that monitoring for speech errors using a 'feedback loop' in the way Levelt proposes in his 'intention-to-articulation' model also involves metonymic processing. In order to detect and correct error a speaker constantly needs to compare the utterances they perform against what they intended to perform. 'Monitoring for differences' is metonymic processing, whether speech is correct or not and whether the speaker is a native speaker or not.

Chapter 8, 'Metonymy and Translation', proposes a Metonymic Theory of Translation which characterizes translation as the exploration of the metonymic relationship between source text and target text. I argue that, as the components of one language rarely correspond exactly with those of another, the relationship between a source text and its translation is neither literal nor metaphoric; instead, the activity of translation is a constant exploration of close relatedness at a number of different linguistic levels between the two different language systems (codes). The theory of translation I present in this chapter combines two areas of translation-studies scholarship—'shift theory' (eg Catford and Vinay & Darbelnet) and writing on the translation of figurative language (eg Baker, Newmark, Dagut and Schäffner). This extends the idea of shift to a general principle of metonymic processing and re-characterizes figurative language as a universal enabler, allowing the translator to compensate for indeterminacy rather than as an occasional irritant encountered when idioms turn up in a text, as it is often portrayed. Metonymy is presented as the means by which translation is possible and the tool which translators can use to compensate for translation loss. I demonstrate that metonymic processing is involved not only in creating a first draft but also when revising a draft to give the final version. Using data collected from professional translators, supported by post-task interviews, I examine the metonymic relations involved in both going from source text to first draft and first draft to final version.

Chapter 9, 'Metonymics', revisits the question of methodology and explores the wide-ranging applications of a metonymic approach. I review the achievements of the monograph as a whole and restate the contribution of this new approach, as well as indicating the direction further investigations in this field might take. This is a 'big idea' thesis in that its central tenet and focus—relatedness—cuts right across human interaction at a very basic level. It deals with a phenomenon which is fundamental in our lives and unavoidable in the living out of our lives. This means that the implications are many and wide ranging. I signpost some practical applications: the training of wordsmiths of various types, such as journalists and editors, the training of language teachers and the training of translators/interpreters. I indicate the direction that further research might take and suggest that the development of ideas presented in this book might profitably lead to the creation of a new area of research in which metonymic principles are developed as an instrument for reframing, analyzing and solving social and theoretical issues. I propose a research programme, for which I suggest the name

Metonymics, which could have applications in fields as diverse as mathematics, arbitration, conflict resolution, diplomacy, complexity theory, biological taxonomy, evolutionary theory and law. I suggest that a theory of knowledge in which metonymic principles play a role could help resolve incompatibilities between competing theories and help partial truths combine together to give unified wholes.

2 Modelling the Linguistic Mind

The purpose of this chapter is to define metaphor. To do so, I present my own comprehensive model of the linguistic mind in order to give a context to this discussion. The model consists of six essential components—grammar, lexis, phraseology, metaphor, pragmatics and coherence—needed by an individual to operate effectively as a language user. Each component is discussed in turn, building up an inclusive model block by block. What is novel about the model is the distinction made between 'stores' and 'skills', that is, between passive information stores, on the one hand, and active skills involved in manipulating and processing language, on the other. This serves to clarify some of the confusion in the complex literature on metaphor while also providing a practical research tool for the investigation of subjects using metaphor. This is then extended to model the bilingual mind, the mind of those who habitually operate with more than one language, such as language learners and translators. It should be noted that the components of the model are not intended to represent discrete physical locations in the brain, but rather, to identify definable linguistic capabilities. The model sets the scene for the chapters to follow, though it is not explored in more depth beyond the present chapter.

GRAMMAR AND LEXIS

I start from a traditional model of language, the most traditional, by characterizing language in terms of grammar and lexis. The first two components of my model are represented by the *Grammar Processor* and the *Mental Lexicon*; the Grammar Processor manages structure while the Mental Lexicon stores information about single words and morphemes:

In this two-part 'grammar and lexis', or 'slot and filler', model, grammar contributes structure and lexis contributes meaning. Creating a string such as *Is that your jacket?* involves selecting words from the lexicon and combining them according to the rules of grammar. Jakobson describes it thus: "the speaker selects words and combines them into sentences according to the syntactic system of the language he is using [. . .] his selection (except for the rare case of actual neology) must be made from the lexical storehouse which he and his addressee possess in common" (Jakobson 1956/1971:72). The grammar/lexis (or syntax/semantics, or words and rules) distinction is so fundamental to linguistic theory, it is hard to imagine a model of language which dispenses with it. It is a principle reflected in Saussurean semiotics, language as a complex system of syntagms and paradigms, of relations *in presentia* and relations *in absentia* (Saussure 1916/1983). But, although the two phenomena can clearly be differentiated, they also overlap: structure is an expression of meaning, a shorthand for general and frequently-occurring concepts. Widdowson puts it thus: "*Grammar* is a device for indicating the most common and recurrent aspects of *meaning* which it would be tedious and inefficient to incorporate into separate lexical items" [my italics] (Widdowson 1990:87). The idea is also fundamental to Hallidayan systemic-functional grammar: "One way of thinking of a 'functional' grammar, like the present one, is that it is a theory of grammar that is orientated towards the discourse semantics. In other words, if we say we are interpreting the *grammar* functionally, it means that we are foregrounding its role as a resource for construing *meaning*" [my italics] (Halliday 1994:15).

While we can say that grammar has meaning, it is also true that lexis has grammar. For Halliday, "the lexicon is simply the most delicate grammar" (Halliday 1978:43). Individual words are stored in the mind with information about their phonology, graphology, denotation, etc, but also their grammatical and morphological behaviour, such as how a stem inflects, how a word behaves colligationally or how theta roles correspond to syntactic positions. Dictionary entries give information about word meaning but also about transitivity, countability, etc; the lemma of each word is assigned semantic as well as grammatical information.

The Humboldtian principle that a limited number of items can combine to create an infinite number of meanings (Humboldt 1836/1999), and that wholes can be analyzed into their parts, and recomposed to achieve wholes again, are basic tenets of generative approaches in grammar (Chomsky 1965), phonology (Kenstowicz 1994) and semantics (Katz & Fodor 1963). Katz & Fodor analyze meaning into bundles of features, while Pustejovsky's 'generative lexicon' is an attempt to codify meaning, each lexical item being assigned information about its 'argument structure', 'event structure', 'qualia structure' and 'lexical inheritance' for computational science (Pustejovsky 1995). Cognitivists have blurred the line between syntax and lexicon even further, seeing language as consisting often of unanalyzable units or 'constructions' on a lexicogrammatical continuum, as in the construction grammars proposed by Kay & Fillmore, Lakoff and Goldberg (Croft & Cruse 2004:257–290). The importance of the 'grammar of lexis' or 'word grammar' is recognized by Lewis, who makes it a fundamental tenet of his 'lexical approach' to language teaching; for him, language is "grammaticalised lexis" more than it is "lexicalised grammar": "Instead of a few big structures and many words, we now recognise that language consists of many smaller patterns [. . .]; in a sense, each word has its own grammar. It is this insight—that language consists of grammaticalised lexis, not lexicalised grammar—which is the single most fundamental principle of the Lexical Approach" (Lewis 2000:137).

While accepting the validity of all these approaches, in the model I am presenting in this chapter, I have retained the idea of a separation between grammar and lexis. My reason for doing so is that I wish to highlight a distinction between *active* skills and *passive* stores. The Grammar Processor carries out a limited number of procedures and does so extremely efficiently, but, like any processor, it cannot operate in isolation; it has to have something to work on, and that something is the information stored in the Mental Lexicon. This distinction between skills and stores is the main thrust of the present chapter, further developed as we move through it. It should be noted here again that the model proposed is a theoretical model rather than a physical one, and that the processing and storage 'modules' identified in it represent functional entities rather than locations in the brain.

PHRASEOLOGY

The next component I am adding to my model of the linguistic mind is the *Mental Phraseicon.* This adds to the model a store of information about lexical phrases. The model now looks like this:

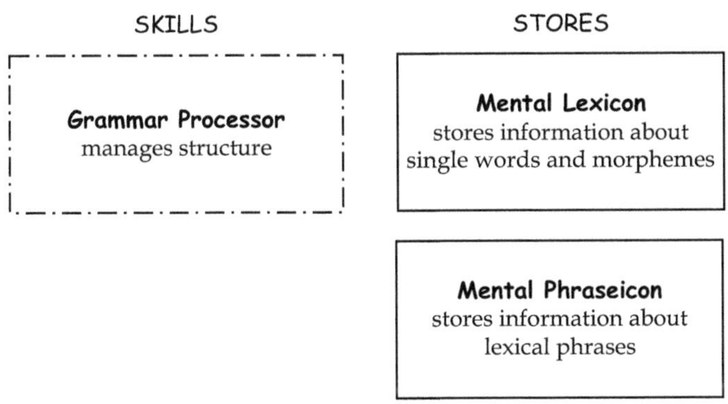

What are lexical phrases? They are prefabricated 'chunks' of language, strings of words which are stored in the mind whole and retrieved whole, and with a meaning of their own which is not merely the sum of their component parts. 'Lexical phrase' is the term preferred by Nattinger & DeCarrico (1992) and is the one I will use in this chapter, but there are many to choose from. Included in the list provided by Wray (1999:214) are: 'chunks', 'collocations', 'fixed expressions', 'idioms', 'formulae', 'multiword units', 'preassembled speech', 'prefabricated routines', 'unanalysed language' and 'sentence builders'; other terms in the literature are 'lexicogrammatical units', 'phrasal lexemes', 'formulaic sequences', 'prefabs', 'ready-made utterances', 'formulaic language', 'composites', 'big words' and 'lexical bundles'. This plethora of terms reflects the intense interest in lexical phrases in fairly recent times. Pawley & Syder (1983), Sinclair (1991), Nattinger & DeCarrico (1992), Lewis (1993), Wray (2002), linguists associated with the Cobuild dictionary project (eg Carter and McCarthy) and other scholars working with corpus data, such as Partington (1998) recognized the importance of lexical phrases both in terms of frequency of occurrence and communicative usefulness. How common are they? Altenberg (1998:102) estimates that lexical phrases account for more than 80% of adult native-speaker production; Hill, that they make up 70% (Hill 2000:53); while Moon (1998) gives a lower estimate. The disparity reflects the inclusiveness/exclusiveness of their definitions rather than any substantive disagreement regarding their importance.

Lexical phrases have been defined in many ways. Sinclair distinguishes between the 'open-choice principle' and the 'idiom principle', taking lexical phrases to be evidence of the latter (Sinclair 1991). Moon classifies lexical phrases into three categories, based on whether the 'idiomaticity' of the string derives from its lexicogrammar, which she calls 'anomalous collocations', its pragmatics, which she calls 'formulae', or its semantics, which she calls 'metaphors' (Moon 1998:83–84). Howarth's 'collocational continuum' includes: 'free collocations', 'restricted collocations', eg *pay heed, give somebody credit*, 'figurative idioms', eg *draw a line* and 'pure idioms', eg *set store by something* (Howarth 1998:28). Wray offers a four way classification: expressions which have 'normal' grammar in their construction, eg *not for me, you bet, isn't it, no way*; expressions which are grammatically idiosyncratic, eg *the long and the short of it, by and large, happy go lucky*; metaphoric expressions which are fairly transparent, eg *we need new blood, to see it on the small screen, pay with plastic*; and metaphoric expressions which are more opaque, eg *go bananas, spill the beans* (Wray 1999:214–216). Classifications have identified lexical phrases as a phenomenon to reckon with, which leads us to ask why they are there and what function they play in communication.

Lexical phrases offer two significant advantages: they extend meaning (because their meaning is more than the sum of their parts) and they make processing easier. Chunking saves us the bother of creating every new utterance from scratch; it allows us to 'cut and paste'. Wray invites us to imagine a situation in a crowded bar where one wants to get past someone, and suggests that *Excuse me!* or *Mind your backs!*, being lexical phrases, are more predictable and therefore easier to process; while a less formulaic utterance, such as *I'm just walking behind you with drinks and need to get by*, would be harder to process, and, interestingly, also more confrontational (Wray 1999:216); a sequence which is predictable comes across as less intrusive. There is empirical psycholinguistic evidence that lexical phrases are processed more quickly by native and non-native speakers (Conklin & Schmitt 2008). It is thought that one of the differences between language learners and mother-tongue speakers is that learners rely more on 'free combination' while native speakers make more use of chunking, and that the process of becoming proficient is linked to the ability to learn lexical phrases and add them to the Phraseicon. It has also been demonstrated that learners have their own chunks, which they drop or modify as learning proceeds (Wray 2002).

Collocation

Implicit in a generative grammar-and-lexis model is that we use free combination to assemble language, but research on lexical phrases indicates that our choices are far more restricted. Lexical phrases present an exception to the generative paradigm as they are 'non-productive'; they cannot be varied much grammatically or lexically if their meaning is to be preserved (Wray 2000:465). Among the huge variety of expressions included under lexical phrases, three axes of variation can be identified, the axes of 'grammaticality', 'transparency' and 'variability'. To clarify these terms: the expression *to spill the beans* is grammatically 'normal' but not very transparent; *happy go lucky* or *the long and the short of it* are grammatically idiosyncratic but fairly transparent; while none of these expressions can withstand lexical variation, eg *She spilled the baked beans*.

It is clear from the discussion above that there is a continuum from free combination, through restricted collocation to lexical phrases. Strictly, then, a separation between the Mental Lexicon and the Mental Phraseicon is an artificial distinction to make, because weak collocations of the sort *the dog barks* and *the plane took off* and strong collocations of the sort *virtually impossible*, *blindingly obvious* and *crushing defeat* represent an area of overlap between the two. Equally, it could be argued that the spectrum is so wide that multi-word units should be seen as ontologically distinct, as they come about differently and behave differently from single words. It is for this reason that I have given the Mental Phraseicon a box to itself, but also in order to acknowledge the relatively recent emergence of studies in this area and the recognition of the importance of lexical phrases in communication. Building further on the model, the next two sections look at the mental processors responsible for managing metaphor and pragmatics.

METAPHOR

The next component I am adding to my model is a 'skill', the *Metaphor Processor*. Its role is to manage metaphoric meaning. The model now has four parts and looks like this:

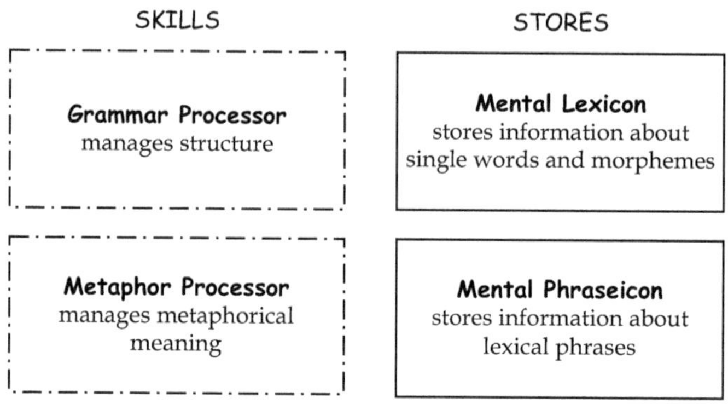

Metaphoric meaning plays a vital role in communication, which is why it merits a 'box' to itself in this model. It contributes to communicative competence in many ways, of which three are: extending meaning, managing imprecision and allowing speakers to be indirect. I consider these in turn below.

Extending Meaning

Metaphor allows us to say things which denotation has not caught up with. It allows us to extend the lexicon beyond the literal via connotation. An expression such as *Less is more* does have meaning, and is not just a contradiction, because both *less* and *more* are understood in a connotational sense; similarly, the expression *Boys will be boys* is not simply a tautology, but again has meaning through connotation. Metaphor allows us to say something in terms of something else and therefore offers infinite possibilities of enriching and extending meaning, and is as much a feature of intimate interpersonal interactions as it is of scientific discourse.

Imprecision

If we had to find the exact words for everything we wanted to express, the demands on our memories and our abilities of recall would be impossible. Instead, we choose the best fit we can find in the given time and rely on the 'tolerance of ambiguity' and ability to infer of our listeners for the rest. Metaphor gives us flexibility by allowing us to be imprecise. For example: what would you call someone who hands out free newspapers at railway stations? They could be referred to as *vendors*, but surely a *vendor* is someone who sells something for money, and these newspapers are free. But *vendor* will do; it is near enough. It gives us access to a sufficient number of the components of meaning of the sense we require for it not to pose a problem. We are all reliant on our speech partners' ability to compensate for unintended imprecision, but this is especially the case with language learners. Their speech is rich in this kind of indeterminate meaning. I think of conversations I have had abroad with taxi drivers or hotel staff. From my perspective, a metaphoric 'haze' accompanies their speech at every level—at the level of phonology, syntax, semantics, discourse—and as a listener I have to compensate by doing extra processing work. It is unintended metaphoricity, for the most part, but that makes no odds; as a listener, I still have to process it as metaphor to understand what is being said.

Indirectness

Metaphor gives us the subtleties we need when interacting with others. It allows us to talk about personal matters safely and tackle delicate topics without losing face or hurting feelings. It allows us to suggest things without saying them explicitly. In public life, incidents often occur in which a public figure insults another using a metaphor. Mio recounts an exchange in which a representative of Russia compares the separation of Lithuania from Russia to a 'divorce'; the representative of Lithuania replies that there had never been a marriage and that Russia's involvement in Lithuania was more like 'rape' (Littlemore & Low 2006b:278). Even when a remark is retracted the insult can still endure. This was the case in 2003 when a German Member of the European Parliament provoked the former Italian Prime Minister Silvio Berlusconi by suggesting that he had passed an immunity law to avoid his own prosecution on bribery charges. Berlusconi replied by saying the German MEP would be well cast for the part of 'capo' in a film currently being produced in Italy about the Nazi concentration camps. In response to the angry reaction, Berlusconi expressed his regrets, but the damage had been done. Berlusconi had both had his swipe and saved face, and enlisted metaphor to do this work for him.

Metaphor Studies

Scholarly interest in metaphor has grown dramatically in recent years: "The study of metaphor has exploded in the last decades" (Cameron & Low 1999a:77); there has been "a rapid burgeoning of interest in and research into the nature and function of metaphor in language and thought" (Ortony 1993b:xiii). Scholars from language philosophy, semiotics, text analysis, discourse analysis, pragmatics, stylistics, computational linguistics, cognitive linguistics, philosophy of science and many other fields have contributed to this ascendancy, summarized in Ortony (1993b), Gibbs (1994) and Knowles & Moon (2006). The result has been that a new field of scholarship has emerged, Metaphor Studies, which, like any new and identifiable discipline, has dedicated to it journals, associations, research projects, communities of scholars, conferences and an extensive literature.

The 'paradigm shift' this development has brought about is to see metaphor as an essential feature of everyday communication, important in all discourses and genres, including the scientific and technical, and no longer as an inessential rhetorical trope, a decorative add-on, encountered predominately in literature. Cameron & Deignan characterize the 'older view of metaphor' as "poetic and decorative uses of language" (Cameron & Deignan 2006:688). For Cameron & Low, metaphor also has a powerful motivating role in forming and consolidating ideas over time: "Metaphor in one form or other is absolutely fundamental to the way language systems develop over time and are structured, as well as to the way human beings consolidate and extend their ideas about themselves, their relationships and their knowledge of the world" (Cameron & Low 1999b:xii). A further aspect of the new view is that metaphor is systematic and predictable rather than unstable and arbitrary. Metaphor is not a licence to make words mean whatever you want them to mean. Just as there is a consensus about the denotational meaning of words in a language community, there is also a consensus about their connotational meaning. The denotation or 'core' meaning of a word is analyzed in the first part of a dictionary entry; the connotational or 'non-core' meaning of a word is often in a dictionary entry too. Denotation and connotation can also be investigated using electronic corpora, such as the *British National Corpus* (www.natcorp.oc.ac.uk). Below are lines from the *Collins Cobuild Corpus* (formerly at www.cobuild.collins.co.uk, accessed 22 May 2006) for the 'node' word *champagne.* In the concordance lines quoted below we find senses which are literal, ie *champagne* as a wine:

They finished one bottle of **champagne** quickly enough, opened a second.
are being pulled out; lobster, pink **champagne**, expense account heaven. Then
15 minute flight they were offered **champagne**, the finest liqueurs and a choice

senses which lie halfway between literal and metaphoric, possibly involving wine but not necessarily champagne:

drink. It's the poor man's **champagne**, though I've never tried it with
said he couldn't go to any of the **champagne** parties laid on for the
two hand-blown, lead-free crystal **Champagne** flutes, imported Icelandic black

and senses which are connotational, such as relating to colour or other associations:

Co, is interlaced highlights in **champagne**, honey and caramel tones
occasional glimpses of Vuitton's **champagne**-colored fur amid the foliage.
to rot in jail; the '**champagne** socialists' who are opposed to
enough to join revellers at the **champagne** socialists ball. Party
meaningless. It also explains the '**champagne** safari', which fairly dripped

From such data one could easily compile a dictionary-type entry for *champagne*, denotational expressions giving literal senses and connotational expressions giving metaphoric senses.

The ease with which we deal with connotation, and the degree of our consensus about it, is shown in an experiment Cameron (1992:82) conducted with university students in the United States of America. The students were given pairs of words—*knife/fork*, *Ford/Chevrolet*, *salt/pepper*, *vanilla/chocolate*—and asked which of the pair was masculine and which feminine. She found not only that the participants could do the task without any difficulty, and did not think it strange to be asked, but that they agreed in their responses. *Knife*, *Ford*, *pepper* and *chocolate* were seen as the more masculine of the pairs, showing that concepts like 'masculine' and 'feminine', which one would expect to find hard to pin down, can easily be manipulated and related to other concepts as shared knowledge. Metaphor shows systematicity not only at the level of individual words but also at a more general conceptual level. Lakoff & Johnson's 'conceptual metaphors' are abstract metaphoric schemata of thought, responsible for generating much of the conventionalized metaphor we find in everyday language (Lakoff & Johnson 1980). The expressions *I'm on top of the world*, *over the moon*, *Things are looking up*, *onwards and upwards*, *I'm up for it!* and *It's the pits*, *down and out*, *down in the dumps*, etc (all of which would be stored in the Mental Phraseicon) reflect a common conceptual schema of the sort GOOD IS UP. The same conceptual metaphor can be called upon to generate, and interpret, novel expressions. What is more, not only is the process by which conceptual metaphors generate language systematic, but the origin of conceptual metaphors themselves is also systematic. For Lakoff & Johnson, conceptual metaphors reflect our bodily experience of the world (in the case of GOOD IS UP, perhaps from early successes as an infant constructing towers from building blocks, pulling up on a table or learning to walk); they are physical experiences which have become encoded, forming part of what Lakoff & Johnson call the 'embodied mind' (Lakoff & Johnson 1999:16–44).

An important observation to make here is that the myriad of theories around metaphor do not in any way compete with each other, though they are often presented as doing so. Instead, each theory has a contribution to make to our understanding of this complex phenomenon and each gives a unique insight. Fauconnier and Lakoff felt exhorted to make a shared statement declaring that there was no opposition between their theories, that it is "a mistaken perception that 'metaphor theory' and 'conceptual blending' are competing views" (Fauconnier & Lakoff 2010). Steen recognizes that metaphor is "not all thought", "not all language" and "not just language and thought", but all of these, and a phenomenon which is interactive and 'emergent' in communication (Steen 2008). Cameron, similarly, characterizes metaphor as being many things—'linguistic', 'embodied', 'cognitive', 'affective', 'sociocultural' and 'dynamic'—and claims that metaphor is "a multi-faceted phenomenon, or perhaps it would be more accurate to say that the idea of metaphor encompasses multiple phenomena" (Cameron 2010:3–7).

To summarize, connotational meaning is not random but encoded and stored as part of the information we have about each word; conceptual metaphor is responsible for sanctioning the use of language in a systematic way; and conceptual metaphors reflect physical experiences of the real world through embodiment. We can add to this the restrictions of 'collocation', 'semantic prosody' (generalized patterns of collocation) and 'colligation', which further refine the way reality is encoded into language (Hoey 2000) and the "relatively stable bundles of patterns of use" which Cameron & Deignan call 'metaphoremes' (Cameron & Deignan 2006). Steen maintains that language use is also 'genre regulated' and that: "people use language on particular occasions in specific roles, for particular goals, about particular topics, in particular settings, and against the background of specific norms and expectations" (Steen 2007:352–353). A picture emerges of language in discourse where little is left to chance!

Types of Metaphor

It could be proposed that every bit of speech or writing we care to examine is metaphoric in one way or another, because each fragment of language exemplifies one of these four types of metaphor: 'historical', 'dead', 'conventional' or 'novel'. Below I explain how I am using these terms.

- **Historical metaphors** are the 'literal' senses of words, which give no indication to the user that they have derived from metaphor. They are metaphoric in the sense that they have metaphor buried in their etymological histories, having derived from other words via metaphoric or metonymic extension over time. Few people are aware of these histories. The word *travel* ultimately derives from a mediaeval three-pronged torture instrument, but few people know that; and although fascinating in their own right, these histories play no significant role in meaning making in everyday communication.
- **Dead metaphors** are metaphors which have become so conventionalized that we are no longer aware of their original literal sense, although we have a sense that there must have been one once, eg *loggerheads* or *tenterhooks.*
- **Conventional metaphors** are metaphoric expressions which have gained acceptance in the shared lexicon of a language community. They are established expressions, so much so that they are reported in dictionaries, such as *spill the beans*, *go bananas*; but unlike dead metaphors, contain elements we know the meaning of, such as *beans*, *bananas*.
- **Novel metaphors** are metaphoric expressions which are not part of a shared lexicon and may never become so. They are original ways of saying something in terms of something else. We can combine words randomly to give us a whole array of novel metaphors, such as *My blouse is an airship*, *Ice-cream is a frigate*, *Wealth is posterity*, *Love is an untidy living room*. How

useful they would be in practice would depend on the context and the degree to which they reflect metaphoric ideas in our conceptual system. Novel metaphors require speakers and interlocutors to work actively to interpret them.

I present this classification in order to make clear in which type of metaphor the Metaphor Processor is involved; it is only involved in the last of the four categories, when processing novel metaphor. Once an expression is conventionalized, it has an entry in the Mental Phraseicon; it is a new sign and the Metaphor Processor does not need to be employed. Wray recounts a story which illustrates this: Kellogg, the breakfast cereal company, asked people in the street what they thought *Rice Krispies* were made of, as part of an advertising campaign (Wray 2002). Nearly all the respondents said they did not know; furthermore, most of them were surprised that the answer was "rice". If a conventional metaphor is extended, however, the Metaphor Processor *is* involved; the expression is analyzed into its components which are exploited metaphorically via core meaning.

What the Metaphor Processor does is in principle simple: it selectively highlights certain meaning components (or 'semes') within words/phrases, and suppresses others. Every time we retrieve a word from the Mental Lexicon, we have equal access to the narrow meaning and the broad meaning (Croft & Cruse 2004:212). Choosing a metaphoric reading over a literal reading is in principle no different from choosing between a narrow and a broad reading. If we imagine each word in the mind to be like a stack of counters in which each counter represents a 'seme' (the counters lower down the stack being denotational and the counters higher up connotational), the difference between a literal sense and a metaphoric sense is that we selectively choose counters only from higher up the stack when we deal with metaphor. To make sense of a novel metaphor, such as *My blouse is an airship*, we ignore certain core components of *airship*, such as being 'large', 'motorized' or 'steerable', and focus instead on a single feature, such as 'air-filled' or 'ballooning'. Similarly, a novel expression involving the word *cat* might be interpreted by ignoring core features, like having four legs, fur, a tail, pointed ears and a meow, and focussing instead on eg agility or mischievousness. Semanticists have tended to put metaphor outside a semantic description of meaning, seeing it as anomalous and not easily described in terms of rules of generativeness or compositionality. I propose instead that metaphor is the best proof we have that words are stored in the mind as meaning components and that metaphor is the most spectacular manifestation of this.

PRAGMATICS

The next component I am adding to the model is also a 'skill', the *Pragmatic Processor*. It has the task of managing meaning in context. The model now looks like this:

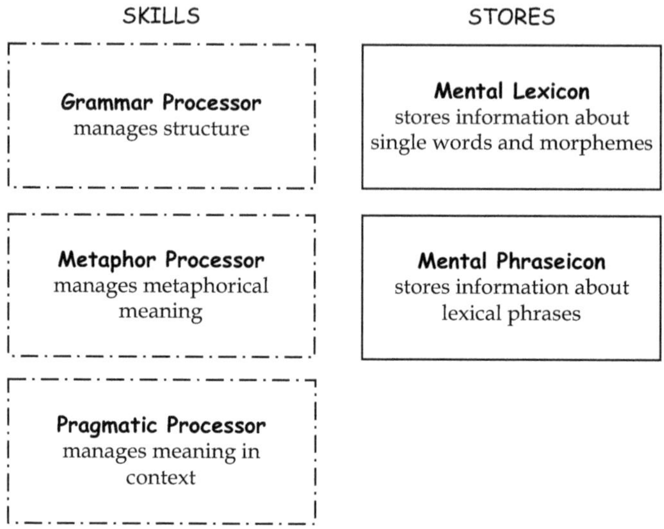

No model of the linguistic mind would be complete without a centre which creates and interprets meaning in context, which compares the propositional 'linguistic' meaning of an utterance with an external physical, psychological or textual reality in which it occurs to arrive at the intended 'speaker' meaning. The Pragmatic Processor starts with a proposition, such as *Is that your jacket?*—created through a collaboration between the Mental Lexicon, Mental Phraseicon, Grammar Processor and Metaphor Processor—adds information about context, and arrives at a 'solution', eg *Is this seat free?* Once a piece of pragmatics is conventionalized, it is stored as an item in the Mental Phraseicon and no longer needs the Pragmatic Processor to work on it. Expressions such as *Would you mind if . . .?* or *Could you pass the . . .?* do not need to be processed anew every time they are encountered, but simply retrieved from the Mental Phraseicon. (We saw a similar pattern with metaphor in the previous section.) The distinction between conventional and novel pragmatics corresponds with Grice's terms 'conventional implicature' and 'conversational implicature' (Grice 1975:45).

The reader might have the impression at this point that the Mental Phraseicon is a repository for quite an assortment of different items; this is indeed the case. Products of all three processors can be found in the phraseicon. It is a storehouse of conventional phrases derived from novel syntactic, metaphoric and pragmatic processing, processes Altenberg refers to as 'grammaticalization', 'lexicalization' and 'pragmaticalization' (Altenberg 1998:121). Or, to say it another way, it is the graveyard for 'dead syntax', 'dead metaphor' and 'dead pragmatics'. It should be also be noted here that although the Metaphor Processor and Pragmatic Processor may seem to be doing the same thing in the sense that they are both giving access to a second order or 'derived' meaning, they are in fact involved in quite different processes. The processes are different with respect to the role of context, the unit of language they operate on, and whether words are understood in their literal sense or not, as I now explain. 1) Pragmatics is concerned with meaning *in context* while metaphor can also be understood *out of context*. 2) The Pragmatic Processor works by resolving implicatures at the level of the *speech act*, while the Metaphor Processor works on a smaller scale, at the sub-word level, the level of the *seme*. 3) Individual words in conversational implicatures are usually intended in their literal sense. If *Is that radiator on?* is said in a context where the intended meaning is "I am cold, please turn the heating up", the words *radiator* and *on* are understood in the literal sense of "heating body" and "not 'off'". Figurative language can be part of a direct speech act; while non-figurative language may involve implicature. Kittay writes: "This is not simply a distinction between literal and figurative language, for there is non-figurative language that has a second-order meaning. Searle's case of indirect speech acts are of this sort—for example, 'Excuse me, you are stepping on my toe'" (Kittay 1987:44).

COHERENCE

The final component I am adding to my model of the linguistic mind is the *Mental Schema Store*, the store of abstract frames of thought and encyclopaedic knowledge. The complete model looks like this:

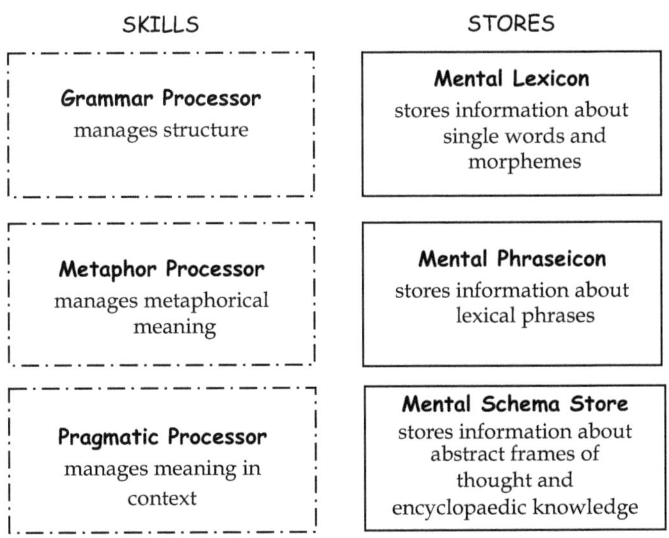

The Mental Schema Store is an important component, perhaps the most important in the whole model, because the knowledge it contains allows us to make sense of the world about us. It stores information about schemata, frames, scripts, genres, discourses, ideologies, narratives and conceptual metaphor; it stores information about mathematics and logic; the principles of pragmatics, eg 'cooperation' (Grice 1975:47), 'politeness', 'interest', 'Pollyanna', 'banter', 'irony' (Leech 1983:79–151) and 'relevance' (Sperber & Wilson 1986); how to construct discourse and text; mythology; narratology; frames for jokes, whether about mothers-in-law or men and lawnmowers; 'urban myths' like 'alligators in the sewer' and 'the baby on the roof rack' (Reeve 2002). It stores cultural knowledge in the broadest sense, ideas and concepts the individual has encountered, memory, identity, what makes you who you are—they are all in the Mental Schema Store. But, are we justified in including this vast store in a linguistic model and claiming it to be part of an individual's language competence? I think we are justified because we cannot do without these schemata, frames and scripts, if we are to operate effectively as language users.

Not only do we need to know the schemata, frames and scripts, but we also need to be able to switch quickly from one to another. Conceptual metaphors are abstract relations deriving from our experience of the world as a biological system, and do not always relate neatly to the rules of mathematics and logic. Sometimes they seem to throw up contradictions, for example: *to fill **in** a form* or *fill **out** a form* are interchangeable; *What is going **on** in here?* and *What is going **off** in here?* express the same idea in different ways in different varieties of British English; in a meeting someone might say *What we need here is an **overarching** strategy*, and, in another, someone may talk of the need for *an **underlying** strategy*. How is it that these expressions mean the same thing, although on the face of it they seem contradictory? This is because they draw on different conceptual metaphors and get at the same idea in different ways: IN and OUT are both involved in form filling; ON and OFF are both part of our conceptualization of something happening; and a structure can unify whether it is ABOVE or BELOW. Another example is the announcement of election results. After votes are counted, the results might be listed alphabetically in order of the candidates' names; they could be announced starting with the least successful candidate and ending with the winner; or they could be announced in the reverse order, starting with the winner, the conceptual metaphors MOST SUCCESSFUL IS FIRST and LEAST SUCCESSFUL IS FIRST both being available to us. Our ability to switch between schemata is so strongly developed, we even switch between them within a sentence. Mixed metaphors are what we have when there are two schemata in the same sentence, eg *Pensions have been plundered sky high* or *If you open a can of worms, they always come home to roost* or *He took the plunge by nailing his colours to the mast*. Mixed metaphors may be looked down upon by some on stylistic grounds, but they rarely pose problems of comprehension to the listener. Instead, they should be admired, as they reflect the fundamental skill of being able to change quickly and effortlessly between schematic frames.

DISCUSSION

Skills and Stores

The model presented in this chapter acknowledges the vital role played by grammar, lexis, phraseology, metaphor, pragmatics and coherence in enabling us to perform effectively as language users. The model is not intended to be controversial, as the six boxes represent six well-established areas of scholarly activity in linguistics. What is thought-provoking and innovative about the model is the distinction made between 'stores' and 'skills'. The stores are passive storehouses, while the skills are active processors. But they are also different in another respect, namely with regard to size: the stores are large, and constantly being added to, while the skills are centres which carry out only a few simple types of manipulation.

In the Mental Lexicon, there is information about individual words, their phonology, graphology, denotation, connotation, the grammatical category they belong to, whether they inflect regularly or not, which words they collocate with and how strongly, their frequency of use, information about register, and so on—all the information involved in 'knowing' a word. The Mental Phraseicon is also large, containing a huge number and variety of lexical phrases, and the Mental Schema Store, as discussed above, is vast. The skill centres only perform a few simple—but vital—types of operation: the Grammar Processor organizes word strings based on dominance and dependence; the Metaphor Processor organizes meaning at the sub-word level by selecting certain semes and suppressing others; the Pragmatic Processor encodes information about context used to 'enrich' propositional meaning. These operations may be few in type and simple in nature, but they are vital. It is because they are essential that the consequences are so great when they go wrong. Broca-type aphasia, the impairment of the ability to structure language, is an example of the disastrous effect of a lesion affecting the Grammar Processor.

But to say the operations are simple is not to underestimate their importance or undervalue the scholarship in these areas, in fact, the x-bar/minimalist approach to syntax (eg Radford 1997) and the single-principle 'relevance' approach to pragmatics of Sperber & Wilson (1986) suggest that scholars in these fields see it this way, too. My 'Stack of Counters model' of the Metaphor Processor, presented in Chapter 3, is also minimalist. It is the economy of the processors which invests them with their generative power. All three processors are generators of language in the Humboldtian sense of "making infinite use of finite means" (Chomsky 1965:8).

Metaphor and Pragmatics Revisited

The model presented in this chapter helps separate out phenomena which in the literature are often confusingly lumped together. It became apparent in the discussion above that metaphor is not a single phenomenon; instead, what

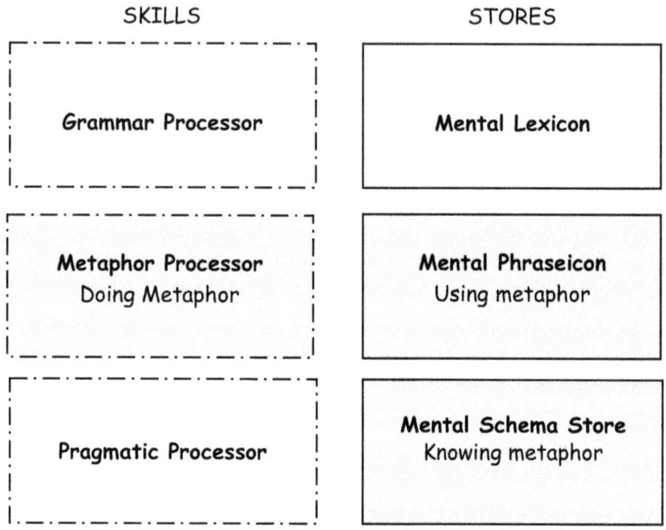

Figure 2.1 'Using', 'doing' and 'knowing' metaphor

Littlemore & Low call 'metaphoric competence' (eg Littlemore & Low 2006b) involves at least three 'boxes': 1) dead and conventionalized metaphor (lexical phrases of metaphoric origin), stored in the Mental Phraseicon—which we could call 'using metaphor'; 2) selectively highlighting and suppressing individual semes of a word/phrase to create novel metaphor, carried out by the Metaphor Processor—which we could call 'doing metaphor'; 3) abstract metaphoric frameworks, conceptual metaphors, such as GOOD IS UP, stored in the Mental Schema Store—which we could call 'knowing metaphor'. It is interesting to note the tendency of different disciplines to focus on different aspects within these: English Language Teaching has been mostly concerned with 'using', ie idioms; literary studies with 'doing'; and cognitive linguistics with 'knowing' metaphor. This pattern of using, doing and knowing is shown in Figure 2.1.

A similar pattern pertains to pragmatics. It is also shared between three components: 1) conventionalized pragmatics in the form of lexical phrases, 'using pragmatics', stored in the Mental Phraseicon; 2) encoding context to enrich the meaning of propositions, 'doing pragmatics', carried out by the Pragmatic Processor; 3) the principles and maxims of pragmatics, 'knowing pragmatics', stored in the Mental Schema Store, shown in Figure 2.2.

Connections and Interconnections

Looking in more detail at the Model of the Linguistic Mind presented above provokes further questions, of which the three considered below are of particular relevance to the present study. They concern Modularity, Connecting to the Outside World and the Bilingual Mind.

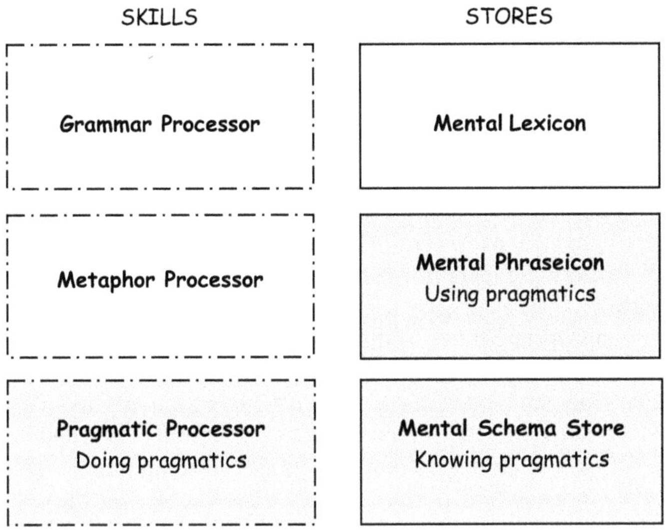

Figure 2.2 'Using', 'doing' and 'knowing' pragmatics

MODULARITY

What connections are there between the different components of the model and to what extent are the components 'modular'?

For the model accurately to represent the linguistic mind, each component will need to interact with all other components. The connections will be between processors, between stores and between stores and processors. If we take the word *green* in the environmental sense as an example, in the mind of the language user there will be information for it in the Mental Lexicon, in the Mental Phraseicon for expressions such as *green issues* and *Green Party*, and encyclopaedic information in the Mental Schema Store, where a whole discourse about green issues is represented in a pre-linguistic form. These are mental representations of the ideas rather than linguistic forms, as the 'green schema' could be expressed visually or gesturally as well as verbally. There would also be connections between the lexical item *green* and equivalents in other languages, if information of this sort had been acquired.

CONNECTING TO THE OUTSIDE WORLD

What connections are there between the six components of the model and the world outside the mind?

When we consider the 'outside world', there need to be connections via the senses to all three stores in order that their contents can be recognized when encountered in speech and writing and so that they can be added to. A connection between the 'outside world' and the Pragmatic Processor is also necessary in order to encode/decode external contexts; and connections between the 'outside world' and the Grammar Processor and the Metaphor Processor are necessary in order that utterances can be decoded. Connections are not needed for 'doing grammar' and 'doing metaphor', as these can occur as mental processes in isolation. Activity in the mind without external stimuli is significant in a broader sense: in work on simulation, the mental activity involved in a subject's imagined and re-enacted physical action (or 'as if' action), was found closely to resemble mental activity during events in which a subject actually participated (Gibbs & Matlock 2008).

This is an appropriate place in this discussion to consider briefly five models of intelligence and cognition in order to situate the Model of the Linguistic Mind in the wider context of cognitive psychology. I discuss the works of Gardner (1983), Sternberg (1990), Anderson (1983), Newell (1990) and Rumelhart & McClelland (1987). Gardner's theory of 'multiple intelligences' is concerned with exploring individual differences more than identifying basic brain functions, and therefore does not have particular resonance with my model (Gardner 1983). The three elements identified in Sternberg's 'triarchic theory of human intelligence', the 'analytic', 'creative' and 'practical' do have a resonance: the analytic element corresponds to an individual's receptive skills and the creative element to productive skills; while the 'heuristics', 'algorithms' and 'problem solving' elements resemble the processors in my model, and the 'expert systems' and 'knowledge organizers' resemble the stores in my model (Sternberg 1990). There is also an approximate correspondence between the 'declarative memory modules' of Anderson's 'Adaptive Control of Thought-Rational' (ACT-R) integrated modular model of the mind and the stores in my model, and between the 'goal modules' and 'production rules' in Anderson's model and the skills in my model (Anderson 1983). All the modules in my model have contact with the 'outside world': it is through auditory, visual, tactile, olfactory and taste sensory perception that new material comes to be included; while input from the immediate environment is required by the processors for online processing. Anderson gives importance to sensory input, represented in his model by 'perceptual motor modules' (Anderson 1983). Newell's theory of cognition is based on generic rules and general problem solving operations similar to the tasks the Grammar Processor, Metaphor Processor and Pragmatic Processor carry out in my model (Newell 1990). Connectionist models are less modular and suggest that processing language is more diffuse and volatile, involving 'spreading activation' rather than discrete locations associated with specific concepts (Rumelhart & McClelland 1987). I have chosen to present the linguistic skills and stores of the mind as modules, though in the physical brain they are probably more accurately represented by 'structured connectionism' and 'spreading activation' of the sort collaborations at Berkeley are exploring in the context of the Neural Theory of Language (Lakoff 2008:18).

THE BILINGUAL MIND

What are the connections between the set of skills and stores for each language in the mind of speakers working with more than one language?

When we turn our attention to the bilingual mind, I envisage a unique set of *stores* for each language but not necessarily a unique set of *skills*. I would speculate that the skills represented by the Grammar Processor, Metaphor Processor and Pragmatic Processor could well be recruited to manage a second or third language. The Mental Schema Store would also be shared, as many schemata are universal 'primary' conceptual metaphors, such as AFFECTION IS WARMTH (Gibbs 1994, Lakoff & Johnson 1999, Kövecses 2005). Many schemata are culturally specific and so many schemata will not transfer: "variation in metaphor appears to be just as important and common as universality" (Kövecses 2005:3). For example, Yasuo Fukuda, the former prime minister of Japan, acquired in some circles the nickname *maguro* (tuna). The connotation in Japanese culture is someone who is lazy and ineffectual, sometimes with a sexual innuendo, but this does not necessarily transfer to other cultures (where the term 'tuna' may have other connotations, such as high price, size, speed and the like). The situation in the bilingual mind proposed above is summarized in Figure 2.3.

The diagram shows the Mental Lexicon and Mental Phraseicon connected via collocation—thus representing the idea of a continuum from free combination to lexical phrases discussed above—and the Mental Phraseicon and Mental Schema Store as contiguous. In addition, the proximity in the diagram of the L1 and L2

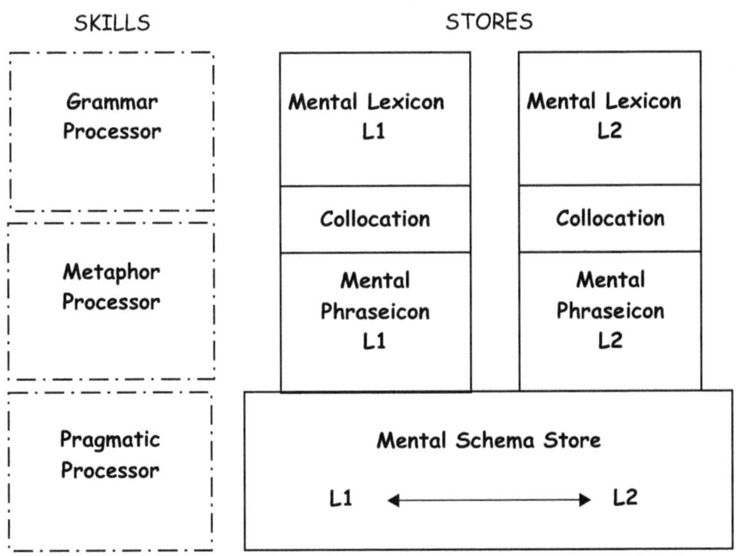

Figure 2.3 Modelling the bilingual mind

lexica and phraseica is intended to indicate that there is interaction between the two. This is compatible with Cook's notion of 'multicompetence', according to which the bilingual mind neither involves 'total separation' of the L1 and L2 mind nor 'total integration', but a collection of interconnections between the two in which continua of associations and gradients of difference exist (Cook 2002). This also aligns with Paradis' model of the bilingual mind in which there are two sets of neural connections, one for each language, as well as other neural networks shared by both (Paradis 2004).

CONCLUSION

Grammar, lexis, phraseology, metaphor, pragmatics and coherence all play an important role in the Model of the Linguistic Mind built up in this chapter. It is suggested that all six components are interconnected and constantly interactive. Clearly, anyone who works with two languages, or more, ie bilinguals, language learners, translators and interpreters, needs to be aware of all six 'boxes', as neglecting any one of them will disadvantage their overall linguistic competence. This chapter, though speculative in nature, aims to offer a practical research tool for investigating the bilingual mind and its application in the areas of text analysis, language learning and translation, and training in those areas, to which I return in Chapters 6, 7 and 8. The next chapter looks in more detail at 'doing' metaphor, our ability to create and understand novel metaphor.

3 The Ability to Metaphorize

Three components of metaphoric competence were identified in the previous chapter. The Model of the Linguistic Mind presented there allowed us to differentiate between 'using', 'doing' and 'knowing' metaphor. This chapter looks more closely at one of these components, 'doing metaphor', the skill of being able to create and understand novel metaphor, the ability to metaphorize. I draw on both traditional and more recent theories of metaphor in order to understand what exactly novel metaphor is in terms of linguistic and cognitive manipulations. I argue that the ability to metaphorize is characterized by feature-level manipulations and that these manipulations have a fundamental role not only within metaphor but also in many other areas of linguistic communication outside metaphor. This is demonstrated in my Stack of Counters model presented here. I also consider literal language and ask how literal comparisons differ from metaphoric comparisons, and survey the functions of metaphor in order to test the Stack of Counters model.

NOVEL METAPHOR IN CLOSER FOCUS

The metaphor literature is vast and ranges over many disciplines, as noted already, metaphor having been taken up by philosophy, poetics, semantics, pragmatics, discourse analysis, stylistics, psycholinguistics, psychology, computational linguistics and, of course, cognitive linguistics. The exciting rise of Metaphor Studies has been well documented and the literature which it has spawned has been well reviewed (especially Ortony 1993b, Cameron & Low 1999b, Cameron 2003, Gibbs 2008 and Cameron 2010). I do not need to repeat what can be found in these overviews; instead, it is my intention to look specifically at what scholars have said about novel metaphor, and in so doing reconcile the multiplicity of approaches found in the literature into a single workable model.

It seems apposite before I do so to recognize the sea-change which Metaphor Studies has brought about by reiterating some of the opinions which scholars have expressed regarding the importance of metaphor. These opinions sit on a spectrum from 'very important' to 'indispensable'. Metaphor is now seen as essential in everyday communication, rather than optional or marginal, and playing a significant role in all types of communication: "figurative language is not deviant or ornamental but is ubiquitous in everyday speech" (Gibbs 1994:16). Deignan maintains that writing about 'life' *without* using language to do with journeys is difficult and that writing about 'feelings' without using an unrelated domain is similarly challenging (Deignan 2005:13–18, 2006). Pinker, in a similar experiment, demonstrates the impossibility of rewriting the American Declaration of Independence without using metaphor (Pinker 2007:235–238). Goddard observes how hard it is to talk about emotions without using metaphor and also observes that many words used to talk about music are personification metaphors, such as *serene*, *melancholy*, *uneasy*, *aggressive*, and many words used to talk about wine are synaesthesic metaphors, such as *cool*, *warm*, *hot*, *peppery*, *tart* (Goddard 2000:148).

Littlemore considers metaphor to be present in all language and communication and "so pervasive in language that it would be impossible for a person to speak without using metaphor at some point whether knowingly or not" (Littlemore 2001b:1). For Cameron & Low, metaphor is "the way human beings consolidate and extend their ideas about themselves, their relationships and their knowledge of the world" (Cameron & Low 1999b:xii). For Chandler "banishing metaphor is an impossible task since it is central to language" (Chandler 2002:126); while for Lakoff, metaphor is important both in everyday conversation and in technical discourse: "much subject matter, from the most mundane to the most abstruse scientific theories, can only be comprehended via metaphor" (Lakoff 1993:244). Jakobson recognizes the equal importance of metaphor and metonymy and that "in normal verbal behaviour both processes are continually operative" (Jakobson 1956/1971:90). But it is in philosophy that we find the boldest claims for metaphor: Johnson considers that "perennial philosophical questions" can't be answered without metaphor (Johnson 2008:40); while Nietzsche famously claims that: "The drive towards the formation of metaphors is the fundamental human drive, which one cannot for a single instance dispense with in thought, for one would thereby dispense with man himself" (Nietzsche 1873/1979).

The Rarity of Novel Metaphor

While there is agreement in the Metaphor-Studies literature that metaphor is vital and ubiquitous, it is acknowledged at the same time that novel metaphor is relatively rare. The distinction here is between metaphor which is original and unfamiliar, on the one hand ('doing metaphor' in the terminology used in Chapter 2), and metaphor which has been conventionalized and is already part of the corpus of the language community, on the other ('using metaphor'). Lakoff expresses this idea thus: "As common as novel metaphor is, its occurrence is rare by comparison with conventional metaphor, which occurs in most of the sentences we utter" (Lakoff 1993:237). A variety of terms has been used in the Metaphor-Studies literature for non-conventionalized,

Table 3.1 Comparison of terms

	Terms corresponding to my category of 'conventional' metaphor	**Terms corresponding to my category of 'novel' metaphor**
Davidson (1979)	DEAD metaphor	LIVING metaphor
Lakoff & Johnson (1980)	LITERAL metaphor	IMAGINATIVE metaphor
Kittay (1987)	DEAD metaphor	NOVEL metaphor
Black (1993)	WEAK metaphor	STRONG metaphor
Searle (1993)	DEAD metaphor	METAPHORIC utterance
Gibbs (1994)	DEAD metaphor	NOVEL metaphor
Goatly (1997)	DEAD metaphor	ACTIVE metaphor
Cameron (2003)	LINGUISTIC metaphor	PROCESS metaphor
Knowles & Moon (2006)	CONVENTIONAL metaphor	CREATIVE metaphor

spontaneous, one-off metaphors. As well as 'novel metaphor' (eg Kittay 1987, Lakoff 1993, Gibbs 1994), we find 'strong' (Black 1993), 'living' (Davidson 1979), 'imaginative' (Lakoff & Johnson 1980), 'alive' (Lakoff 1987b), 'metaphoric' (Searle 1993), 'active' (Goatly 1997), 'creative' (Knowles & Moon 2006:5) and 'process' (Cameron 2003). These terms are contrasted with 'conventional' (Knowles & Moon), 'weak' (Black), 'dead' (Davidson, Kittay, Searle, Gibbs and Goatly) and 'linguistic' (Cameron). These terms are summarized in Table 3.1.

Many attempts have been made to quantify the frequency of metaphor. Hoffman estimates that a speaker of English on average produces 3,000 novel metaphors a week (Littlemore 2001b:1). Graesser et al found political commentaries and debates on TV to contain a 'unique' metaphor every 25 words (Whitney 1998:224). Pollio et al found five examples of figurative language per one hundred words in counselling data of which a third were novel and estimate that an L1-speaker uses about 10 million original metaphors and 20 million conventional metaphors in a lifetime (Pollio et al 1977). More recently, Steen, from his study of metaphor occurrence in various genres (academic discourse, news discourse, fiction and conversation) using British English and Dutch corpus data, found that fewer than 1% of the metaphors were novel, ie not already in the conceptual system (Steen 2008:220). Such quantitative measures indicate the relative infrequency of novel metaphors and may explain why conventional metaphors have been studied so much more intensely. Added to this, there is a tendency for individuals to favour conventional language and processing which is automatic over conscious choices as "metaphorical thought is unavoidable, ubiquitous, and mostly unconscious" (Lakoff & Johnson 1980/2003:272). It is therefore perhaps understandable that creative uses have been neglected. Aitchison sees conventional 'automatic' language as being one which is encouraged by the educational system: "Education channels children towards conventional usages and less colourful speech" and the use of novel language "fades fastest among children who attend reputedly 'good' schools" (Aitchison 1994:154). My interest here is with this less prioritized area of production and reception, because, I feel, in spite of it seeming marginal, in fact it has a greater impact on everyday communication than has been acknowledged.

In Chapter 2, I offered a four-term classification of linguistic metaphor into 'historical', 'dead', 'conventional' and 'novel'. This is based on the degree of conventionalization, which determines how that expression is processed. Historical metaphors do not offer any potential for metaphoric extension because there is not a more basic 'physical' meaning available to the speaker. Similarly, 'dead metaphors', such as *to be on tenterhooks*, *to be at loggerheads*, *to cock a snook*, cannot easily be extended, but there is a sense they could be were the speaker to know what the terms *tenterhooks*, *loggerheads* and *snooks* originally meant. In data from my notebooks, a radio presenter explicitly asks this: "We are all on tenterhooks here at BBC London, whatever tenterhooks are. What are tenterhooks?" (*The Late Show*, BBC London, 20 January 2008). Black does not consider the term 'dead metaphor' useful and avoids it, as for him "a so-called dead metaphor is not a metaphor at all" (Black 1993:25). Lakoff also recommends either avoiding the term 'dead metaphor', as it is confusingly used to refer to four different phenomena exemplified by *pedigree*, *dunk*, *comprehend* and *grasp* (Lakoff 1987a:146), or reserving it for words such as *pedigree*, where neither conceptual mappings nor linguistic mappings exist (Lakoff 1987a:147). For me, the distinction between historical and dead metaphor is useful, for although historical and dead metaphors are retrieved from the Mental Lexicon as ready-made signs without the need for them to be processed by the Metaphor Processor, dead metaphors can be explored and 'interrogated' in a way that historical metaphors cannot.

Conventional metaphors, such as *to spill the beans*, *to see light at the end of the tunnel* or *to go bananas*, are also processed as ready-made signs, but retrieved from the Mental Phraseicon rather than the Mental Lexicon. Research from psychology suggests that idioms are more likely to be processed as chunks 'straight off', rather than decomposed into their literal elements and interpreted metaphorically to fit the context in which they occur. Gibbs reviews the relevant evidence for this claim (Gibbs 1994, 2008), and suggests, contrary to Bobrow & Bell's 'idiom-list' or 'literal-first' hypothesis, that "literal processing is not a default mode of understanding normal discourse" where idioms are concerned (Gibbs 1986:28). But although it seems that conventional metaphors are processed as chunks, there is encoded in them the potential for metaphoric extension, achieved by analyzing the expression to access literal senses from the same domain and then exploiting the connotations of those senses, as in these examples:

> We are getting on like a house on fire, or rather a house quietly smouldering.
> (Data Notebooks)

> Some of my father's ideas are half baked, or not even baked at all. In fact, sometimes he hasn't even got the ingredients together.
>
> (Data Notebooks)

> He's got egg on his face. He's got egg on more than his face—he's got it on his hair, his hands, his clothes. His whole body's got egg on it.
>
> (Data Notebooks)

> I'm not a one-trick pony. I'm not a ten-trick pony. I've got a whole field of ponies waiting to literally run towards this.
>
> (*The Apprentice*, BBC1 TV, 8 December 2010)

> I have a fabulous support network here—people who want to help me through this and make sure I don't completely lose my marbles. I am sure I have lost a few. They are rolling around on the floor, and I'll find them when I am packing up to leave.
>
> (Flat out at Work, C. Neilan, *FT Magazine*, May 6/7 2006, p.7)

The fourth category, novel metaphor, expressions such as *Libraries are goldmines*, *Friends are anchors*, *Jobs are jails*, *Alcohol is a crutch*, *Surgeons are butchers* and *Vision is like a tap*, is quite different. They require to be processed as metaphors and involve manipulations of the Metaphor Processor in their creation and interpretation, or as I have named it above, 'doing metaphor'. The 'paradox of metaphor' Steen identifies is that what we generally call metaphor does not involve cross-domain mapping and, in an attempt to resolve this paradox, he introduces the term 'deliberate' metaphor, defined as metaphor which changes "the addressee's perspective [. . .] by making the addressee look at it from a different conceptual domain" (Steen 2008:222). Gibbs questions the notion of 'deliberate' metaphor, arguing that it is far from clear when metaphor is used deliberately, as it is hard to assess what is in fact performed consciously; that cross-domain processing may well be involved in non-deliberate metaphor; and that the 'tuning devices' used to signal metaphor are often also employed to signal non-figurative language (Gibbs 2011). Nonetheless, it is this ability to perform cross-domain manipulations, whether they are consciously performed or not, an ability we undoubtedly possess, which is the principal concern of this chapter and this book as a whole. I argue in the chapters which follow that these manipulations are important not only in metaphoric meaning making, but also more generally across other linguistic phenomena, and help explain the subtlety of expression achieved by language and its fitness for purpose.

It is important to note here that, for the purposes of the present discussion, I am including 'simile', 'metaphor' and 'analogy' as types of metaphoric comparisons, notwithstanding that many scholars argue for them being distinct (reviewed in Steen 2007). What distinguishes similes from metaphors is the inclusion of the marker *like*, but the metaphoric idea is the same—compare *Billboards are like warts* and *Billboards are warts*. Holme calls similes 'marked metaphors' (Holme 2004:89). I should add that while considering the metaphoric idea to be the same, I acknowledge that any differences between two strings of words, however small, such as the addition of a word, may result in the two strings being processed differently and potentially giving different meanings. There is nothing unusual about signalling a comparison linguistically. Signalling can take the form of a single word, such as *like*, or it can be a performative verb, eg *Shall I compare thee to a summer's day*, or even an elaborate sentence with numerous hedges such as, *It could be said that in a certain sense some features of the present conflict in the Far East can be seen as having similarities with the situation in Northern Ireland.* All these set up metaphoric ideas. Analogies are also metaphoric ideas, but presented as an explicit relationship between four elements of the sort "A is to B as X is to Y" (sometimes notated as A:B::X:Y). Analogies, like comparisons, can be literal or metaphoric. If they are metaphoric, A and B are from the target domain and X and Y from the source domain; if intended as literal, such as lawyer:client::doctor:patient, the elements are taxonomically more closely related.

The four categories discussed above closely resemble Deignan's categories of, what she calls, 'metaphorically-motivated linguistic expressions', namely 'historical', 'dead', 'conventionalized' and 'innovative' metaphors (Deignan 2005:39). But while Deignan is interested in permanence and frequency of particular usages as evidenced by corpus data, basing her distinction between 'conventional' and 'dead' metaphor on relative 'coreness' and 'dependency' (Deignan 2005:42), my concern is with mental processing and the involvement of the Metaphor Processor. Goatly has five categories: 'active', 'tired', 'sleeping', 'dead' and 'dead and buried' (Goatly 1997:34), a useful refinement but one which I will not pursue, as the categories of novel versus conventional are sufficient for my purposes. The categorizations of Deignan, Lakoff and Goatly, and my own, are on what Deignan describes as a cline from the metaphors you notice to those you do not notice (Deignan 2006) and represent classifications based on current or 'synchronic' use; but it is clear that an historical or 'diachronic' progression is also envisaged here, whereby expressions start life as novel, then progress to become conventional, and then perhaps become dead or even historical. Bowdle and Gentner are scholars of this longitudinal change in status of metaphoric expressions, referring to it as the 'career of metaphor' (Bowdle & Gentner 2005, Gentner & Bowdle 2008). Handl, too, investigates the conceptual principles involved in the conventionalization of metaphoric and metonymic expressions, and, using corpus data, speculates why it is that certain expressions become conventionalized and others not (Handl 2011).

Whether an expression is perceived as conventional assumes a certain degree of conformity across a speech community, but a single expression can of course be perceived differently by individuals and show variation across idiolects. The varying status of a single expression has been explored by applied linguists, such as Littlemore (2001b) and Holme (2004). Littlemore observes that what is conventional for one speaker is not necessarily conventional for all speakers, and that language learners will often process conventional metaphor differently from the way in which non-learners do: "What is a frozen metaphor to a native speaker is a novel metaphor to a language learner when he or she encounters it for the first time" (Littlemore 2001b:1), and, for this reason, 'familiar' and 'unfamiliar' may be more useful terms in this context than 'conventional' and 'novel'. Holme introduces the term 'inadvertent metaphor' for expressions which a learner uses thinking them to be standard or conventional but which require native speakers to process them as novel (Holme 2004), an idea I return to in Chapter 7.

In the remainder of this section, I consider individual accounts of scholars who have made a particularly valuable contribution to understanding metaphor in communication. They are Lakoff, Fauconnier & Turner, Steen, Deignan and Cameron. Although focussing mainly on conventional metaphor, 'using metaphor', these studies take us nearer to understanding what goes on when we create novel metaphor, 'doing metaphor', offering insights into what is at the core of our ability to metaphorize and the active use of the Metaphor Processor.

Lakoff

Whether we consider the original exposition in *Metaphors We Live By* (Lakoff & Johnson 1980) or later works by Lakoff (eg Lakoff 1993), the linguistic metaphors which are considered are almost entirely conventional. The concern is with how embodied associations between domains in the brain are manifest in conventionalized language, rather than whether these embodiments are expressed through novel or conventionalized language. The Neural Theory of Language (NTL), the product of the collaboration between Lakoff and Berkeley neuroscientists (particularly Feldman) reinforces this (Lakoff 2008). According to the NTL, conceptual metaphors are replaced by neural mappings, metaphors being relatively simple neural circuits in which connections are created and strengthened by repeated activation of the brain in two places at the same time (Fauconnier & Lakoff 2010:2). Even the novel metaphors characteristic of literature are understood by Lakoff & Turner to come about through the combination of conceptual metaphors already in existence in the conventional metaphors system (Lakoff & Turner 1989). For Lakoff, novel metaphors, when they do occur, come about in three ways: from the extension of conventional metaphors (used here to mean conceptual metaphors, such as LIFE IS A JOURNEY), from generic-level metaphors (eg EVENTS ARE ACTIONS), and from image metaphors (Lakoff 1993:237). 'Image metaphors' are usually based on resemblances in physical shape, created when you "map one conventional mental image onto another" (Lakoff 1993:229). They are 'one-shot' metaphors in that they are "used for one term only" and as a result are not productive and systematic in the way 'rich' metaphors are (Lakoff 1987a:144), though, I would argue, being visual does not make them any less conceptual. Lakoff gives the example *My wife . . . whose waist is an hourglass*, where the hourglass shape is mapped onto the wife's waist (Lakoff 1993:229), and *dunk* in basketball, where the rim of a cup is mapped to the rim of the basket and the pastry is mapped to the ball (Lakoff 1987a:144).

Fauconnier & Turner

While Lakoff explains how our conceptual system is structured with regard to metaphor, Fauconnier & Turner's 'blended space' theory offers a model of how metaphoric meaning is construed 'online' (in other words, in real time) in serving participants at particular moments in face-to-face interaction (Fauconnier & Turner 2002). It is thus a more dynamic and temporal approach to construal and less concerned with the systematicity of metaphor, and therefore very relevant to the study of novel metaphor. For Fauconnier & Turner, a unique 'blended space' emerges from the interaction between two 'input spaces', via mappings to a 'generic space' (Fauconnier & Turner 2002). Comparing it to Lakoff's Conceptual Metaphor Theory approach, 'blended space' theory has a wider scope, applying to all types of blend, not just metaphoric blends but also literal blends. The blend between BREAKFAST and LUNCH to give *brunch* (Radden 2008a:398) and the concept of *Jewish Pizza* (Lakoff & Johnson 1980/2003:263) are literal blends. Because blends other than metaphoric blends are included, and because many input spaces can concurrently combine in creating a blend, in blended space theory there is no emphasis on directionality.

I now turn to three scholars, Steen, Deignan and Cameron, whose work is characterized by an interest in the emergent meaning of metaphor in discourse. Theirs are what might be called 'discourse-analysis approaches'. Their work is of interest in the present argument as all three combine an awareness of Cognitive Metaphor Theory and traditional metaphor theory with an understanding of discourse and genre. They also have in common that they use empirical data to support their hypotheses.

Steen

Steen investigates metaphor not in isolation but in the context of the 'genre event' in which it is found, seeing the use of metaphor as goal-directed, situated in practice and regulated by genre knowledge (Steen 2008). Research studies at the Vrije Universiteit Amsterdam have analyzed empirical data and revealed that 99% of the examples of metaphor across various genres were conventional and that few of these (one in a thousand) were expressed in a classic 'A is like B' form, "the arena in which the fiercest battles about psycholinguistic models of metaphor are fought" (Steen 2008:227). This presents a paradox to Steen: it means that most metaphors are not processed as metaphors in the sense of involving two domains and cross-domain mapping (ie 'doing metaphor'), in spite of this being central to definitions of metaphor (Steen 2008).

To resolve this, Steen recommends a 'three-dimensional model' of metaphor. Steen argues that metaphor is not all language, as relevance theorists would have us believe ('contra-relevance' hypothesis); not all thought, as cognitive linguists would have us believe ('contra thought'); and not all thought and language, as some discourse analysts would lead us to believe ('contra language and thought'). Steen also reminds us that there are two senses of 'metaphor as thought': 'thought' in the sense of semiotic knowledge, knowledge of mental concepts and how they are organized in the mind; and 'thought' in the sense of mental processing in a psycholinguistic sense. The three dimensions of Steen's model are 'language', 'thought' and 'communication', which he tags 'naming', 'framing' and 'changing' (Steen 2008:230). He identifies the function of each of these dimensions as follows: "The linguistic function of metaphor is to fill lexical [. . .] gaps in the language system [= 'naming']; The conceptual function of metaphor is to offer conceptual frameworks for concepts that require at least partial indirect understanding [= 'framing']; The communicative function of metaphor is to produce an alternative perspective on a particular referent or topic in a message [= 'changing']" (Steen 2008:231).

The third dimension, metaphor as communication, resolves the paradox of metaphor, but also invites Steen to introduce a new pair of terms, 'deliberate' and 'non-deliberate' metaphor, which he considers are more useful in this context than 'novel' and 'conventional' (Steen 2008:237). In 'deliberate metaphor' the "communicative function is to shift the addressee's attention to another domain and set up some cross-domain mapping", while with 'non-deliberate metaphor' the "communicative function is not a matter of cross-domain mapping in symbolic structure or in cognitive processing and representation" (Steen 2008:227). But this is not just a renaming of novel and conventional, as conventional and non-deliberate are not equivalent terms because, as Steen explains: "It is quite possible for people to use conventional metaphor very deliberately [. . .]. Examples of such usage can be found on the sports page of any newspaper, where deliberate metaphor use is signaled by word play and other added rhetorical devices" (Steen 2008:223).

Deignan

Deignan takes a similar approach; for her, metaphor is "a textual and social phenomenon as well as a cognitive one" (Deignan 2008:280). Metaphor emerges in interactions because it is a text resource, a discourse resource and a cognitive resource. Cognitive Metaphor Theory (CMT), though presented as if it were contemporary, is in fact quite traditional, according to Deignan, in that it focusses on representation rather than interaction (Deignan 2006). When authentic data are analyzed, metaphor appears to be set up or 'primed' both conceptually and linguistically, conceptual metaphor being the more generalized motivation, adapted in specific ways when expressed linguistically: "What are found [. . .] are metaphorically and metonymically used words that seem to develop their own life and linguistic associations in the target domain" (Deignan 2005:222).

Deignan likens our linguistic metaphor system to a street map, where the streets are not organized in neat blocks as CMT suggests, but involves backruns and alleyways, "not the logical grid networks of planned modern cities, but collections of different sized and merging villages, with interconnecting roads" (Deignan 2005:222). Deignan demonstrates this using corpus data, certain expressions being nearly always used with metaphoric meanings, such as *shoot down in flames*, *all guns blazing*, *heavy blow* and *pay a high price* (Deignan 2008:287); while other expressions, such as *keep an eye on* have different degrees of metaphoricity depending on their collocates, eg *children*, *housing association flats*, *progress* (Deignan 2008:292). For Deignan lexical priming is as important as conceptual priming: "In common with other features of language in use, metaphors are shaped by their linguistic context, genre, culture, and ideology as well as their informational content" (Deignan 2008:293). Deignan argues that true ambiguity is rare in naturally-occurring language because there is so much contextualization both from the situation and the text itself, semantic and sociolinguistic indicators serving to signal whether metaphor is intended or not (Deignan 2005:217). Although the data studied by Deignan are conventional metaphors, the approach which emphasizes face-to-face interaction is a useful tool for investigating novel metaphor.

Cameron

Like Steen and Deignan, Cameron is concerned with the dynamic role played by metaphor in discourse and its use in creating emergent meaning 'online' in face-to-face talk. Cameron employs data from reconciliation dialogues between Jo Berry and Pat Magee, the daughter of a man murdered by the IRA in Ireland and his murderer (Cameron 2008, 2011). Cameron looks at sections of the dialogues where 'metaphor density', calculated as the number of linguistic metaphors per 1,000 words, is particularly high (Cameron 2008:199). Like Steen, she finds that the metaphors she identifies, although rarely novel, are used deliberately: "Novel metaphors—which seem to occur quite rarely in spontaneous talk—are deliberate, since some kind of search for an appropriate expression must have preceded production" (Cameron 2008:202); and that metaphor has a significant role in managing discourse: "The creativity of metaphor in talk appears less in the novelty of connected domains and more in the use of metaphor to shape a discourse event and in the adaptation of metaphor in the flow of talk" (Cameron 2008:197). Discourse events are managed by the use of metaphor to make difficult topics approachable, conventional metaphor being used in these dialogues to 'distance' or 'de-emphasize' "when the topic of talk is uncomfortable" (Cameron 2008:203).

An important point Cameron makes is that conventionalization is a process which can take place between two people within a single interaction, not only within a larger speech community over a longer period of time. She also observes that a conventionalized use once established between two speakers in one interaction may be taken up again in a subsequent interaction: "Conventionalization is a dynamic process that takes place within the talk of a discourse community and from which emerges a metaphor that can act as common currency in future talk" (Cameron 2008:202). Like Deignan, Cameron sees language as having a 'life' independent of thought in the sense that there may be systematicity within language which does not reflect cognitive systematicity. Cameron introduces the concept of a 'systematic linguistic metaphor', that is, the recognition of metaphoric patterns of use, such as *RECONCILIATION IS CONNECTION* in her data, without actually constituting conceptual metaphors (Cameron 2008:208). For Cameron, discourse-analysis studies have the merit of not claiming to generalize beyond what is offered by the data, leaving broader conclusions and generalizations, gained from abstracting away from the data, to cognitive linguists (Cameron 2008:208).

The work of Steen, Deignan and Cameron, considered in this section, prioritizes conventional metaphor over metaphorization. Their work is germane to the present study, as it emphasizes emergent and creative meaning and the use of metaphor as a flexible resource in discourse. In the next section, I identify three themes which recur in the Metaphor-Studies literature, and which I pursue in order to arrive at an even more precise ontology of novel metaphor and a better understanding of what is involved when the Metaphor Processor is in active use.

A MORE PRECISE ONTOLOGY OF NOVEL METAPHOR

The metaphor literature offers a plethora of different theories on what metaphor is and how it is used, some of which have already been referred to in this chapter. 'Different' here could be understood to mean 'competing', but what we have in fact is a constellation of different but compatible 'takes' on metaphor, each offering a particular emphasis and reflecting the discipline which inspired it. In this section, I look across the theories of metaphor in order to identify common themes which will allow us to arrive at a more precise ontology of novel metaphor. The themes I identify are that: 1) metaphor involves two domains; 2) metaphor involves a transfer between these two domains and in one direction; and 3) certain contents are selected for transfer while others are suppressed. I look at these in turn below.

Two Domains

Traditional scholars and cognitive linguists concur that it is necessary to have two unrelated entities in order to create metaphor. For both, metaphor is seeing one thing in terms of another, but while traditional scholars identify these as linguistic components, cognitive linguists identify them as primarily conceptual. There is agreement that metaphor generally goes from a more physical source domain to a more abstract target domain, eg TIME IS MOTION (Lakoff 1993:216–218). Traditional scholars refer to the two entities variously as 'tenor' and 'vehicle' (Richards 1936), 'frame' and 'focus' (Black 1962), and 'topic' and 'vehicle' (Leech 1969); while cognitive linguists refer to them as 'target domain' and 'source domain'

(Lakoff & Johnson 1980) or 'trigger' and 'target' input spaces (Fauconnier & Turner 2002). Littlemore & Low, in their consideration of educational discourse, adopt a combining approach, using 'source' and 'target' to refer to both linguistic expressions and conceptual domains: "we use the labels 'source' and 'target' here for both linguistic and conceptual metaphors" and "talk of 'domains' in both cases" (Littlemore & Low 2006b:290). This, I think, is a useful solution. Cognitive linguists have refined what is meant by a 'domain' by adding 'basic', 'abstract', 'simple', 'complex' and 'matrix' to the terminology. For Langacker, a 'basic' domain indicates a domain which derives from a directly-embodied human experience and an 'abstract' domain, one which does not (Langacker 1987:148–150). Langacker refers to 'simple' domains and a complex 'matrix' of domains to indicate an integrated collection of domains, such as the parts of the body making up the matrix BODY (Langacker 1987:152). Croft uses the terms 'domain' and 'domain matrix' (Croft 1993); Lakoff refers to an 'Idealized Cognitive Model' (ICM) and 'complex ICM' (Lakoff 1987b:282); while Kövecses extends the idea to event structure, and uses the term 'event ICM' and 'complex event ICM' (Kövecses 2002:152,161).

Cognitive linguists also make refinements regarding different types of conceptual metaphor. The distinction Grady makes between 'primary' and 'complex' metaphors is the most significant (Grady 1997). Primary metaphors are more basic than complex metaphors and involve basic notions such as time, causation, events, emotions, etc (Lakoff & Johnson 1980/2003:257): "There are hundreds of [. . .] primary conceptual metaphors, most of them learned unconsciously and automatically in childhood simply by functioning in the everyday world with a human body and brain" (Lakoff & Johnson 1980/2003:256–257). The combining of primary metaphors to form complex metaphors is compared by Grady to atoms combining together to form molecules (Lakoff & Johnson 1999:46). This agglutination has consequences for how metaphors appear in different cultures. Primary metaphors derive more directly from bodily experience and are more likely to be universal, whereas complex metaphors, being made up of a combination of primary metaphors, are more likely to be culturally specific (Kövecses 2005:11, Yu 2008:248). Fauconnier & Turner see complexity in terms of 'multiblends', where outputs become inputs for new cross-space mappings, creating networks, such as those around 'Dracula', the 'birth stork' and the 'grim reaper' (Fauconnier & Turner 2002:279–295).

Directional Transfer

The compatibility of traditional theories and theories from cognitive linguistics is also to be seen when we consider transfer between domains. The traditional 'comparison theory', which goes back to Aristotle, is not inconsistent with the wording of Goatly's definition, "A metaphor occurs when a unit of discourse is used to refer to an object, concept, process, quality, relationship or world to which it does not conventionally refer" (Goatly 1997:108–109), or this statement from Lakoff & Johnson: "The essence of metaphor is understanding and experiencing one kind of thing in terms of another" (Lakoff & Johnson 1980:5). The 'interaction theory', developed by Black, in which an 'implicative complex' is created by the interaction of the first and second subject (Black 1962), is not far away from Fauconnier & Turner's notion of a 'blended space' (Fauconnier & Turner 2002), or even the 'ad-hoc concept' of Sperber & Wilson (Sperber & Wilson 2008:102). There is also agreement that the interaction between the domains is directional, from source to target, not in reverse; thus, *Butchers are like surgeons* and *Surgeons are like butchers* are two different metaphoric ideas.

Selection

Finally, this directional transfer between the domains is 'partial', as only certain 'mappings' are permitted: "Metaphors are mappings across conceptual domains. Such mappings are asymmetric and partial" (Lakoff 1993:245). In the example Black uses, *A battle is a game of chess*, some features of *battle* are transferred, such as SPEED, POSITION and CASUALTIES, while others are ignored, such as WEATHER, WEAPONS and SUPPLIES (Goatly 1997:117–118). Reddy, in his detailed analysis of the 'conduit metaphor' (communication is like the flow of water in a pipe), shows not only the mappings which occur between CONDUIT and LANGUAGE, but also the potential mappings which do not occur (Reddy 1993). For Ortony, a significant feature of metaphor is that mappings are multiple and transfer does not involve just a single feature (Ortony 1975:50), while Lakoff emphasizes that mappings are set by conceptual metaphors and cannot be varied, referring to this as the 'invariance principle' (Lakoff 1993:215).

Evidence offered by the lexicographer Ayto demonstrates that although the invariance principle may well apply, certain lexical items can have a very rich spectrum of features from which to choose (Ayto 1986). Ayto identifies the features of *cat*, as: FELINE, QUADRUPED, PET, MOUSE-CATCHING, SOFT, DOCILE, AGGRESSIVE, SPITEFUL/MALICIOUS, SKILFUL AT ESCAPING DANGER, DEATH-DEFYING, SEEING WELL IN THE DARK, ALOOF/SELF-CONTAINED, LITHE/AGILE, GRACEFUL, STEALTHY, HAVING NON-HUMAN UNDERSTANDING (Ayto 1986:53), all of which have expression in the lexicon, a phenomenon which poses no problem of ambiguity or confusion in use. Ayto makes a distinction between heavily-weighted prototypical features of a word and lighter features, and suggests that heavier features are not transferred, which is why the features which are discarded are often basic ones, such as FOUR-LEGGEDNESS in *He's a pig* or gender in *He's a bit of an old woman* (Ayto 1986). "When a metaphorical transfer occurs, the prototypical features of the word being used metaphorically are mapped onto those of another in such a way that those which do not match, typically the *more heavily weighted* ones, are discarded, and the light ones come to the surface" (Ayto 1986:51). In practice, especially when metaphors are recontextualized and extended, matching can reveal inconsistencies, as Semino et al show in their analysis of the 'vaccine' metaphor and 'Holland' metaphor in the texts and online postings they examine (Semino et al 2013). In this section, I have shown that metaphorizing involves the processes of transfer and selection.

In the Stack of Counters model presented in the next section, I focus my attention on this second process, selection.

THE 'STACK OF COUNTERS' MODEL

The Stack of Counters model presented in this section is a feature model; it offers a way of recording which features are selected during metaphorization and where they occur on the denotational-connotational continuum. Numerous feature models have been proposed in semantics to represent word meaning, eg Katz & Fodor (1963), Talmy (1985), Jackendoff (1990) and Pustejovsky (1995). Feature models have also been used in applied linguistics, Nida, for example, adopting a componential-analysis approach in his theory of translation (Nida 1975). In the cognitive sciences, Chandler in his 'connectionist' model of metaphor comprehension analyzes word meaning into a set of auditory, olfactory, tactile, gustatory, visual and kinesthetic features and relations (Chandler 1991). The contributions of Tversky (1977), Ortony (1975, 1993c), Glucksberg & Keysar (1990) and Glucksberg (2001) have been particularly significant in understanding figurative language in terms of semantic features. Tversky uses 'feature matching' in his model of similarity; Ortony explains metaphor in terms of highlighting 'non-salient predicates'; while Glucksberg & Keysar and Glucksberg use 'salient properties' to explain metaphor. It is at the level of features we need to look in order to understand what is involved in the ability to metaphorize, because feature analysis takes us below the level of whole-word meaning and closer to the finely-tuned meaning making we find in novel metaphor.

The Stack of Counters model assumes that information about each word, and each sense of a polysemous word, is stored as features in an encyclopaedic entry in the Mental Lexicon. Each entry is pictured as a stack of counters in which each counter represents a semantic feature. The features are in a continuum from denotational, or 'core', features at the base of the stack to connotational, or 'non-core', features at the top. The 'stack of counters' image is used to emphasize that there is a particular sequence in the order in which features are stored in the mind of an individual, that the features at the base of the stack are more 'stable' than those further up, and that each feature is independent and can be picked off individually. I propose that metaphoric meaning is created by manipulating these 'counters', highlighting some from the connotational end of the stack (of the source term) and suppressing others, almost invariably from the denotational end.

Two comments should be made at this point. Firstly, the principles of pragmatics apply here as much as they do for any utterance or text. I am taking for granted that the manipulations involved in the model I am presenting here are occurring within a pragmatic context. I am using the term 'pragmatic context' to include: a cognitive context (ie which cultural frames are chosen); an ideational context (ie which real or imagined worlds are invoked); an interpersonal context (who the participants are and what their relationship to each other is); and a textual context (what information is contributed by the accompanying co-text). Within these contexts, the usual pragmatic principles, such as the Gricean maxims, the principle of relevance, etc, apply. Secondly, this is a theoretical model, and I do not suggest that it reflects the physical reality of features stored in the brain. Physical storage is likely to be more diffuse and less neat in the brain than my model, and to involve networks of connections rather than linear arrangements.

In Chapter 2, I gave an example of how an encyclopaedic entry for *champagne* could be built up using corpus data. Corpus data supplemented with data from dictionary definitions would give a set of features for the item *champagne* which could be ordered from core to non-core in a way which would reflect its use within the speech community from which the data were collected. The list might look something like this: 1 WINE, 2 WHITE, 3 FRENCH, 4 SPARKLING, 5 CHARACTERISTIC BOTTLE AND CORK, 6 EXPENSIVE, 7 USED FOR MAKING COCKTAILS, 8 LUXURY ITEM, 9 ASSOCIATED WITH THE 'HIGH LIFE', 10 USED FOR CELEBRATIONS, 11 USED FOR NAMING SHIPS, 12 SPRAYED BY WINNING RACING DRIVERS. The labels used in this list will probably not coincide exactly with the features as mental entities in the mind. They are expressed using everyday language for convenience and are in small caps, following the convention in semantics to indicate predicates rather than lexical items. Also, I have arranged the list in the order I felt appropriate following my intuition. This again is approximate, but could be refined by asking a panel of subjects from the speech community being investigated to decide the order through consensus. This would be a reasonable expectation, as research suggests that both native and learner speakers have a strong sense of which meanings are basic (James Hampton, personal communication, 2006).

I now take a metaphoric use of *champagne* in the expression *champagne lifestyle* to demonstrate the model. In this noun-noun compound, *lifestyle* is the head (target or topic) and *champagne* the modifier (source or vehicle). It is a conventionalized expression, but if heard for the first time, we can imagine that from the list of features offered by the item *champagne*, the connotational features EXPENSIVE, LUXURY, HIGH LIFE would be highlighted, and the denotational features WINE, WHITE, FRENCH and SPARKLING (and the remaining connotational features) suppressed. If we consider *champagne* used in a literal sense, such as *I bought a bottle of champagne*, this is reversed, the denotational features being highlighted and the connotational features suppressed. These two examples are illustrated in Figure 3.1.

The next expression I wish to consider in order to test the model is an expression which is likely to be a novel metaphor for most people, *Vision is like a tap*. This was taken from a text on how to see without spectacles (*Seeing: The Bates Method*, www.seeing.org, accessed Jan 2008) in which it is stated that tension 'turns off' vision and relaxation turns it 'on': *Tension turns it off, relaxation turns it on*. Vision is compared to a tap. *Vision* is the target, and is used literally, and *tap* is the source, used metaphorically. In this metaphoric use, the core features of *tap*, 1 MADE OF METAL, 2 USED ON PIPES, 3 USED FOR WATER, 4 USED FOR GAS,

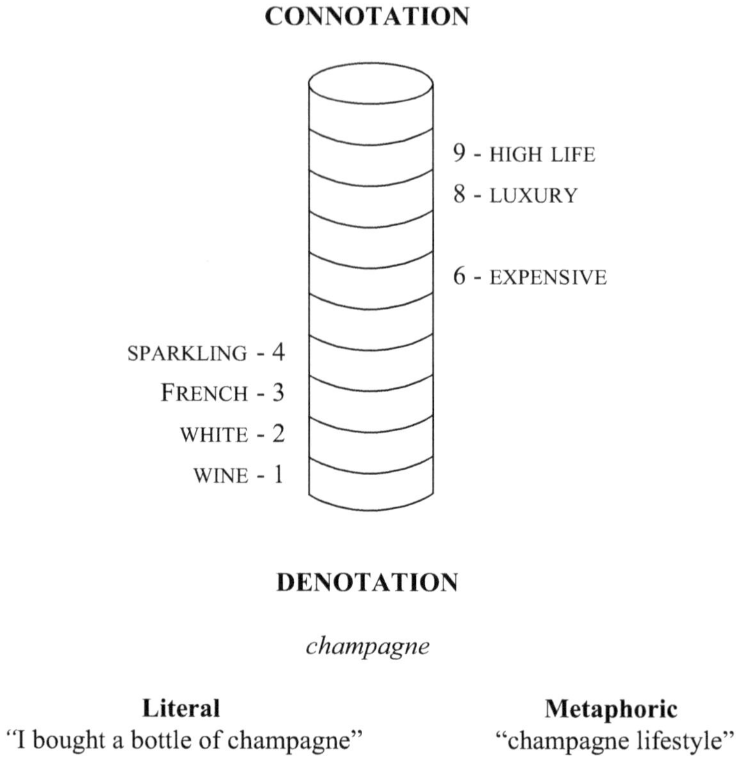

Figure 3.1 Stack of Counters for *champagne*

are suppressed, while features higher up the stack are transferred, as illustrated in Figure 3.2.

It could be argued that 6 TURNING ON and 7 TURNING OFF are denotational features of tap, just as core perhaps as MADE OF METAL, USED ON PIPES, but it is access to the metaphoric sense of turning on/off which is significant here. This example is further complicated by a metonymic step which conflates WATER and TAP, as the metaphor is really that vision is like water and taps allow water to flow.

The evidence from the examples above is at odds with the claims of literalists, such as Davidson, that metaphor does not belong to a compositional/generative description of language. Davidson claims that there cannot be a 'compositional semantic theory of metaphor' to explain how metaphoric meaning is achieved through compositional rules acting on a finite set of simple meanings (Stern 2008:266). It would seem to me that metaphor demonstrates this very notion. It is an excellent demonstration that word meaning operates at the level of individual features, otherwise how can we explain that words are 'picked apart' in the way that occurs during metaphorization? Not only do manipulations occur below the level of the word, but they occur with

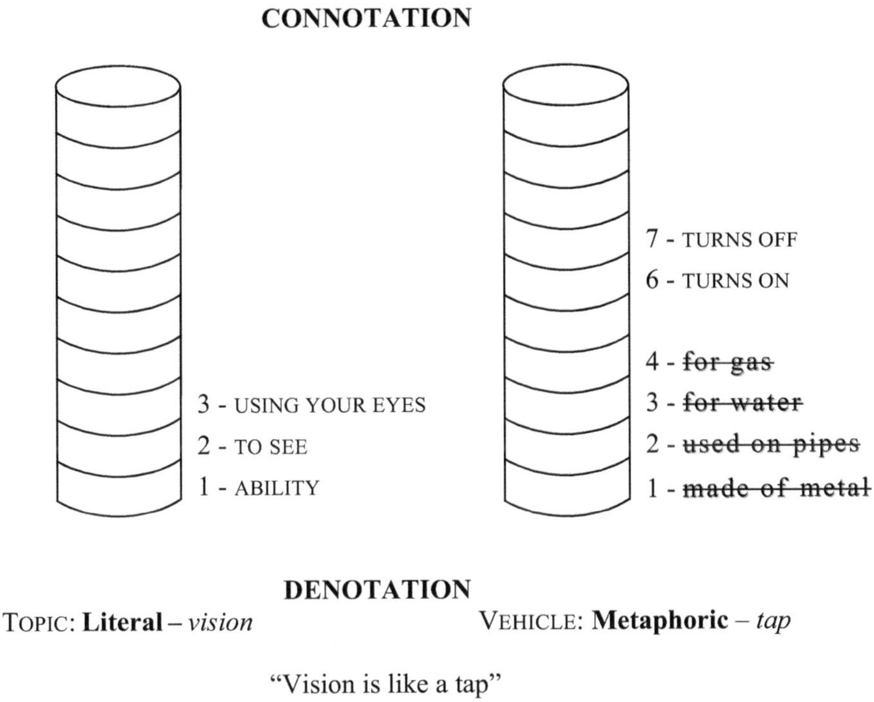

Figure 3.2 Stack of Counters for *vision* and *tap*

predictability. This is because the information used in metaphorizing is already there in the encyclopaedic entries. Searle is also a literalist, but his denial of there being metaphoric meaning in the code itself is argued differently. Searle states that "in a genuine metaphorical utterance, it is only because the expressions have not changed their meaning that there is a metaphorical utterance at all" (Searle 1993:90). His reason for arriving at this conclusion is that he sees metaphor as purely a pragmatic phenomenon; my conclusion is that it is because of the stability of meanings of words in the language code that metaphorizing is possible.

Metaphoric Comparisons and Literal Comparisons

In this section, I examine the difference between literal and metaphoric comparisons in order to test further the Stack of Counters model presented above. Above, comparing two unrelated domains was given as one of the key characteristics of metaphor—along with 'directional transfer' between the domains and 'selection'—but comparisons can be made which are not metaphoric. It is the difference between these two, metaphoric comparisons and literal comparisons, to which I now turn.

It is appropriate to comment on two assumptions implied in the paragraph above: 1) that metaphors are comparisons, and 2) that metaphoricity can be characterized as opposite to literality. Lakoff questions both. He eschews the idea of metaphors as comparisons, considering them instead to be "mostly based on correspondences [. . .] rather than on similarity" (Lakoff 1993:245). In my use of the term 'comparison' in the present work I intend nothing more than the notion of bringing together two domains into juxtaposition. Lakoff also objects to the second assumption, that 'literal' is the opposite of 'metaphoric'. He considers the term 'literal' confusing, as it has come to refer to four distinct phenomena: standard language; language used conventionally to talk about a particular subject; truth-conditional meaning; and nonmetaphorical meaning (Lakoff 1986:292). Lakoff suggests 'literal' is best either avoided or reserved for the fourth sense, 'nonmetaphorical meaning' (Lakoff 1986:293). Although Lakoff claims metaphor is central and pervasive in our conceptual system, he does not claim that our conceptual system is entirely metaphoric: "Though much of our conceptual system is metaphorical, a significant part of it is nonmetaphorical" (Lakoff 1993:244). What is more, he recognizes that the part which is not metaphoric is essential in the grounding of metaphoric thought (Lakoff & Johnson 1980:56–68, Lakoff & Johnson 1999, Lakoff 1987b): "Metaphorical understanding is grounded in nonmetaphorical understanding" (Lakoff 1993:244).

What then is the difference between novel metaphors and literal comparisons? I explore this below by first considering the work of Glucksberg and Ortony on this question and then giving my own account, using the Stack of Counters model. In order to make clear what I mean by novel metaphors and literal comparisons, first I give a list of examples of each, drawn from my own data and various discussions in the literature (eg Ortony 1993a, Glucksberg 2001, Forceville 2008). Literal comparisons are: *Blackberries are like raspberries*, *Wasps are like hornets*, *Tin is like copper*, *Encyclopaedias are like dictionaries*, *Hotels are like motels*, *Harvard is like Yale*, *Canada is like the USA*, *Spain is like Italy*, *India is like China*—though many such expressions can, in certain circumstances, be understood as metaphoric comparisons. Novel metaphoric comparisons (expressed as similes for the sake of conformity) are: *Billboards are like warts*, *Encyclopaedias are like goldmines*, *Libraries are like goldmines*, *Friends are like anchors*, *Lectures are like sleeping pills*, *Jobs are like jails*, *Alcohol is like a crutch*, *Brains are like computers*, *Butchers are like surgeons*, *Surgeons are like butchers*, *Vision is like a tap*. The first scholar I consider is Glucksberg.

Glucksberg

Glucksberg follows rhetoricians in characterizing metaphor as "two *unlike* things compared, as in *some jobs are jails*" and literal comparisons as "two *like* things [compared], that is, things that belong to the same taxonomic category (eg *wasps are like hornets*)" (Glucksberg 2001:61). He identifies three differences between literal and metaphoric comparisons: firstly, that literal comparisons have features in common as well as features which are not shared, while metaphors only have one or two features in common and differences are ignored; secondly, that literal comparisons are reversible, while metaphors are not; thirdly, that literal comparisons cannot be expressed without a signalling device, such as 'like', while metaphors can (Glucksberg 2001:30–37). Glucksberg notes that literal comparisons can be asymmetric, the nature of the comparison being influenced by the term which comes first, as this emphasizes salient characteristics of the first term by virtue of its position, thus *Canada is like the USA* would perhaps activate the concept of the linguistic minority in Quebec, while *The USA is like Canada* would not (Glucksberg 2001:32).

Ortony

Metaphor, for Ortony, comes about through the elimination of 'tension' created when topic and vehicle are brought together, resulting in a 'distinctive set' of appropriate characteristics being constructed from all the features available (Ortony 1975:48). Ortony is influenced by Tversky's 'contrastive model' in which a measure of similarity is achieved by looking at shared features, metaphor being understood "by scanning the feature space and selecting the features of the referent that are applicable to the subject" (Tversky 1977:349). Ortony prefers the term 'predicate' to 'feature', and refers to those predicates which are important and necessary in identifying an item (ie which would define it) as 'high-salient predicates' (Ortony 1993c:346). Ortony reports on an experiment where subjects were given lexical items, eg *encyclopedias*, *billboards*, *warts*, and asked to list predicates for them. On average six predicates were given by the subjects. Subjects were then asked to rank them and say which of them were necessary in order to identify the item to somebody who did not know it. On average, three predicates were used to do this. These particular items were chosen as they appear in novel metaphors considered in the experiment, eg *Billboards are like warts*. Ortony found that UGLY was a high-salient predicate of *wart* but a low-salient predicate of *billboards*, and that metaphor as a result could be defined in terms of the highlighting of non-salient features (Ortony 1993c:351).

Ortony argues that literal and nonliteral comparisons both involve 'predicate selection' (Ortony 1993c:352), and that the difference between the two is that in metaphor there is "virtually no common salience", while in literal comparisons many salient predicates are shared (Ortony 1993c:350). Consider a construction of the sort *A is like B*: a literal comparison is one where high-salient predicates of A and high-salient predicates of B are the same; a nonliteral comparison is one where high-salient predicates of B are the same as less-salient predicates of A, and there are high-salient predicates of B which do not apply to A (Ortony 1993c:349): "in [metaphor], high-salient predicates of the vehicle are low-salient predicates of the topic, [. . .] this distinguishes [metaphor] from literal comparisons, where the match is of high to high-salient predicates" (Ortony 1993c:354). Ortony also comments on reversibility, maintaining that "nonliteral similarity statements will tend to be much less reversible than literal similarity statements" (Ortony 1979:179), for the reason that in nonliteral comparisons "terms have nonoverlapping sets of salient predicates" and therefore are asymmetric to begin with (Ortony 1993c:351), and that even if there are asymmetries, it is less obvious because many other salient predicates are shared (Ortony 1993c:352). If terms are reversed, the change in meaning for metaphor is greater than that for literal comparisons (Ortony 1979:179). This model of predicate selection encourages Ortony to see literal versus nonliteral more as a question of degree rather than one of essential difference: "The position that I have adopted is still basically one that denies any fundamentally important difference in the processing of literal and nonliteral comparisons. I am inclined to believe that this is true for literal and metaphorical uses of language in general" (Ortony 1993c:353).

In order to illustrate my own account of the difference between a literal and metaphoric comparison, I look at an example of each, using the Stack of Counters model. Earlier in this section, the selection of a distinctive set of predicate features from the vehicle/source term was illustrated for the expression *Vision is*

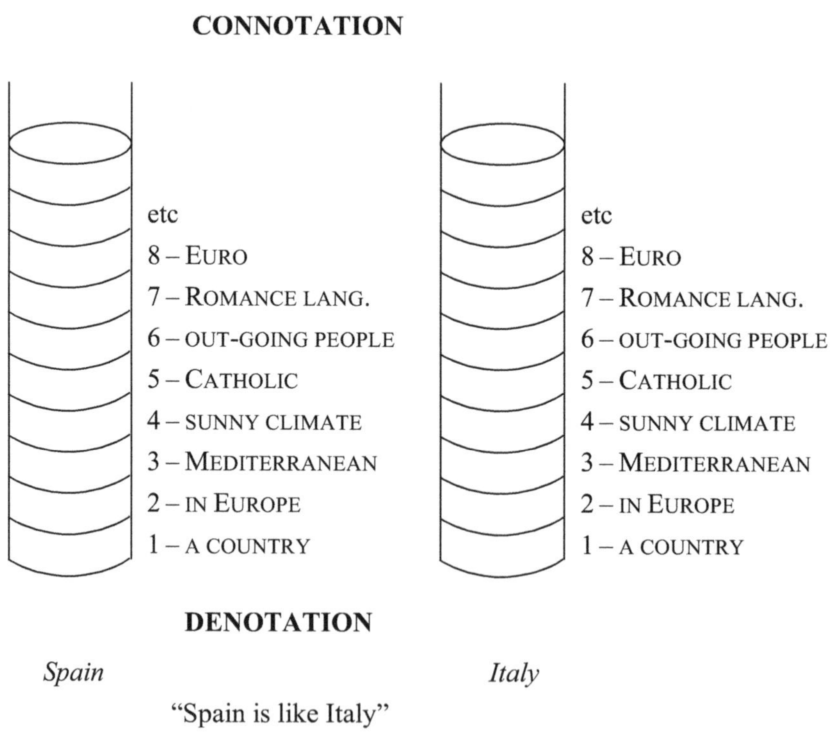

Figure 3.3 Stacks of Counters for *Spain* and *Italy*

like a tap. In order to illustrate a literal comparison, I have chosen the sentence *Spain is like Italy*. *Spain* and *Italy* share many features. They are both countries in Europe, located on the Mediterranean, both have sunny climates, Catholicism has been dominant in their histories, their people are thought to be outgoing, the dominant languages, Spanish and Italian, are from the same language family, the currency is the Euro, and so on. The exact nature and order of these features in the encyclopaedic entries could be determined through experimentation, but I will simply leave them as approximations here. What is illustrated in Figure 3.3 conforms with the accounts of Ortony and Glucksberg, that is: similar sections of the two encyclopaedic entries are used in literal comparisons; the comparison involves numerous features, not just one or two; and the order of the two items can be reversed, so that in this case *Italy* could come before *Spain* (though putting *Spain* first will inevitably make it the theme, the 'standard' against which the comparison is made).

THE FUNCTIONS OF METAPHOR

In this section, I look at the functions of metaphor in discourse. My purpose for doing so is to show that the wide range of functions which metaphor can express is enabled through a single common mechanism, the 'selection of features'. Much has been written on the subject of the function of metaphor in discourse. What emerges from these studies is the vast array of different functions which metaphor exhibits and that these functions are so diverse that they include those with an effect in discourse directly opposite to other metaphor functions, such as 'cultivating intimacy' versus 'discouraging intimacy', 'inclusion' versus 'exclusion', 'making meaning more specific' versus 'making meaning less specific'. I review the classifications of metaphor function compiled by Ortony (1975), Low (1988), Gibbs (1994) and Goatly (1993, 1997), and studies on the role played by metaphor in structuring discourse by Lerman (1985), Drew & Holt (1988, 1998) and McCarthy (1998) in order to demonstrate this variance. I then offer my own synthesis of these findings into a Cartesian 'grid' of functions and use this to argue that the many and diverse functions of metaphor are proof that the 'selection of features' aspect of metaphor is primary to metaphorizing, while the transfer of that information to the target domain is secondary. This overview of the functions of metaphor provides a proof for the Stack of Counters model presented in the previous section.

Typologies of Metaphor Function

Many attempts have been made by scholars to classify the function of metaphor in discourse. Ortony identified three functions: 'compactness', 'expressibility' and 'vividness' (Ortony 1975). These are extended by Low, Gibbs and Goatly. Although Low modestly describes his classification as an attempt to list "a few of the major functions of metaphor", it still stands as a pretty comprehensive overview of metaphor function (Low 1988:127–129). His functions are: Making it Possible to Talk about Something, such as describing musical pitch, particles in physics, the nature of religion; Demonstrating that Things in Life are Related and Systematic, using linguistic metaphors to make conceptual metaphors explicit; Extending Thought, using metaphor to provide models and generate new hypotheses, eg *The brain is a computer*, *Atomic particles have colour*; Compelling Attention by Dramatizing, making utterances more vivid (close to Ortony's 'vividness' function); Prevaricating or Denying Responsibility for Something, allowing the speaker distance or avoiding explicit reference, eg by commenting metalinguistically or quoting someone else's words; Allowing the Speaker to Discuss Emotionally Charged Subjects and Problematic Topics, including euphemism, eg *seeing a man about a dog*; Compressing, Summarizing and Buying Time, expressing things in a more concise manner (close to Ortony's 'compactness' function) or buying time by being more vague.

The functions Low identifies are diverse. Even if we categorize them within the functional framework of Hallidayan systematic functional grammar, we see that they do not belong to just one metafunction; some are ideational ('Making it Possible to Talk about Something', 'Demonstrating that Things in Life are Related' and 'Extending Thought'), while some are interpersonal ('Compelling Attention by Dramatizing', 'Prevaricating and Denying Responsibility' and 'Allowing the Speaker to Discuss Emotionally Charged Subjects'). Low remarks on this paradox, that a single phenomenon, linguistic metaphor, can give rise to opposing functions in discourse with regard to 'clarity': "Metaphor thus has the intriguing attribute of having two central but opposing roles. On the one hand, it promotes greater clarity in what is said, while, on the other, it serves with quotations, jokes, and stories, to create what Lerman [. . .] calls a 'shielded form' of discourse" (Low 1988:129). Low also comments that if we accept the Canale-Swain-Bachman model adopted by many language teachers and testers, that 'communicative competence' consists of a linguistic, sociolinguistic, discourse and strategic component, then metaphor is involved in all four (Low 2008:221).

Gibbs refers to the functions of metaphor in his typology as 'social functions' (Gibbs 1994:134–140). They are: Reinforcing intimacy, Expressing one's own attitudes and beliefs indirectly, Relating the attitudes and beliefs of others, Signalling formality/informality, Signalling hostility, Indicating membership to a group, Giving judgments without offending, Releasing emotion, Avoiding unpleasant emotions (such as hospital slang, eg *beached whale*, *apple bobbing*, *a Betty Crocker*), Manipulating status within a group (such as American college slang, eg *to do the nasty*, *to play hide the salami*, *to do the bone dance*) and Conceptualizing in science, art and the law. Here again some functions are ideational and others interpersonal. Gibbs is perhaps more concerned with the interpersonal usefulness of metaphor, those functions which relate to politeness, showing regard for the feelings of others, and establishing and maintaining interpersonal rapports, but he also recognizes the ideational function of metaphor in conceptualizing in science, art and the law.

Goatly has published two classifications of metaphor function (Goatly 1993, 1997). The 1997 classification is more comprehensive and is the one I look at here, considered for the contribution it makes to the topic and also as a framework for summarizing the work of Low and Gibbs. Goatly acknowledges that his classification is similar to Low's: "Low [. . .] gives a list of the functions of metaphor which more or less coincide with some of mine" (Goatly 1997:332). In it, he lists twelve 'functional varieties' of metaphor (Goatly 1997:148–163), assigning each to one of four functional categories, IDEATIONAL, INTERPERSONAL, TEXTUAL or PHATIC, or a combination of categories, ie IDEATIONAL and INTERPERSONAL (Goatly 1997:166):

IDEATIONAL

Filling lexical gaps: providing a term where none is available, eg *light year*; when a term is only partly appropriate, eg *He put his face in the water and half-gulped, half-ate it*; or when a term is modified to make it more precise, eg *My cry for help was the cry of the rat when a terrier shakes it.* **Explanation and modelling**: explaining something which is unfamiliar; theory-constitutive metaphors, eg explaining electricity in terms of waterflow, light in terms of waves and particles, the human brain as a computer. **Reconceptualization**: changing how we see the world and modifying how we see it, in both science and literature.

IDEATIONAL AND INTERPERSONAL

Reasoning by analogy: used as an analogy in argumentation. (No equivalent in Low's classification.) **Ideology**: defining and maintaining power relations through metaphors. (No equivalent in Low's classification.)

INTERPERSONAL

Expressing emotional attitude: conveying attitudinal meaning that cannot be conveyed by literal language, eg *hell*, *bugger*, *piss off.* **Decoration and disguise**: to decorate, entertain, grab attention and disguise, as in euphemism, eg *He fell asleep* and *to cross over the great divide.* **Metaphorical calls to action and problem-solving**: according to Goatly, this is more an aspect of other functions than a function on its own, eg *Don't think of it as you are seeing it but simply as a mountain to be climbed.* (No equivalent in Low's classification.)

TEXTUAL

Text structuring: an analogy can run through a text and help give it coherence. (No equivalent in Low's classification.) **Enhancing memorability, foregrounding and informativeness**: making an utterance stand out and be more memorable, eg *He moved to a private bar upstairs and trouble erupted.* (Goatly sees Foregrounding as equivalent to Low's 'Compelling attention by dramatizing'.)

PHATIC

Cultivating intimacy: inclusion through shared knowledge. (No equivalent in Low's classification.) **Humour and games**: jokes, puzzles and conundrums. (No equivalent in Low's classification.)

Other important studies look at the role of metaphor in structuring and managing discourse, such as those of Lerman, Drew & Holt and McCarthy. Lerman identifies the use of metaphor in avoiding direct reference, or 'masking', in interviews with the US President Nixon (Lerman 1984), and dealing with problematic, or 'P', topics in Nixon's political speeches and the media reporting of them, eg *heavy weather*, *weather the storm*, *take the heat off* (Lerman 1985). Drew & Holt reveal that conventional and novel metaphor are particularly abundant when giving praise and making critical assessments about grievances, using data from business meetings and psychotherapy sessions (Drew & Holt 1988). In another study, using data from recorded telephone calls, they show that conventional metaphor is frequently used (ten examples per hour of recording) in making topic transition, that is, signalling the end of a topic and inviting the speech partner to move to another topic (Drew & Holt 1998). McCarthy in his analysis from the CANCODE corpus identifies four functions of conventional metaphor: making an evaluation, giving an opinion, showing membership and negotiating meaning (McCarthy 1998). Cameron talks of conventional metaphor in classroom discourse 'adding value' along three axes: positive and negative evaluation, the speaker aligning themselves with or distancing themselves from their conversational partner, emphasizing and de-emphasizing (Cameron 1999:126–127). But it is Goatly's typology which makes the most useful contribution to the present argument by demonstrating the multitude of functions made available through the single operation of metaphor. Though Goatly, Gibbs, Low and the other scholars considered above are mainly describing conventional language, I feel it is not too speculative to suggest that the functions they identify can be proposed for novel metaphor as well.

A Two-Axis Typology of Metaphor Function

In order to test further the idea that metaphor is not tied to any one function, I offer my own typology. I place the functions discussed above, plus further functions mentioned in Davitz (1969), Eder (1990), Moon (1994), Petrie & Oshlag (1993), Pollio et al (1977) and Sticht (1993), along two 'axes'. I am testing this hypothesis further to demonstrate how powerful the seemingly unremarkable ability to select at feature level is in linguistic processing. The axes are:

- whether the message is made *more* or *less specific* through the use of metaphor
- whether the message expressed by metaphor concerns *transaction* or *interaction*, that is, whether it is content-based or to do with social relations/personal attitudes in Brown & Yule's sense (1983:1–4).

I have chosen these axes as I see them as representing fundamental dichotomies in language and they serve here to show up opposing functions maximally, creating a Cartesian grid with the greatest possible extension. This creates four functional domains, which I name *New meaning*, *Detachment*, *Additional meaning* and *Vagueness*, as shown in the four quadrants of the grid below (Table 3.2).

The next four paragraphs show in detail how the academic writing on metaphor function can be mapped onto the four quadrants of the grid. It should be noted that the literature rarely differentiates between novel and conventional uses.

NEW MEANING is the functional category with the coordinates of 'specific' and 'transactional' and includes: **Organizing discourse**, structuring text (Goatly), text coherence (Sticht), organizing discourse (Moon); **Explaining**, filling lexical gaps (Goatly), making it possible to talk about something (Low), explaining the unfamiliar (Petrie & Oshlag), describing intellectual history (Pollio et al), explaining and modelling (Goatly), indicating comprehension (Sticht), providing additional vocabulary (Pollio et al); **Expressing feelings**, being expressive (Ortony), describing emotional states (Davitz), releasing emotions (Gibbs); **Problem solving**, problem solving (Sticht, Goatly), problem solving by analogy (Pollio et al), reasoning by analogy (Goatly); and **Conceptualizing**, extending thought by providing models (Low), demonstrating that things in life are related and systematic (Low), reconceptualizing to change how we see the world, eg scientific theory (Goatly), creating a fictional world to say something about the real world, eg literary analogy (Goatly), conceptualizing in science, the arts and law (Gibbs).

DETACHMENT is a functional category with the coordinates 'unspecific' and 'transactional' and includes: **Expressing emotional states**, expressing opinions (Moon), expressing emotional attitudes (Goatly), expressing attitudes and beliefs—in the context of transaction (Gibbs); **Commenting**, commenting on something (McCarthy); **Summarizing**, compactness (Ortony), compressing and summarizing (Low); **Managing topic change**, structuring discourse—the mechanics of changing topic in what are otherwise interactional encounters (Drew & Holt).

ADDITIONAL MEANING is a functional category with the coordinates 'specific' and 'interactional' and includes: **Cultivating closeness**, cultivating intimacy (Goatly), reinforcing intimacy (Gibbs), creating a sense of camaraderie (Moon), aligning speaker and listener (Cameron), indicating membership to a group (Gibbs), 'membershipping' participants (McCarthy), signalling formality/informality (Gibbs); **Decoration**, decoration (Goatly), ornament (Pollio et al); **Language play**,

Table 3.2 Four domains of metaphor function—as a grid

	More Specific	Less Specific
Transactional	**New meaning**	**Detachment**
Interactional	**Additional meaning**	**Vagueness**

humour and games (Goatly), punning (McCarthy); **Highlighting**, enhancing memorability (Goatly), making vivid and memorable (Ortony), making vivid, interesting and appealing (Moon), compelling attention by dramatizing something (Low), dramatizing (Lerman), giving emphasis (Moon, Cameron), foregrounding (Goatly); **Asserting yourself**, threatening face (Eder), signalling hostility (Gibbs), trivializing a political opponent (Lerman), manipulating status within a group (Gibbs), establishing and maintaining ideological power relations (Goatly).

VAGUENESS is a functional category with the coordinates 'unspecific' and 'interactional' and includes: **Politeness**, providing a mask (Pollio et al), masking reference to problematic topics (Lerman), avoiding unpleasant emotions (Gibbs), avoiding precise reference (McCarthy), negotiating meaning to be indirect (McCarthy), informing others of attitudes and beliefs in an indirect manner (Gibbs), discussing emotionally charged subjects and problematic topics (Low); **Avoiding commitment**, denying responsibility for something (Low), buying time (Low), distancing (Cameron); **Expressing approval**, expressing approval or admiration (Moon), praising (Drew & Holt), conveying thanks or refusals (Moon); **Expressing disapproval**, expressing disapproval (Moon), expressing criticism (Moon), making critical assessments, complaining (Drew & Holt), giving a negative judgment without offending (Gibbs), expressing an evaluation (Cameron, Moon, McCarthy).

The information on metaphor function from the academic literature overviewed above is further summarized in Table 3.3.

Table 3.3 Four domains of metaphor function—summary

	More specific	Less specific
Transactional	**New meaning** Metaphor is used for: organizing discourse, filling lexical gaps, explaining the unfamiliar, indicating comprehension, describing emotional states, problem solving, reasoning by analogy, reconceptualizing, creating fictional worlds, conceptualizing scientific theory.	**Detachment** Metaphor is used for: expressing opinions, expressing emotional states, expressing beliefs, commenting, summarizing, compressing, managing topic change.
Interactional	**Additional meaning** Metaphor is used for: cultivating intimacy, reinforcing intimacy, indicating membership, signalling formality and informality, decoration, language play, enhancing memorability, making vivid and memorable, dramatizing, foregrounding, emphasizing, asserting yourself, signalling hostility, establishing and maintaining power.	**Vagueness** Metaphor is used for: avoiding unpleasantness, avoiding precise reference, negotiating meaning, informing others of attitudes and beliefs, discussing problematic topics, avoiding commitment, expressing approval or disapproval, criticizing, complaining, evaluating.

CONCLUSION

The aim of this chapter has been to identify the central defining characteristic of metaphor in the sense of being able to metaphorize (create and interpret novel metaphor), the ability to select certain features (mappings) and deselect others. The Stack of Counters feature model I have presented in this chapter goes some way towards understanding metaphoric processing and therefore the capabilities within the Metaphor Processor which characterizes its operation. The idea that metaphor is capable of creating diametrically-opposed functions was developed into a proof that 'selection', rather than 'transfer', is primary in defining metaphor in the sense of 'doing' metaphor. An in-depth examination of the discourse functions of metaphor, as presented in the academic literature, was used to support the idea that, although the effects are hugely diverse in communicative terms, a single common linguistic operation is behind the ability to metaphorize. The function a metaphor has in discourse is determined by choice of lexis, which in turn determines which conceptual domain is accessed, but it is the selective choice of features and the de-selection of others which is unique to novel metaphor. As selection is so powerful, in the next chapter, I focus on 'selection' isolated from 'transfer', and explore the myriad of verbal and non-verbal phenomena where selection plays a role in communication.

4 The Vital Role of Metonymy in Conceptualization and Communication

This chapter moves the argument from metaphor to metonymy. In the previous chapter, I demonstrated that 'doing metaphor' in the sense of managing novel metaphor receptively and productively—the ability to metaphorize—involves the selection of features, the recognition of part-whole relations between signs and parts of signs. This is the essence of metonymy and is the sense I shall be using for the remainder of this book. Recognizing that metonymy is a stage, or 'sub-process', *within* metaphor allows us to draw the conclusion that metonymy is more fundamental as a phenomenon than metaphor, and for this reason it is appropriate that metonymy now becomes the focus of the present study. In this chapter, I develop a General Theory of Metonymy by demonstrating the significance of metonymy across a whole range of linguistic and multimodal phenomena. I show that metonymy has a far wider 'reach' than just the creation of lexical formulations used for referring; it plays a vital role at every level of the language hierarchy, from phonemes to pragmatics, as well as serving a whole variety of essential communicative functions. I argue that metonymy offers a means by which existing semiotic resources can be exploited to give salience and nuance, and that it is here we find the explanation of language's great subtlety, flexibility and fitness for purpose.

METONYMY IN THE LANGUAGE SYSTEM

I am defining *metonymy* in this chapter as the highlighting of relatedness, usually part-whole, between closely-related concepts, things and signifiers. Whether we are concerned with a physical part, eg *give me a hand*, a part in the sense of an attribute, eg *the small screen*, or a part in the sense of an effect, eg *smoke* standing for FIRE, they have in common that they involve 'relatedness' and it is this which distinguishes metonymy from metaphor. Definitions of metonymy and relatedness will be examined in detail in the next section; in this section I outline the vital role metonymy plays in the language system itself and in our conceptual system in general. I consider a whole range of linguistic phenomena which all have in common that, to operate, they rely on the recognition of part-whole relations. I consider the following headings in turn below: 'sense and reference', 'literal language as metonymic', 'defining categories', 'etymology' and 'pragmatics'.

Sense and Reference

The distinction between *sense* and *reference*, identified by Frege and explored by later language philosophers, such as Russell and Strawson, involves the distinction between the generic meaning of a word, its 'sense', and a specific use of it when representing an entity in the real or an imagined world, its 'reference' (Frege 1892/1960). Sense is close to what a lexicographer tries to encapsulate in a dictionary definition, such as "A *ball* is a round object used in a game or sport . . ."; while reference reflects the meaning of a word in actual utterances, such as "Alex is holding a *ball*". Sense is the 'full' meaning of a word, while reference is a 'partial' meaning. Given this whole/part relation, it is reasonable to suggest, as Radden does, that sense/reference relations are inherently metonymic (Radden 2008b, 2009) and that moving between them involves the cognitive ability to process metonymically.

The sense/reference distinction has close parallels with other key concepts in language studies, namely, Saussure's distinction between 'langue' and 'parole' (Saussure 1916/1983) and Chomsky's similar distinction between 'competence' and 'performance' (Chomsky 1965). They concern the difference between the idealized knowledge of a language and the ability to use it. The relationship between the idealized systems of a language and how a language is actually used is a metonymic relation, and this, to my mind, is a more significant feature of the langue/parole and competence/performance (and I- /E-language) distinctions than those more usually cited, such as syntactic incompleteness and grammatical incorrectness in performance.

The effortlessness with which a speaker goes back and forth from sense to reference belies the complexity of the information contained in encyclopaedic entries stored for a lexical item in the mental lexicon. How complex and inclusive 'sense' is can be demonstrated by the difficulty in defining even (or especially) common objects. Lexicographers can have a challenging task to 'pin down' meaning, as this entry for *door* below, from the third edition of *Webster's New International Dictionary*, demonstrates.

> **Door** [n]: a movable piece of firm material or structure supported usu. along one side and swinging on pivots or hinges, sliding along a groove, rolling up and down, revolving as one of four leaves, or folding like an accordion by means of which an opening may be closed or kept open for passage into or out of a building, room or other covered enclosure or a car, airplane, elevator or other vehicle . . .
>
> (Hanks 1979:32)

The entry verges on the comical in its attempt to include all possible cases and this extract does not even consider the materials from which a door can be made or the connotations of *door*.

Not only do speakers/listeners move effortlessly between sense and reference, and thus between ideas and their articulation in words, but also between 'generic reference', the abstract reference to a whole category, and 'real reference', the indication of a real instance (Radden 2009). Radden describes the generic-for-specific relationship as a TYPE FOR TOKEN metonymy (Radden 2005:13), and sees generic reference in English as motivated by INSTANCE FOR TYPE and TYPE FOR SUBTYPE metonymies (Radden 2009:201–202). The INSTANCE FOR TYPE metonymy "evokes the generic type" (Radden 2009:223), while the TYPE FOR SUBTYPE metonymy "serves to restrict the generic referent to prototypical members of the type" (Radden 2009:223). For example, if a shop assistant were to say "This jacket is our best-selling item", we would understand this as an instance standing for a type, where the type is that model of jacket; if a client in a car showroom points to a car and says "I like this car", we would understand this both as instance and type (Radden 2008b). We are aware when we buy an item on the internet that what we are being offered is a generic type, not the specific item in the photo, unless it is a public auction website such as *eBay*, in which case it will often be the actual item (Radden 2008b). Misunderstandings in respect to sense, generic reference and real reference occur only rarely and are quickly corrected, suggesting that these metonymic steps are a highly-practised part of our repertoire and are there out of necessity.

Literal Language as Metonymic

In Chapter 3, I demonstrated that the selection of features, metonymy, is the fundamental operation within metaphor, and that metaphor involves the recognition of part-whole relations in selecting certain aspects and ignoring others. Here I wish to propose that the processing of 'literal language' also involves metonymy. To give an example, if we take the adjective *red* and use it to qualify various nouns, such as *red carpet*, *red lorry*, *red apple*, in each case, a different quality of RED is understood. There are reds of different hues, intensities and reflectiveness, so a prototypical carpet, lorry or apple will reflect a particular constellation of qualities within these categories. Thus each word-pair selects certain aspects from the full sense of *red* and excludes others which are inappropriate in that context. The meaning of a word is modified from the generic or prototypical sense by the words it combines with and the co-textual context in which it is found. When a word is apparently used literally the meaning is metonymic because it expresses a specific or narrowed sense.

As strings of words are built up into paragraphs, and paragraphs into whole texts, the process of 'metonymic narrowing' is multiplied, with meanings construed by the reader becoming ever more specific. The longer the text, the more this accumulative 'narrowing' is involved in interpreting it. Miller illustrates this with the novel *Walden*:

> When I read the first sentence [of *Walden*] and encountered Thoreau borrowing an axe, I used that information to narrow down the variety of possible

> states of affairs to just those that included Thoreau borrowing an axe. When I read next that he went down to the woods by Walden Pond, I narrowed the potential set even further, now to those that included Thoreau with his axe walking to the woods by Walden Pond. By the time I finished, I had narrowed down this set considerably, but there were still indefinitely many alternatives left.
>
> (Miller 1993:360)

The text builds up in the reader's mind a specific image of the protagonist, Thoreau, the axe he borrows, the wood he walks towards and the pond he sees. It is a specific set of mutually coherent images, which still leaves scope for further narrowing as the prose progresses. The words on the page give access to the general sense associated with those words and 'metonymic processing' narrows them down to the specific image that the reader constructs for that particular reading.

Defining Categories

Because the relationship between superordinates (general categories) and hyponyms (sub-categories) involves part-whole relations, metonymy is very well suited to identifying general categories which do not have convenient labels. Departments within retail stores and sections of supermarkets, for example, can be identified in this way. In data from my notebooks, I noted that in a branch of the UK supermarket *Tesco*, the section for pharmacy products was identified metonymically by 'Aches and Pains' (metonymic because products for treating ailments other than pain and products of general hygiene are found there), alongside sections identified using literal superordinates, such as 'Canned Goods', 'Household Goods' and 'Soups'. In another UK supermarket, *Morrisons*, the term 'Medicines' was used for this section. In both cases, the term 'Pharmacy' was perhaps not used because it was considered to sound too medical or it suggested that a trained pharmacist was on hand, though it is the term used by another UK supermarket chain, *Waitrose*.

Many languages have a single word standing for both superordinate and hyponym, eg in the Native American Indian language Hopi, the word for 'cottonwood' means both 'deciduous tree' and 'cottonwood tree' (the most common deciduous tree in this region); and in the Native American Indian language Shoshoni, the word for eagle means both 'eagle' and 'large bird' (Glucksberg 2001:39). The relationship between these words is metonymic. In sign languages, salient features are used to identify celebrities, such as 'big ears' for Prince Charles and 'opening a trouser zip' for Bill Clinton. In American Sign Language, many superordinate categories do not have their own sign, so, for example, 'furniture' is achieved by 'chair-table-bed etc' (signed rapidly with the sign for 'etc' "crisply executed"), thus, to express "I lost my **furniture** in the house fire, but one thing was left, the **bed**", 'bed' would appear twice: once as part of the signing to express the superordinate 'furniture' and again to express the hyponym 'bed' (Glucksberg

2001:39), establishing metonymic relations between the different senses represented by 'bed'.

I now turn to 'prototype effects' in understanding categories. A 'prototype' is understood to be an idealized example of a category, the 'best fit'. In her experiments with university students in California, Rosch found, when asked to rank exemplars of a category from most to least prototypical, eg for BIRD: *robin, sparrow, owl, eagle, ostrich, emu, penguin . . .*, that they were not only able to carry out the task but concurred in the rankings they gave (Lakoff 1987b:44). The relationship between an idealized prototype of a category and real exemplars of a category is metonymic, because there is an overlap between the characteristics of the prototype and the exemplar. Kövecses & Radden claim that metonymic relations are involved in constructing prototypes (Kövecses & Radden 1998), while Gibbs maintains that prototypes are 'stand for' categories and metonymic for that reason (Gibbs 1999:66); and for Lakoff "metonymic models of various sorts are the sources of a wide variety of prototype effects" (Lakoff 1987b:203).

For the cognitivists Brugman & Lakoff, 'prototype effects' are not limited to single lexical categories but also operate in 'radial networks', where the various senses of a polysemous word, such as *over*, share some but not all features (Brugman & Lakoff 2006). For Lakoff, 'radial categories', such as compounds of *mother*, eg *adoptive mother, birth mother, surrogate mother*, are related more by having 'family resemblances' than being hyponyms of a central category (Lakoff 1987b:84). For Al-Sharafi, all categorization is metonymic, because to categorize is to see something as a "kind of" thing and therefore to relate it metonymically (Al-Sharafi 2004:57). For Langacker, prototypes are involved in grammatical categories and constructions, prototypes being the "highest level schema" of a grammatical category or construction, and are involved in all essential operations in conceptualizing and articulating concepts in language (Langacker 1990:3, 17). Prototype effects also operate in phonology, the category 'phoneme' having a prototype structure by being a collection of allophones, thus making phonological categories also inherently metonymic (Radden 2005:13–14).

The meaning relationships considered in the traditional study in linguistics of 'relational semantics', such as 'hyponymy', 'superordinacy', 'synonymy' and 'antonymy', are necessarily metonymic, because meaning relations described by them must involve some degree of semantic overlap. The relationship between the superordinate *vehicle* and its hyponyms, eg *car, bus, lorry, van,* is metonymic; the relationship between the synonyms *little/small, over/above, expert/specialist* etc is metonymic, because synonym pairs share denotational meaning, if not connotational meaning; and the relationship between 'complementary antonyms', such as *on/off, open/closed, dead/alive*, 'gradable antonyms', such as *big/little, fat/thin, rich/poor* and 'reversive antonyms', such as *start/stop, husband/wife, borrow/lend,* are metonymic, as they also share complementary features.

Fillmore's concept of the 'frame', closely equivalent to terms favoured by other scholars, such as 'schema', 'script', 'scenario' and 'cognitive model', is a theory of understanding categories which relies on metonymic processing. For Fillmore, a frame is a collection of interrelated concepts: "I have in mind any system of concepts related in such a way that to understand any one of them you have to understand the whole structure in which it fits"; and access to one of them allows access to the others: "when one of the things in such a structure is introduced into a text, or into a conversation, all of the others are automatically made available" (Fillmore 1982/2006:373). It can be seen from this discussion that categorization is recognized independently by many scholars in linguistics as metonymic, and the manipulation of categories in communication as a metonymic process.

Etymology

When we look at meaning relations historically, diachronically rather than synchronically, again we see metonymy at work. Metonymic and metaphoric shifts are the two processes most evident in historical semantics when explaining the change of word meaning over time. The noun *buff*, for example, ultimately derives from 'buffalo': the skin of a buffalo is a yellowy-brown colour, hence the use of *buff* to mean colour, as in *buff envelope*. This was the colour of the uniforms of volunteer firemen in New York, hence the sense of *buff* as expert, eg *film buff*. Another line of derivation goes from the sense of skin being visible, as in *to be in the buff*, ie naked; while yet another comes from the smoothness of a buffalo's skin, as in *to buff up*, meaning to make shine, and to the more recent sense, *to be buff*, meaning fit/good looking. The animal standing for its skin; the skin standing for the colour; the colour standing for the clothing; the clothing standing for the profession; the profession standing for expertise, are all metonymic steps; and skin standing for unclothed; skin standing for shininess; shininess standing for the process by which you make something shiny; and shininess standing for 'fitness', are also all metonymic. The change of part of speech which *buff* undergoes in its history from noun to adjective, from adjective to noun, from adjective to verb, etc, ie 'zero derivation' ('conversion'), is also a metonymic rather than a metaphoric process. Sometimes a number of metonymic steps results in a shift which is metaphoric, as is the case with the Arabic idiom *kathīr al-ramād*, "He has a lot of ash", cited by Al-Sharafi (Al-Sharafi 2004:26). This idiom means "to be generous", explained by this chain of metonymies: A LOT OF ASH STANDS FOR COOKING → A LOT OF COOKING STANDS FOR A LOT OF FOOD → A LOT OF FOOD STANDS FOR A LOT OF GUESTS → A LOT OF GUESTS STANDS FOR GENEROSITY (Al-Sharafi 2004:60).

Pragmatics

For Radden, metonymy is present "at all levels of linguistic structure: phonology, lexical semantics, lexical grammar, morphology, grammar, and pragmatics" (Radden 2005:11). It is the pragmatic level I now turn to and the role of metonymy in understanding deixis and inference. Deixis is metonymic because it allows speakers to refer to the same entity using different frames, frames which depend on the speaker's perspective with regard to space (*this chair here* versus *that chair there*), person (*my timetable* versus *your timetable*), time (*this meeting now* versus *that meeting then*), etc. The 'indirect speech acts' of Austin/Searle involve inferencing from a logical form to a function which is not typically associated with that form. Radden explains indirect speech acts (ISAs) in terms of part-whole relations between sentence meaning and utterance meaning: "The indirectness of a speech act resides in the incongruity between the intended illocution and the utterance meaning, which only partly renders the full speech act meaning" (Radden 2005:22).

Gibbs recognizes that "speaking and understanding indirect speech acts involves a kind of metonymic reasoning, where people infer wholes (a series of actions) from a part" (Gibbs 1994:352). Panther & Thornburg also recognize that ISAs involve metonymic reasoning (2003, 2009). 'Conversational implicatures' of Grice involve a process by which propositional meaning is enriched by information from the (cognitive, physical, interpersonal and textual) environment in order to arrive at the secondary derived, intended 'utterance meaning'. Thus, *Why don't you finish your drink and leave?!* is more likely to be a threat than a suggestion; *Who do you think you are?*, a challenge rather than a request for information; *Whose car is that parked in front of the gate?*, a complaint rather than an enquiry; *Have you seen my keys?*, an entreaty to join in the search rather than a question designed to elicit a 'yes' or 'no' answer. It is possible for us to arrive at these secondary 'derived', or 'conversational', meanings by virtue of them being sufficiently closely related to be retrievable (inferred) using the context and our knowledge of the world to resolve incongruity.

Radden discusses the role of metonymy in implicature (Radden 2000:98–101). For him, "The conceptual relationships between a named and an implicated entity are based on contiguity, or metonymy" (Radden 2000:98). He identifies 'sequential events', 'event and result' and 'place and activity' as three metonymic relationships which "are particularly prone to evoking conversational implicatures" (Radden 2000:98). Gibbs calls this inferencing 'metonymic reasoning' (Gibbs 1999:72), though Radden calls it 'metonymy-based inferencing': "Indirect speech acts represent a particularly convincing case of metonymy-based inferencing" (Radden 2005:22). Ruiz de Mendoza also recognizes the role of metonymy in pragmatic inferencing (Barcelona 2005:31), as do Panther & Thornburg and authors in the volume edited by them, *Metonymy and Pragmatic Inferencing* (Panther & Thornburg 2003). Barcelona goes further: "The inferential nature of metonymy, ie, its role in activating the implicit pre-existing connection of a certain element of knowledge or experience to another one, also explains its ubiquity and its multilevel nature (from morphemes in some cases to text)" (Barcelona 2005:42). Barcelona claims that metonymy is "primarily *inferential* in nature rather than primarily referential" (Barcelona 2005:42). Metonymies "basically have an inferential function" and "their referential and motivational functions are consequences of their inferential function" (Barcelona 2009:391), while adding that there is more to inferencing than metonymy (Barcelona 2009:394).

Although they do not describe it as such, Sperber & Wilson's 'relevance theory' is essentially also a metonymic theory of inference (Sperber & Wilson 1986). It is metonymic because utterances are incomplete representations of intentions, external manifestations of assumptions the speaker wishes to communicate. 'Ostensive behaviour', central to relevance theory, is behaviour which indicates that an implicit idea is being made explicit; it draws the hearer's attention to an assumption the speaker wants to communicate. Carston observes that explicatures are inferentially developed from partial, conceptual representations: "An explicature is an ostensively communicated assumption which is inferentially developed from one of the incomplete conceptual representations (logical forms) encoded by the utterance" (Carston 2002:377). It is a metonymic process which takes the speaker from the intended meaning to the incomplete logical form and the hearer from the incomplete logical form to the inferred message.

THE PARTIAL NATURE OF THE SIGN

It is a basic assumption behind all linguistic theory that words represent things (real, abstract or imagined) and clauses represent events (who does what to whom and in what circumstances); but such a determinist 'encoding' view of language soon becomes inadequate when we go from an idealized model of language to language in use. Many approaches have been adopted to explain what else is involved beyond one-to-one representation when we look at language use in the real world. The contributions phraseology, metaphor, pragmatics and cognition make to extending meaning have been discussed in Chapter 2 in the context of my Model of the Linguistic Mind presented there. Sociolinguistics, discourse analysis and cognitive linguistics are other approaches which help explain indeterminism, focussing respectively on language variation, meaning at the level of the whole text and the relationship between language and thought. In this section, I explore the insights which Metonymy Studies give to the question. An approach focussing on metonymy puts into relief a basic characteristic of language as a semiotic system, namely, that language under-refers/under-determines, that 'the message' is always more than 'the text', that what is being said is only a partial representation of what exists, that, as Kress suggests, "All representation is always partial" (Kress 2010:70).

The logical consequence of language being a sign system is that language is metonymic: "Since we have no other means of expressing and communicating our concepts than by using forms, language as well as other communication systems are of necessity metonymic" (Radden & Kövecses 1999:24). Kress eschews the term 'metonymy', not finding it useful (personal communication, 2009), but uses 'metaphor' instead to cover phenomena I would consider to be metonymic, when he writes: "all signs are metaphors, always newly made, resting on, materializing and displaying the interest of the maker of the sign" (Kress 2010:71). Because language is metonymic, representation is not only possible but also flexible. It is possible, because without metonymy there would be no signs to begin with; it is flexible, because if partial correspondence, rather than one-to-one correspondence, is the principle at the centre of communication (semiotic work), then that partiality can be exploited to give infinite grades of meaning, a potential which can be used for highlighting and giving salience. As Kress states: "At the moment of the making of the sign, representation is always partial [. . .]. It is *partial* in relation to the object or phenomenon represented; it is *full* in relation to the sign-maker's interest at the moment of making the sign" (Kress 2010:71). Thus, the partial nature of the sign allows the full expression of meaning as it emerges in discourse; and if meaning making were not partial, 'full' expression could not be achieved.

For Langacker, this interface between fixed coded meaning and unfixed intermediate meaning is made possible through metonymic processing, as metonymy is a 'reference-point' or 'active-zone' phenomenon, where explicit indications "merely provide mental access to a desired target" (Langacker 1993:30–31), the reference point entity serving as a 'vehicle'. Langacker observes that cognitive linguistics constantly discovers metonymic dualities: "I have been struck by the number of clearly essential notions involving an entity that is somehow 'prominent' or 'focused' within a more inclusive 'dominion'. This is reflected in such terminological pairings as profile vs. base, trajector vs. landmark, participant vs. setting, immediate scope vs. overall scope, objective vs. subjective, autonomous vs. dependent, and thing vs. relation" (Langacker 1993:35). He also observes that grammar is metonymic for the same reason, that it offers broad rather than precise indications: "grammar [. . .] is basically metonymic, in the sense that the information explicitly provided by conventional means does not itself establish the precise connections apprehended by the speaker and hearer in using an expression" (Langacker 2009:46).

In the discussion so far, I have been talking of 'signs' and have been using the term for what Peirce calls 'symbol' in the three aspects of the sign identified by him—icon, index and symbol (Hawkes 1977:128–130). Peirce did not intend this as a classification of signs, though it is often presented as such. It is the *index* which metonymy is most usually identified with, indexical representation, eg "smoke standing for fire", being seen as quintessentially metonymic. In fact, metonymy is involved in all three aspects, with symbols, as already discussed in this section, with indices, as in the example above of smoke representing fire, but also with icons which I will demonstrate now. If we take the famous London Underground *Tube Map* as an example, in the edition I have to hand (April 2011), a wheelchair icon is used to indicate wheelchair access, but the icon is only supplying information that there is something here to do with wheelchairs; we have to infer that this is not, for example, a sales point for purchasing or hiring a wheelchair or that it signifies there is room for one wheelchair only (as such a sign might on the side of a train). In fact, the key to the map reads "step-free access between the platform and the street", giving more explicit information than the icon offers. The icon is only *part* of the message, the rest of the message is supplied by the reader; thus even an icon is processed metonymically. Another example: readers at the British Library in London are given instructions as to what they may or may not take into the reading rooms on the plastic carrier bags they are given to put their belongings in. On it, there is a combination of signs, some iconic, some indexical and some symbolic. These are sometimes used in combination; so, for example, an iconic representation of a pair of hands is accompanied by a text, *Wash hands*, hands being represented twice (pictorially and verbally), washing only once.

The partial nature of meaning making is well illustrated by examining 'naming' across languages. This shows up the different strategies independently adopted by different speech communities in the evolution of how things are named. Kress illustrates this with the name for 'light bulb' in German, *Glühbirne*, observing that in German this object is conceived as having the shape of a 'pear' (*Birne*) rather than a 'bulb', and emitting a 'glow' (*Glühen*) rather than 'light' (Kress 2010:103). Radden compares three objects, *push chair*, *seat belt* and *hiking boots*, in Spanish and English, and observes that whereas in English the actions of 'pushing', 'sitting' and 'hiking' are emphasized, in Spanish, 'walking' *silla* ***de paseo*** (chair **of walk**), 'safety' *cinturón* ***de seguridad*** (belt **of safety**) and 'mountains' *botas* ***de montaña*** (boots **of mountain**) are salient (Radden 2005:20). The different words used in different languages for the place where you get on and off a train also show a difference of perspective: the German word *Gleis* emphasizes a track or route; the Italian word *binario* emphasizes the pair of metal rails the train runs on; while the English word *platform* gives salience to the structure adjacent to the train which allows you to board. In all these examples, one can see how the conceptual metonymy SALIENT PART FOR WHOLE was instrumental in giving origin to these words and expressions. I explore this phenomenon in more detail below in a study in which I compare names for body parts and common electrical devices across languages.

A Study of Naming Across Languages

In this study, my informants were applied linguistics students on MA courses at a London university. In the context of a practice workshop they were asked to give translations in their first languages for the two anatomical structures, *floating rib* and *rib cage*, and two electrical devices *answering machine* and *mobile phone*. Anatomical structures were chosen because the design of the human body is universal; electrical devices were chosen because their design is also fairly universal but terms for them have a shorter history. Data collected during this workshop were added to by data given by via email over a period of three weeks in 2008. The twenty-two informants were all non-native speakers of English and represented the following languages: Arabic, Chinese, Dutch, Finnish, French, German, Greek, Italian, Polish, Portuguese, Russian, Spanish and Urdu. The informants were asked to rely on their first-language knowledge but were also invited to research further, if they wished, eg via the internet, friends and reference sources. Where more than one informant gave data for the same language, I collated these to give a single version after discussing any contradictions or inconsistencies with the informants via email first. For each item, the informants were asked to give:

- The English term
- The language being documented—their first language
- A translation of the English term into the language being documented, choosing an everyday term rather than a medical or technical term, if there was a choice available, and using a transliteration into the Latin alphabet, if the language being considered used another script
- An 'interlinear translation' of the translation, ie an explanation of what each morphemic/lexemic element meant in the order they came. Some gave fuller explanations than this.

For the first term, *floating rib*, the data revealed an interesting phenomenon, that across the languages considered, only three broad but distinct semantic categories were represented. In all the languages for which data were obtained, the word for RIB was modified by a term from one of these three meaning areas, FLOATING, FREE and FALSE, as shown in Table 4.1. Arabic, Dutch, French, Italian and Spanish make salient the sense of FLOATING or SWAYING; Chinese, French (*flottante* appears twice, the word in French meaning both 'floating' and 'loose', according to my informants), German and Polish make use of the FREE or UNATTACHED aspect; while Greek, Russian and Spanish make use of FAKE or FALSE. Here we see a clear demonstration of metonymic, or 'partial', meaning making at work in the creation of terms for *floating rib* across these languages.

The second term considered in this study was *rib cage*. Here, the same principle applies but the situation is more complex as the data fall into six categories, RIBS, RIB CHEST, RIB CAGE, THORACIC CAGE, THORACIC BOX, CHEST CAGE, as shown in Table 4.2. Here, the idea of CAGE, modified by RIB, THORACIC and CHEST, accounts for seven of the languages represented in this study: Arabic, Chinese, French, German, Greek, Italian and Russian; while the idea of BOX is the aspect used in Spanish; and RIBS, without any modifier, in Polish. Meaning making through metonymy allows the selection of certain aspects and the disregarding of others, such that if there are enough aspects to choose from, it is possible for two languages to have arrived at terms which do not share any components, as is the case if we compare the English term *rib cage* and the Spanish *caja torácica* (literally 'thoracic box').

The third term for which data were collected was *answering machine*. Here three semantic categories emerge, representing the aspects of ANSWER, RECORD and SECRETARY, as shown in Table 4.3. Arabic, French, German, Spanish, Russian and Urdu all use the aspect of ANSWERING, either modified by the equivalent of—ER (French, German and Spanish) or expressed as a THING or MACHINE which ANSWERS (Arabic, Russian and Urdu). Chinese is the only language in the data to take the aspects of the device being a TELEPHONE and one which RECORDS; while the Greek, Italian and Portuguese terms approach the meaning through personification, an

Table 4.1 'floating rib'

FLOATING	FREE	FALSE
Arabic *athlae aema* rib floating	Chinese *fú-dòng-de lèi-gŭ* unfixed rib	Greek *nothos plevra* fake rib
Dutch *wevende ribbe* swaying rib	French *côte flottante* rib loose	Russian *lozhnoey rebro* false rib
English ***floating rib***	German *frei Rippe* free rib	Spanish *costilla falsa* false rib
French *côte flottante* rib floating	Polish *żebro wolne* rib free	
Italian *costola flutuante* rib floating		
Spanish *costilla flotante* rib floating		

Table 4.2 'rib cage'

RIBS	THORACIC CAGE	CHEST CAGE
Polish *żebra* ribs	French *cage thoracique* cage thoracic	Arabic *kafas sadri* cage of-chest
RIB CHEST	Greek *thorakikos klovos* thoracic cage	German *Brustkorb* chest cage/basket
Dutch *ribbekast* rib chest	Italian *gabbia toracica* cage thoracic	Russian *grudnaya kletka* chest cage
RIB CAGE	**THORACIC BOX**	
Chinese *lèi-gŭ lóng-zi* rib cage	Spanish *caja torácica* box thoracic	
English ***rib cage***		

'answering machine' being an automatic, electronic or telephonic SECRETARY or TELEPHONIST.

The fourth term considered in this study was *mobile phone*. Here, again, the data grouped into three distinct semantic areas, CELLULAR, PORTABLE and SMALL, as shown in Table 4.4.

Table 4.3 'answering machine'

ANSWER	**RECORD**	**SECRETARY**
Arabic *Alat Alrad* machine of answering	Chinese *lu yin dian hua* record telephone	Greek *aftómatos tilefonitís* automatic telephonist
English ***answering machine***		Italian *segreteria telefonica* secretary's office telephonic
French *répondeur* answerer		Portuguese *secretária electrônica* secretary electronic
German *Anrufbeantworter* call answerer		
Spanish *contestador* answerer		
Russian *avtootvetchik* auto answer thing		
Urdu *machine-e-jawaab* machine of answering		

Table 4.4 'mobile phone'

CELLULAR	**PORTABLE**	**SMALL**
Arabic *telephone khilyawi* telephone cellular	**English** ***mobile phone***	Chinese *shou ji* hand machine
English *cell phone*	Finnish *matkapuhelin* travel phone	German *Handy* handy
Italian *cellulare* cellular	French *portable* portable	Italian *telefonino* telephone little
Polish *komórka* cell	Greek *kinitó* mobile	
Portuguese *celular* cellular	Spanish *móvil* mobile	
Russian *syotovoy telefon* honeycomb telephone	Urdu *haatif saafaree* telephone travelling	

Arabic, Italian, Polish, Portuguese and Russian highlight the CELLULAR nature of the mobile-phone network; Finnish, French, Greek, Spanish and Urdu highlight the PORTABILITY of a mobile phone, the fact you can carry it with you; while Chinese, German and Italian highlight its SMALL size. These are three distinct areas of meaning, each one offering only a partial representation of the concept of 'mobile phone'. It is interesting to note that Italian has two terms for 'mobile phone', *cellulare* and *telefonino*, one belonging in the CELLULAR group, the other to SMALL. This is so also for English, where *mobile* and *cell phone* belong to the PORTABILITY and CELLULAR groups. A further category for mobile phone, which has not so far been included in this discussion, is exemplified by a now outdated term used in Chinese, *da ge da*, which means, literally, 'big brother big', coming from a time when mobile phones were new and associated with flash entrepreneurs and gangsters. This is a cultural association with mobile phones which is also available for use in metonymic meaning making and which at the time in China was presumably thought to be salient.

Dictionary definitions, a context where you would expect to find complete semantic descriptions, surprisingly, are also partial, offering only certain aspects of the items/concepts they define. The *Longman Dictionary of English Language and Culture* defines a mobile phone in terms only of PORTABILITY: "a telephone which one can carry with one"; the entry in the *Macmillan English Dictionary* uses two aspects to define the mobile phone, PORTABLE and SMALL: "a small phone that you can carry around with you"; while the *Cambridge International Dictionary of English* uses characteristics of the network and portability, but not size: "telephone which is connected to the telephone system by radio, rather than by a wire, and can therefore be used anywhere where its signal can be received". Thus, the three aspects identified in the data discussed above across languages, CELLULAR, PORTABLE and SMALL, are not all found in any one of the dictionary definitions given above, demonstrating that the principle of metonymic meaning making applies as much to the evolution of a term in a language as it does to post hoc semantic descriptions in dictionaries.

METONYMY IN CLOSER FOCUS

The huge growth in interest in metaphor, since the publication of Lakoff & Johnson's seminal *Metaphors We Live By* (Lakoff & Johnson 1980), has resulted in the emergence of a massive literature on the subject and the birth of a coherent discipline which has come to be called Metaphor Studies, discussed in the previous chapter. From this academic interest in metaphor, a burgeoning interest in metonymy has emerged over recent years, especially the last fifteen, resulting in the formation of an impressive body of research, almost entirely from a cognitive linguistics perspective, enshrined in the volumes edited by Panther & Radden (1999b), Barcelona (2000), Dirven & Pörings (2002), and Panther, Thornburg & Barcelona (2009). These collections contain both reprints of classic articles (eg Goossens 1990, Croft 1993, Kövecses & Radden 1998) and new papers published in these volumes for the first time (eg Radden 2000, Riemer 2002b, Taylor

2002, Langacker 2009). Further articles, not in these volumes, also contribute to the body of metonymy literature (eg Langacker 1993, Radden 2005). Seen collectively, the new writing on metonymy shows a consensus around a number of claims: that metonymy, like metaphor, is a conceptual phenomenon; that metonymy, like metaphor, is ubiquitous and plays a central and crucial role in conceptualization and communication; and that metonymy and metaphor can be identified as distinct, though related, phenomena. Metonymy is seen by some metonymy scholars not only to be *as* important but *more* important than metaphor. Radden considers metonymy to be "an even more pervasive phenomenon than metaphor", being present "at all levels of linguistic structure" (Radden 2005:11). Taylor sees metonymy as "one of the most fundamental processes of meaning extension, more basic, perhaps, even than metaphor" (Taylor 2002:325), and for Barcelona metonymy "is probably even more basic than metaphor in language and cognition" (Barcelona 2002:215).

The plan of this book, moving as it does from a discussion of metaphor in Chapters 2 and 3 to a discussion of metonymy in Chapters 4 and 5, reflects these developments and the position I take in their regard. The idea that metonymy is the more fundamental of the two concepts is supported by the Stack of Counters model of metaphor proposed in Chapter 3, in which metonymy, the ability to recognize part-whole relations, is shown to be the mechanism behind metaphor and the ability to metaphorize. In later chapters, I make the case that this position has implications for text analysis and editing (Chapter 6), language learning (Chapter 7) and translation/interpreting (Chapter 8). Radden observes that "the ubiquitous nature of metonymy has only recently been noticed" (Radden 2005:11), and Barcelona that "*metonymy* has not received as much attention as metaphor in cognitive linguistics" (Barcelona 2002:215). But if metonymy is so basic, why did the metonymy literature emerge so much later than the metaphor literature, and why has there been less interest overall? The answer may be that it is often the case that more basic phenomena are discovered only when more complex and evident phenomena have been explored first. Exactly this occurred within Metaphor Studies: after publishing *Metaphors We Live By*, Lakoff & Johnson realized that in order to explain fully their 'contemporary theory of metaphor', it was necessary to introduce a concept more fundamental than conceptual metaphor, namely the 'image schema'. Image schemas are the schematic representation in the mind of repeatedly encountered physical experiences, defined by Gibbs & Colston as "dynamic analog representations of spatial relations and movements in space" (Gibbs & Colston 1995:349). This concept allowed Johnson and Lakoff to explain how 'source' domains are mapped onto 'target' domains without flouting the principle of 'invariance': experiencing the world sets up schematic representations in the mind (image schemas) which help form the more detailed 'cognitive models'; connections between cognitive models create conceptual metaphors via specific mappings; these are then expressed through lexicogrammar or multimodally. Both authors examine image schemas in depth in the volumes they published independently in 1987 (Johnson 1987, Lakoff 1987b). Schemas are cognitive 'primitives', but it was conceptual metaphor to which Johnson's and Lakoff's attention was drawn first.

Metonymy is present in this discussion in a further sense, as metonymy itself turns out to be one of the image schemas discussed by Johnson, PART-WHOLE being an image schema discussed along with CONTAINMENT, CENTRE-PERIPHERY, PATH, LINK, BALANCE, CONTACT, SURFACE, FULL-EMPTY, MERGING, MATCHING, NEAR-FAR, MASS-COUNT, ITERATION and SUPERIMPOSITION (Johnson 1987). Image schemas are few in number because they are so basic, and in any analytical framework fundamental units tend to be few in number. Gibbs & Colston suggest there are "over two dozen different image schemas" when considering the work of Johnson and Lakoff together (Gibbs & Colston 1995:347), while Taylor identifies nine in his summary: CONTAINMENT, JOURNEY (origin-path-destination), PROXIMITY/DISTANCE, LINKAGE/SEPARATION, FRONT/BACK, PART-WHOLE, LINEAR ORDER, UP-DOWN ORIENTATION and MASS/MULTIPLEX (Taylor 2002:337–338). Even in Taylor's overview where only nine image schemas are listed, part-whole is one of the nine, giving further confirmation that metonymy is recognized as fundamental to conceptualization. This leads us next to explore in more depth what the common and essential features of this basic phenomenon are. In order to arrive at a more precise ontology of metonymy and identify what distinguishes it from metaphor, I devote the remainder of this chapter to a discussion of the three areas: Domain Theory, the Metonymy-Metaphor Continuum and Metonymy Typologies.

Domain Theory

There is agreement in the literature that metonymy differs from metaphor in involving a single domain, while metaphor involves two domains. This is called 'domain theory' in the Cognitive Linguistic Theory of Metaphor and Metonymy (Dirven 2002a:15). For Lakoff, "metonymic mapping occurs within a single conceptual domain" (Lakoff 1987b:288), while metaphor involves "cross-domain mapping" (Lakoff 1993:203). Lakoff & Turner maintain that "metonymic mapping occurs within a single domain, not across domains" (Lakoff & Turner 1989:103). Kövecses & Radden (1998), Radden & Kövecses (1999) and Panther & Radden (2005:3) do not depart from this in their definitions but use a combination of terminology from traditional studies, ie 'vehicle' and 'target', alongside terms from cognitive linguistics, such as 'cognitive process', 'conceptual entity', 'mental access' and 'idealized cognitive model': "Metonymy is a cognitive process in which one conceptual entity, the vehicle, provides mental access to another conceptual entity, the target, within the same domain, or ICM" (Kövecses & Radden 1998:39), "within the same idealized cognitive model" (Radden & Kövecses 1999:21). Warren also makes a connection back to traditional studies of figurative language, recasting 'contiguity' as 'similarity in dissimilarity': "the approach presented here is a further development of the traditional view that metonymy involves contiguity, whereas metaphor involves seeing similarity in dissimilarity" (Warren 2002:126).

Croft's much-cited paper attempts to refine this, suggesting that both involve mapping between domains, but that they are domains from the same 'domain matrix' in metonymy, and between different—and therefore unrelated—domains/domain matrices in metaphor (Croft 1993:348). Croft introduces the term 'domain matrix' here from Langacker in order to recognize that concepts are complex and represented in the mind by clusters of related domains; thus *We need new blood in this company* involves mapping between the two domains of BLOOD and PERSON, but this is metonymic because the domain BLOOD is within the domain matrix of PERSON, along with other domains, such as ARM, HEAD, SKIN, FINGER. Croft characterizes the nature of the mapping in metonymy as 'highlighting', reserving the term 'mapping' for metaphoric projections (Croft 1993:348). Barcelona uses the term 'mapping' for both, otherwise his definition accords with Croft's: he defines both metonymy and metaphor as involving the mapping of a conceptual 'source' domain onto a conceptual 'target' domain, but distinguishes between them on the basis of whether the source and target are in the same 'functional domain' and whether they are linked by a 'pragmatic function'; thus, in metonymy, "source and target are in the same functional domain and are linked by a pragmatic function"; while in metaphor, source and target are either "in different functional domains" or "not linked by a pragmatic function" by being "in different taxonomic domains" (Barcelona 2002:246).

There are two significant differences between metonymy and metaphor which have not been emphasized so far in this discussion, both of which concern the nature of mappings: in metonymy there is usually just one mapping, whereas metaphor has several mappings; also, the mapping in metonymy can usually operate in either direction (source and target domains can be interchanged), while metaphoric mappings are strictly unidirectional (the source domain remaining constant). The computational linguist Barnden uses 'complexity of mappings' and 'imaginary' versus 'real' as criteria for distinguishing between metonymy and metaphor (Barnden 2006). Metaphoric mappings go from (usually) a more concrete source domain to a more abstract target domain, eg LIFE (target) IS A JOURNEY (source), while for metonymy, if a PART-WHOLE relation can be recognized, then the reverse, WHOLE-PART, will usually also be available. This is not always the case. Barcelona states simply that "a large number of metonymies are reversible" (Barcelona 2002:221).

For Kövecses & Radden, in their classification of metonymies into 'sign', 'reference' and 'concept' metonymies, that is metonymies operating at each of the three points of the semiotic triangle, only 'concept metonymies' are reversible (Kövecses & Radden 1998:46). Radden & Kövecses base their definition of metonymy on the notion of the Idealized Cognitive Model (ICM), understood here to be the encyclopaedic knowledge of a domain as well as "the cultural models they are part of" (Radden & Kövecses 1999:20). They define metonymy as a phenomenon which occurs *within* an ICM (Radden & Kövecses 1999:21). Each ICM offers three 'ontological realms', representing the three points of the semiotic triangle: 'the world of reality' (things and events), 'the world of conceptualization' and 'the world of language' (forms), all of which can give rise to metonymies (Radden & Kövecses 1999:20). "These realms roughly correspond to the three entities that comprise the well-known semiotic triangle as developed by Ogden and Richards [. . .]: thought, symbol and referent" (Radden & Kövecses 1999:23). The computations of these three ontological realms result in three types of metonymy, 'sign', 'reference' and 'concept' metonymies, and six metonymic relations within them: 'sign metonymies' (FORM FOR CONCEPT), 'reference metonymies' (FORM/CONCEPT FOR THING/EVENT; FORM FOR THING/EVENT; CONCEPT FOR THING/EVENT), and 'concept metonymies' (FORM/CONCEPT FOR FORM/CONCEPT; FORM/CONCEPT FOR CONCEPT) (Kövecses & Radden 1998:41–48; Radden & Kövecses 1999:28–29). Kövecses & Radden note that 'sign' and 'reference' metonymies do not offer bidirectional variants, while 'concept' metonymies do, and suggest that this is because concept metonymies do not cut across ontological realms in the way that sign and reference metonymies do (Kövecses & Radden 1998:46).

The distinctions discussed above, particularly the idea of metonymy involving connections within a single domain and metaphor involving connections between unrelated domains, are all ultimately reflections of the work of Jakobson and the distinction he made in his influential article of 1956 between relations of 'contiguity' and of 'similarity' (Jakobson 1956/1971). For Jakobson, 'the metonymic way' involves the combination of syntagmatically-associated items resulting in relations of contiguity; while 'the metaphor way' involves selection from among paradigmatically-associated items resulting in relations of similarity (Jakobson 1956/1971). On closer examination, equating syntagmatic relations to metonymy and paradigmatic relations to metaphor is just confusing (Dirven 2002b:87), as both relations are always present in all language items at all levels, whether metaphor, metonymy or literal language is involved. As Jakobson himself claims: "in normal verbal behaviour both processes are continually operative" (Jakobson 1956/1971:90). Lodge observes that although Jakobson argues that metonymy and metaphor are "opposed", being "generated according to opposite principles", they are related on a pragmatic level as both involve the principle of substitution (Lodge 1977:76). Towards the end of this essay, Jakobson seems to be giving in to this confusion by explaining metonymy in terms of selection rather than combination: "Jakobson ends up interpreting metonymy as relying on a 'paradigmatic' association by contiguity!" (Blank 1999:172). The term favoured by Jakobson to describe the nature of the relationship between vehicle and topic in metonymy is 'contiguity' (Jakobson 1956/1971). Langacker considers the term 'contiguity' too vague and attempts to analyze it further in terms of features such as centrality vs. peripheralness, profile vs. base, basic vs. abstract (Croft 1993:345). The term I have chosen with which to characterize metonymy is 'relatedness'. Like contiguity, it is not a precise term, but it has enough precision to define metonymy while being loose enough to embrace all the phenomena I wish to consider together.

The Metonymy-Metaphor Continuum

Here, I consider whether metonymy and metaphor, though related, are ultimately distinct phenomena, or whether there is a metonymy-metaphor continuum with intermediate points along it. Riemer refers to this debate as the 'demarcation question' (Riemer 2002b:380–388). For many scholars, metonymy is not even distinct but simply a type of metaphor, classified by subsuming it under the heading of metaphor. Aristotle identifies four types of metaphor in his famous definition in the *Poetics*, but three of these, 'genus to species', 'species to genus' and 'species to species', are strictly speaking metonymies, only the fourth, 'analogy', being true metaphor (Al-Sharafi 2004:13). Searle sees metonymy and synecdoche as "special cases of metaphor" and adds them to his "list of metaphorical principles" (Searle 1993:107). Halliday's discussion of 'grammatical metaphor' is really a discussion of metonymy in grammar in the sense of zero derivation (Halliday 1994:342). It is Jakobson who reduces the list of classical tropes to two in his famous essay on aphasia (Jakobson 1956/1971), but although he presents metaphor and metonymy as opposing 'poles', entitling the explorative Section 5 of his essay 'The Metaphoric and Metonymic Poles' (Jakobson 1956/1971:90), Jakobson is more concerned with keeping them apart than exploring the metonymy-metaphor continuum. As Dirven observes: "Jakobson was far more interested in opposing metaphor and metonymy and, in fact, he did not much bother about the idea of a continuum, on which metonymy and metaphor can be supposed to meet and to develop" (Dirven 2002a:4).

How can we distinguish between metonymic and metaphoric linguistic expressions? This question has been extensively covered in the literature. I will review some of the answers found there and then give my own view. Gibbs offers a test in order to distinguish between the two, his 'like' test, for which expressions are reformulated by adding 'like' (Gibbs 1994:322). If the expression still makes sense, we are dealing with metaphor, if not, it is metonymy. Thus, *It is **like** a chest cage* (in the example for 'rib cage' given earlier) makes sense, but CREDIT CARDS are *like plastic*, does not (they are made of plastic); similarly, a TV is not *like* a *small screen*, it has a small screen as one of its parts; nor is the ROYAL FAMILY like *Buckingham Palace*, but rather the building is used to stand for the family. There are many other ways of signalling metaphor other than *like*, eg *as if, so to speak, metaphorically speaking, the proverbial*, etc (Goatly 1997:168–197). Also, although Gibbs' 'like test' is useful, it is suited to nouns, other tests being needed for other parts of speech: for example, for verbs, the 'as if' test, and for adjectives, the 'as if it were' test (Glucksberg 2001:50). Even for nouns, *like* is not unproblematic. As Glucksberg observes, both metaphor and metonymy involve the concept of 'likeness', the difference between them being a matter of degree, ie *how* 'like' they are (Glucksberg 2001:40). To compare two things is to look for 'likeness' between them, but metonymy is a comparison between two concepts which are already alike, while metaphor is a comparison between two concepts which are not alike.

In the colloquial use of *like*, such as "It is **like** we went to the shopping mall and **like** met up with friends", *like* is used to indicate metonymy. We can conjecture that a speaker who uses *like* in this way intends to give the impression that the activities they are engaging in are 'something like' rather than exactly those stated, perhaps because simply "going to the mall and meeting up with friends" sounds too banal, too 'uncool'. Also, because there can be degrees of likeness, examples will emerge which are intermediate, such as *cherry tomato*. Is this metonymy or metaphor? 'Cherries' and 'tomatoes' are both foods, round, red, shiny and juicy (thus related metonymically because they share certain characteristics) but different in other respects, such as size, sweetness, internal structure, lobing, etc (making comparisons between them metaphoric). Radden proposes another test, the 'but test', where a clause with *but* is added to introduce a counter expectation, thus "Sheila is a mother of three children but she doesn't work" provides unexpected information, because WORKING is not a prototypical attribute of *mother* and could therefore not be used to access MOTHER metonymically (Radden 2005:12–13).

The idea that there can be degrees of relatedness has prompted scholars, such as Al-Sharafi (2004), Deignan (2005) and Radden (2000), to propose the existence of a metonymy-metaphor continuum, and to verify that this continuum exists by looking for points intermediate along it. Radden gives five examples with *high*, which form a cline from literal through metonymic to metaphoric; they are: *high tower/high tide/high temperature/high prices/high quality* (Radden 2005:24). For him, *high tower* is literal, *high temperature* is metonymic and *high quality* is metaphoric; while *high tide* is intermediate between literal and metonymic and *high prices* is intermediate between metonymic and metaphoric. This is a successful approach, I feel, as although *high* is polysemous, and this is what these examples show, graded meaning is revealed through the combinations it forms.

The metonymy-metaphor continuum can be illustrated by the behaviour of words in various noun-noun compounds. If we rank noun-noun compounds of *champagne* from the most literal to the most metaphoric, we would get a sequence like this: LITERAL (a glass of) *champagne/champagne cocktail/champagne flute/champagne breakfast/champagne pullover* (ie colour)/*champagne lifestyle/champagne socialist* METAPHORIC (examples from the Cobuild corpus, accessed 9 November 2006). Similarly, compounds of *sandwich* give a sequence like this: LITERAL *sandwich filling/sandwich knife/sandwich shop/sandwich counter/sandwich man/sandwich board/sandwich course* METAPHORIC (ibid). Warren points out that noun-noun compounds tend not to be compositional because metonymic narrowing has already been set up in creating the compound; as Warren says for her example *foxholes*: "not all holes which have foxes in them are foxholes" (Warren 1999:125). This, it seems to me, offers evidence enough that metonymy and metaphor are related phenomena and that there is a metonymy-metaphor continuum with intermediate points along the continuum.

Scholars who have explored phenomena intermediate between metonymy and metaphor include Goossens (1990), Bartsch (2002), Riemer (2002a, 2002b) and Dirven (2002b). Goossens investigates the interaction between metonymy and metaphor in conventionalized figurative expressions and identifies four categories of 'metaphtonymy' in his data: 'metaphor from metonymy', 'metonymy within metaphor', 'metaphor within metonymy' and 'demetonymization in a metaphorical context' (Goossens 1990). Goossens has observed that many metaphoric expressions clearly derive from metonyms, such as *close-lipped* (to mean secretive), *tongue in cheek* (not in earnest), etc, and has coined the term 'metaphor from metonymy' to describe them (Goossens 1990). Here, the physical reality of having 'lips which are close together' or 'your tongue in your cheek' are part and parcel of the behaviour associated with the expressions. 'Metaphor from metonymy' is the most common category of Goossens' four categories of metaphtonymy according to Deignan's study of corpus data (Deignan 2005). Another of Goossens' metaphtonymy categories is 'metonymy within metaphor', where a metonymic element is embedded in a metaphoric expression, eg *to shoot your mouth off*, in which mouth stands for speech (metonymy) and the expression as a whole means to reveal a secret (metaphor). 'Metonymy within metaphor' is not intermediate between metonymy and metaphor, but rather where both metonymy and metaphor coexist in the same expression while remaining distinct (Goossens 1990). In fact, in all his examples, metonymy and metaphor remain distinct phenomena appearing together, and so do not contribute to our understanding of the metonymy-metaphor continuum. This is so too for Bartsch who identifies, 'double metonymy', a combination rather than a blending of tropes, eg *Wall Street is in panic*, where a 'metonymic chain' can be identified within the same expression, namely PLACE FOR INSTITUTION FOR PEOPLE (Bartsch 2002).

Though Goossens' work looks at conventional expressions, and so is less concerned with metonymic processing in interaction than the evidence of metonymic processes having taken place in the past, two of the categories of metaphtonymy discussed above help highlight important phenomena: the metonymic basis of metaphor, eg *tight lipped* and *beat your breast* ('metaphor from metonymy'); and the embedding of metonymies in metaphoric expressions ('metonymy within metaphor'), eg *the hand* (= person) *that rocks the cradle rules the world* (Goossens 1990). Metaphor from metonymy is an idea which Kövecses & Radden explore, claiming that "many conceptual metaphors derive from conceptual metonymies", such as ANGER IS HEAT (Kövecses & Radden 1998:61), which Kövecses understands as coming about through a chain of conceptual metonymies: ANGER CAUSES BODY HEAT, BODY HEAT CAUSES HEAT (Kövecses 2002:156). Radden sees the embodiment of experience of the world as motivating this process and involving particularly 'primary metaphors', and that "Basically all the metaphors which Lakoff claims are grounded in our experience can be traced back to a metonymic basis" (Radden 2005:25).

Riemer, in his attempt to understand the metonymy-metaphor continuum, identifies points which are intermediate between 'plain' metonymy and 'plain' metaphor (Riemer 2002a, 2002b). The terms he coins in the first article both involve the process of conventionalization: 'hypermetonymy', the extension of the meaning of a metonymy through conventionalization without invoking a metaphoric process; and 'hypermetaphor', the extension of the meaning of a metaphor through conventionalization without invoking a metonymic process (Riemer 2002a). In the second article, he proposes further terms which involve modification through generalization and conventionalization: 'post-metonymy', a generalization of a metonymy beyond its normal use, eg *Don't knock it until you've tried it*; and 'post-metaphor', an expression which loses metaphoric qualities through conventionalization, eg *kick someone out of his flat* (Riemer 2002b). Dirven presents Riemer's categories diagrammatically on a cline—metonymy/post-metonymy/post-metaphor/metaphor—but also adds further points along the cline—'literalness', 'modulation' and 'frame variation' (Dirven 2002b:107), concluding that one principle, 'conceptual closeness/distance', is enough to place all these phenomena, convincingly illustrated through the use of data around the lexeme *tea*: "the distinction between conceptual closeness and conceptual distance seems to be powerful enough to account both for the different levels of figurativity within metonymy and for those between metonymy and metaphor" (Dirven 2002b:99). What is important to recognize in Riemer's rather complicated accounts is the significance of 'metonymy in metaphor', the move from metonymy to metaphor through conventionalization, as this is a widespread phenomenon. To use my own example, the expression *man of the cloth* to mean PRIEST may once have been metonymic, in that priests were perhaps those members of a community who were able to wear clothes made of fine cloth and that this was something which distinguished them. Now the expression is a 'dead' metonymy, in that it is no longer transparent, understood metaphorically, as priests nowadays are just as likely to wear tracksuits.

In this context, I propose that a test for measuring metonymic processing effort could be developed. This would take the form of an 'overlap coefficient', a measurement of the degree of similarity between (real or virtual) utterances. This measurement of the 'strength' of a metonymy could be judged by a panel of informants, the 'degree of overlap' being expressed on a scale from 1 to 5. This could also be used to test for 'break points', ie where the overlap coefficient is so small that the link between source and target can no longer be identified and the connection cannot be processed metonymically. This is similar to a technique used by Gibbs & Colston in an experiment in which they asked participants to assess the degree of relatedness between thirty-two senses of the lexeme *stand* relative to five image schemas (Gibbs & Colston 1995:352–353).

Metonymy Typologies

Many attempts have been made to classify metonymies, eg Lakoff & Johnson (1980), Nerlich et al (1999), Radden & Kövecses (1999) and Kövecses (2002). One can assume these scholars are working from the premise that making a complete list of possible metonymic relations is part and parcel of achieving an understanding of what metonymy is. While the cognitive approach to metaphor is a relatively recent development, the literature on metonymy has always taken what might be called a 'cognitive' approach, though traditional rhetoricians would, of course, not have referred to it as such, in that even earlier work on metonymy attempted to classify metonymy into types rather than considering them merely as individual linguistic items. Radden & Kövecses suggest that the names given to types of metonymy by traditional rhetoricians are not unlike the terms given by cognitive linguists now: "Unlike metaphor, metonymy has always been described in conceptual, rather than purely linguistic, terms. In analyzing metonymic relationships, traditional rhetoric operated with general conceptual notions such as CAUSE FOR EFFECT, CONTAINER FOR CONTENTS, etc." (Radden & Kövecses 1999:17). The difference is that cognitivists see these classes as mental categories which connect to other cognitive processes (and have the potential of being expressed multimodally), while more traditional approaches see them as classifications of linguistic items occurring in speech and text and no more.

Typologies abound in the literature. Schifko classifies metonymies into 'spatial', 'temporal' and 'causal' (Blank 1999:169); Al-Sharafi lists nine types (Al-Sharafi 2004:3); Norrick lists eighteen (Nerlich et al 1999:363–364); while Radden & Kövecses calculate that linguists/cognitive linguists propose as many as forty-six different types (Radden & Kövecses 1999). These taxonomies show the variety of metonymic relations which exist and demonstrate how heterogeneous 'contiguity' is, classifying metonymies into broad relational categories, such as PART FOR WHOLE, PLACE FOR THE EVENT, EFFECT FOR CAUSE, CONTROLLER FOR CONTROLLED, PRODUCER FOR PRODUCT, AGENT FOR ACTION. It would be hard to tell whether this is a list compiled by a traditional rhetorician or a modern-day cognitive linguist; rhetoricians and cognitive linguists have in common that they have explored the systematicity of metonymy.

Blank offers a 'cognitive typology' of metonymy in which different types of contiguity are explored (Blank 1999); while Seto uses spatial, temporal and abstract E- and C-relations (a distinction between metonymic, or 'category', and synecdochic, or 'entity' relations) as the basis for his classification (Seto 1999). Nerlich et al cite nine classifications, including those of Nyrop, Esnault, Stern and Ullmann, though favouring the typology of Norrick as being most complete:

> Group I: CAUSE—EFFECT, PRODUCER—PRODUCT, NATURAL SOURCE—NATURAL PRODUCT, INSTRUMENT—PRODUCT; Group II: OBJECT—ACT, INSTRUMENT—ACT, AGENT—ACT, AGENT—INSTRUMENT; Group III: PART—WHOLE, ACT—COMPLEX ACT, CENTRAL FACTOR—INSTITUTION; Group IV: CONTAINER—CONTENT, LOCALITY—OCCUPANT, COSTUME—WEARER; Group V: EXPERIENCE—CONVENTION, MANIFESTATION—DEFINITION; Group VI: POSSESSOR—POSSESSION, OFFICE HOLDER—OFFICE.
>
> (Nerlich et al 1999:363–364)

There are seven categories of metonymy in Lakoff & Johnson's list, part for whole, producer for product, object used for user, controller for controlled, institution for people responsible, place for institution and place for event (Lakoff & Johnson 1980:38). These are not only categories of metonymy but conceptual metonymies themselves. Kövecses adds a further six relations to Lakoff & Johnson's list: whole for the part, instrument for action, effect for cause, destination for motion, place for product and time for action (Kövecses 2002:145), and gives a list in his index of conceptual metonymies and metaphors (Kövecses 2002:281–285). We also find a "Metonymy and Metaphor Index" at the end of the Panther & Radden volume (Panther & Radden 1999b:419–423) and at the end of the Panther et al volume (Panther et al 2009:403–406). In the Panther et al index, there are more than 100 conceptual metonymies listed in the 'Metonymies' section (Panther et al 2009:403–405). Can we consider this list to be complete? Probably not, as this list was compiled for the purpose of indexing the conceptual metonymies discussed in the volume, not to provide a comprehensive list. Also, as Brdar observes, conceptual metonymies, like conceptual metaphors, are not necessarily universal, so identifying conceptual metonymies in one culture does not necessarily mean they will apply cross-culturally (Brdar 2009:261). Like Kövecses and Panther & Radden, Panther et al use the convention whereby metonymies are named in the format source for target, while in a separate list metaphors are named in the format target is source (Panther et al 2009:403).

Among the metonymies are being at a location for movement to the location, capability to do action for action, concept for ideology, destination for motion, fruit for fruit tree, non-control for problematic collective action, relation for concomitant sub-relation and soul for emotions, though the authors add that these hundred plus metonymies are essentially of three overall categories, whole for part, part for whole and part for part: "Most metonymies in this index are of the WHOLE FOR PART, PART FOR WHOLE, or PART FOR PART types, but are not classified into these types because this classification is normally quite obvious and because not all metonymies can be grouped under these types" (Panther et al 2009:403). A limitation of these taxonomies is that they are not comprehensive and never will be, as there will always be new associations to add to the list. Also, classification gives an artificial sense of categories being clear-cut, while utterances often fall into more than one category, eg 'blood' in *We need new blood* could be seen as both a part or an aspect. Taxonomies can also distract us from questions of more consequence, such as attempting to understand the mechanism and motivation behind metonymy—the main concern of this work. For the present study, the problem is not so much classifying metonymies into types but making a distinction between conventional and novel use. Most of the discussions in the literature concern ready-made signs, that is, words, compounds or phrases which are already part of the corpus of a language. While these are certainly of great interest in revealing metonymic processes which have occurred in the past, they tell us little about the mental process in communication. As Gibbs observes, "People may [. . .] comprehend conventional metonymic language without necessarily drawing metonymic mappings" (Gibbs 1999:74). A similar observation was made regarding metaphor in Chapter 3, which led to identifying metonymy as the mechanism behind active metaphorization.

CONCLUSION

This chapter has developed a General Theory of Metonymy. I have shown that the ability to recognize relatedness has a wide reach, playing an important role in conceptualization, in the language system and in face-to-face interaction using language. Metonymy is important in defining categories, in pragmatic inferencing and in realizing literal and metaphoric meaning, as well as metonymic meaning. I have developed a more precise ontology of metonymy in this chapter by exploring domain theory, the metaphor-metonymy continuum and typologies of metonymy. In the next chapter, I look at the role played by the active use of metonymic mapping in communication and the strikingly conspicuous role metonymy plays in various cultural and social activities, which seem to have no purpose other than to fulfil a ludic or recreational function, a sense of play and enjoyment in metonymy for its own sake.

5 Metonymy in Culture and Recreation

The previous chapter has considered metonymy as a phenomenon in conceptualization, in the language system and in communication. In this chapter, I look at metonymy in a number of specific contexts. I look first at the use of metonymy in giving nuance, emphasis and spin. I suggest that processing near equivalents and partial matches is the key to explaining the flexibility of linguistic communication and why language is so well suited to the social purposes to which it is put. I then look at the conspicuous role played by metonymy in personal and popular culture and recreational activities. I consider pursuits such as games, puzzles and jokes, activities which are inessential in a sense but nonetheless important in our lives, certainly when we consider them in terms of the time, money and enthusiasm invested in them. They have in common that they have at their centre the exploration of metonymic processing for its own sake. I consider the following phenomena: TV quiz shows, lookalikes, humour, formal metonymy, alternative names, in-family expressions and avoiding cooperation, and suggest that the surprising prominence of metonymy in these activities indicates an emotional acknowledgement of the importance of metonymy in many practical aspects of our lives.

THE USE OF METONYMY TO GIVE NUANCE, EMPHASIS AND SPIN

In the introduction to this book, I gave examples of metonymy occurring in everyday interactions which I had collected in my field notebooks during a two-day period over New Year 2010. They included a discussion about the short form of a name, the solutions to crossword clues, the etymology of the word *buff*, and so on. All involved the identification of part-whole relations for their success. Here, I offer some further examples, again taken from my data notebooks. These illustrate just how widespread and diverse metonymic processing is in everyday interaction. These data include conventionalized expressions, such as *pay with plastic*, *the small screen*, *white-collar worker*, *scratch card*, *go for a bite*, *a roof over your head*, *fight tooth and nail*, *head for the door*, *win hearts and minds*, *go under the knife*, *slap and tickle*, *bums on seats*, *get money from the hole in the wall*; expressions, such as *prick and ping* 'ready meals' (the containers are 'pricked' with a fork and the microwave 'pings' when the meal is ready); and proverbs, such as *The pen is mightier than the sword.*

There are also shop names in my data, where a salient feature is used to identify the type of business, such as *Fags and Mags* (tobacconist/newsagent), *Scissors* (hairdresser) and *Wasabi* (Japanese food outlet); publications, such as *Decanter* (about wine), *Bricks and Mortar* (about property) and *Click!* (about IT); and product slogans, such as "Snap, Crackle and Pop" for the breakfast cereal *Rice Krispies*. There is the method of naming in the comedy TV series *Friends*, whereby each episode is identified via a salient feature, eg "The one where Ross finds out", "The one where Joey speaks French" and "The one with the male nanny". The Reg Keeland English translations of Stieg Larsson's trilogy have metonymically-related titles—*The Girl with the Dragon Tattoo, The Girl who Played with Fire, The Girl who Kicked the Hornet's Nest*—although the originals do not. Individuals become associated in the public's mind with particular incidents giving rise to expressions, such as *do a Ratner*, after the jewellery-chain owner Gerald Ratner joked that his products were "total crap", causing the company to suffer losses; *do a Burberry*, to turn a company around in the way the designer Christopher Bailey took Burberry from a traditional clothing company to a fashionable designer label; *do a Cantona*, after an incident when the former Manchester United footballer Eric Cantona attacked a rival fan with a karate kick; and *do a Suarez* after the footballer Luis Suarez bit an opponent during a World Cup game. Gibbs and Aitchison give *do a Liz Taylor* and *do a Napoleon* as typical examples (Gibbs 1993:261, Aitchison 1994:154).

Original metonymies like these are understood because any complex entity offers a number of features, each of which can potentially be isolated and used to give access to the entity as a whole. Metonymy allows the speaker to construe meanings which reflect different viewpoints from which a situation is viewed. Langacker sees metonymy as an 'active-zone' or 'reference-point' phenomenon, one which allows the speaker to highlight a particular aspect of a complex entity (Langacker 1993:30–31); 'explicit indications' allowing mental access to concepts rather than being determinist encodings of them: "Explicit indications evoke conceptions that merely provide mental access to elements with the potential to be connected in specific ways, but the details have to be established on the basis of other considerations" (Langacker 2009:46). Radden sees this as following a general metonymic principle of SALIENT PROPERTY FOR A BUNDLE OF PROPERTIES (Radden 2005:19). Choosing a single feature to identify a concept or entity gives that feature salience. Each of the various words and expressions which accesses the schema for a 'film' (ie what is shown in a cinema) has a slightly different emphasis: *movie*, gives salience to the representation of moving rather than still images (as does *motion picture*); the roll of translucent material through which light is projected to display the images is highlighted with *film*; *celluloid* is the material that the roll of film is made of; *the flicks* gives salience to an earlier technology which did not make the transition from frame to frame seamless; *the talkies* gives salience to the speech accompanying the images (in contrast to *silent films*); while seeing a movie *on the big screen* or *on the silver screen* or *in Technicolor* have other emphases. The gesture used in the game 'charades' to indicate the category 'movie' acts out turning a crank handle on an old-fashioned camera, a different emphasis again. Cruse gives the example of *car*, which combined with different verbs emphasizes the exterior in "wash a car", the interior in "vacuum-clean a car" and the motor-vehicle mechanics in "service a car" (Taylor 2002:325). Taylor gives the example of *door*, which can be given the emphases of door as 'an aperture', as 'a physical plane', and as 'a means of entry/exit', depending on the verb it is combined with, ie *walk through a door*, *paint a door* and *lock a door* (Taylor 2002:326–327). Sense relations expressing relative meaning can also employ metonymy for their construal, offering alternatives to core words such as *small*, *medium*, *large*. For example, for coffee sizes, the UK company *Costa Coffee* uses *primo*, *medio*, *massimo*; *Seattle's Best Coffee* uses *tall*, *grande*, *grande supremo*; while *Starbucks* uses *tall*, *grande*, *venti*, and were also reputedly testing 'trenta'; while the difficulty levels of Sudoku puzzles in newspapers are expressed variously: *easy*, *moderate*, *challenging* in *Metro* and *moderate*, *tough*, *killer* in *The Daily Telegraph* (Steven Wootton, personal communication, 2012).

To give further examples of my own: organizers of public events have the option of selling tickets which are numbered or unnumbered. There is a whole variety of ways in which we could express the idea of unnumbered tickets, thanks to our ability to process metonymically. It can be expressed as: *free seating*, *unreserved seats*, *unnumbered tickets*, *general admission*, *no seat allocation*; more conversationally as, *tickets sold on a first-come-first-served basis*, *sit anywhere*; or even more informally *a free for all*. On tickets for an event I attended recently, the organizer had printed *General Admission* on the ticket, a choice probably motivated by a wish to avoid the negative connotations of 'un-' (eg *unreserved*) or 'no' (eg *no seat allocation*), to avoid the potentially misleading association of 'free' (eg *free seating*), and to benefit from *general admission* sounding 'official'. Another example: the practice of selling food and drinks on trains from a trolley pushed along the aisle can also be expressed in a variety of different ways, *refreshment service*, *trolley service*, *aisle service*, *seat-side service*, all identifying a salient feature and giving mental access to the phenomenon as a whole. The usage I noted in my data for one UK train company was *at-seat service*—"An at-seat service of light refreshments is available on board this train".

Metonymy gives alternative ways of saying things. The expression *dual fuel* in eg *dual fuel cookers* (gas hob and electric oven) and *dual fuel energy bills* (a company supplying both gas and electricity) is one of many possible ways of expressing this idea; the expression *kerbside collection* for the collection of waste for recycling by local authorities from each house rather than a common drop-off point is again just one of many possible ways of describing this practice; *cash for crash* has come into use to describe scams involving bogus road-traffic-accident insurance claims; and *booze cruise* for a trip made to France from the UK to buy alcohol in bulk more cheaply. It is of interest in these examples, *dual fuel*, *kerbside collection*, *cash for crash* and *booze cruise*, that these particular choices are motivated by a further layer of metonymy; there is a phonic overlap between the two elements of the expression. The expressions are related in form (their sound) rather than function. I will be calling this 'formal metonymy'. The idea of rhyme as metonymy, and calling this 'formal metonymy', are explored later in this chapter.

Metonymy clearly has an important role in referring; and for some scholars, metonymy is no more than referring. For Knowles & Moon, it is simply "about *referring*: a method of naming or identifying something" (Knowles & Moon 2006:54); but as early as *Metaphors We Live By*, Lakoff & Johnson recognized that metonymy does more than refer: "metonymy is not merely a referential device. It also serves the function of providing understanding. [. . .] Which part we pick out determines which aspect of the whole we are focusing on. When we say that we need some *good heads* on the project, we are using "good heads" to refer to "intelligent people". [. . .] The point is not just to use a part (head) to stand for a whole (person) but rather to pick out a particular characteristic of the person" (Lakoff & Johnson 1980:36). As Gibbs states, "Metonymy is a fundamental part of our conceptual system: People take one well-understood or easily perceived aspect of something to represent or stand for the thing as a whole" (Gibbs 1994:319–320). Similarly, for Langacker: "A well-chosen metonymic expression lets us mention one entity that is salient and easily coded, and thereby evoke—essentially automatically—a target that is either of lesser interest or harder to name" (Langacker 1993:30). The great power of metonymy is its use in *focussing* and picking out particular characteristics. This applies as much to actions and events as it does to entities, in other words, verb phrases as well as noun phrases. Radden uses the term 'referential metonymy' for an entity described by a noun phrase and 'event metonymy' for an action or event described by a verb phrase (Radden 2008b). Lakoff gives examples of how you might describe how you got to a party, eg *I hopped on a bus*, *I borrowed my brother's car*, *I just stuck out my thumb*, observing that they all rely on the identification of a sub-event within the event for their representation (Lakoff 1987b:78–79). Gibbs makes the same point with the exchange, *"How did you get to the airport?"*, *"I waved down a taxi"*. (Gibbs 1994:327). Seto gives examples of expressions which represent being ill and being well metonymically: *She can hardly get out of bed* and *to be up and about* (Seto 1999:106).

We have seen above that metonymy can choose one of a number of the different parts of a complex phenomenon in order to identify that phenomenon. This is useful in naming, but it is also useful in another respect. The fact that there is a *choice* of element opens up a hugely powerful tool; it means that a wide spectrum of subtle and closely nuanced meanings is made available to the speaker, as each metonymic choice represents a different emphasis/focus within a more generalized domain. Radden compares expressions meaning 'to drive' and observes that *sitting behind the steering wheel* has a different emphasis to *having wheels*; the former emphasizes the monotony of driving, while the latter emphasizes mobility and freedom (Radden 2008b). A similar contrast can be seen in examples from my own data, *I am moving house* and *I am being re-housed*, where the former suggests autonomy, the latter passivity, choosing where to live on the open market versus being given a home by the state when one becomes available. It gives politicians and journalists the opportunity to give 'spin': a government policy has been described in the UK in terms of *efficiency savings* and *swingeing cuts*, depending on the point of view; another policy has been called a *spare room subsidy* or a *bedroom tax*, the same concept/entity talked about in different terms. Other examples of event metonymies giving emphasis to a particular aspect: the press referring to Barack Obama's inaugural ceremony, "When he goes up those steps to the Capitol"; England rugby team members, when interviewed about qualifying for a European rugby tournament to be held in Spain spoke about their hopes of "getting on that plane to Spain". Other examples, both of which emphasize the physical action of doing something rather than a mental effort include "I'll just get your details up on screen" and "You've only got to pick up the phone" (Croft & Cruse 2004:215).

This emphasis could be called 'fine-tuning', 'nuance' or 'spin', but whatever we call it, I believe it is this resource which gives language its huge flexibility and expressive range. Metonymy multiplies the possibilities of what can be expressed while remaining within the conventionalized linguistic resources of ready-made signs. It is working at the same time within and beyond the 'code'. It also gives us strategies for making meaning by extending the lexicon when ready-made signs are not available, or simply covering over gaps because existing signs cannot be retrieved in time or have not yet been learnt. As Nerlich et al put it: "Metonymies are used by children to cover up gaps in their tiny lexicons, whereas creative metonymies are used to express something new by not using the already available words in their lexicons" (Nerlich et al 1999:367). Metonymy thus makes a virtue of indeterminacy. It makes accessible the 'middle ground' between deterministic encoding/decoding, of which there is a component enshrined in every language, and the extensions of the lexicon achieved by making associations between things which are unrelated, ie metaphor. It makes fine-tuning possible; Langacker describes it as allowing us to access the right house not just the right district: "Explicit linguistic coding gets us into the right neighborhood [. . .] but from there we have to find the right address by some other means" (Langacker 2009:46). Indeterminacy is hard to avoid because it "rears its ugly head even in mundane examples of the most basic and seemingly straightforward constructions" (Langacker 2009:48), but it should also be welcomed, as "metonymy [. . .] should not be seen as a problem but as part of the solution" (Langacker 2009:69).

Metonymy in Context

To show how powerful a tool metonymy is in more pragmatic 'meaning in situation' contexts I give further examples from my data notebooks. A passenger asking a bus driver "Do you go down Oxford Street?" intends with this to ask whether the *bus* will go down Oxford Street; a customer asking a shop assistant "What time do you close?" is asking what time the *store* closes; a customer speaking on the phone to the switchboard of a department store who asks "Could I speak to cookers, please" means 'could I speak to someone in the department selling cookers?'; a mother might explain "I have three children, 13, 7 and 5", meaning their ages, not their names. In another context she might have said her children were "clarinet, guitar and piano" or given the names of the schools they attend to identify them, if these characteristics had been salient in that context. These are all examples of commonly-used, situationally-motivated metonymies: PERSON FOR VEHICLE, PERSON FOR ESTABLISHMENT, PERSON FOR DEPARTMENT, AGE FOR PERSON, OCCUPATION FOR PERSON, etc. They are so common that many would be surprised to have them identified as instances of figurative language at all, but what shows them to be figurative is that they can often be 'unpicked' by being taken literally, as I will demonstrate in the section on Avoiding Cooperation later in this chapter. Often they are shorthand versions of ideas which would take longer utterances to express but which metonymy allows us to 'skip over'. Radden & Kövecses give the example *lighting the Christmas tree* for 'lighting the candles on the Christmas tree', observing that this "does not strike us as unnatural" (Radden & Kövecses 1999:31). The use of a characteristic of a person to get their attention is another common use of situational metonymy, such as *Hey Diana Ross!* or *Hey Smiler!* The characteristic of the person—looking like the singer Diana Ross or smiling a lot—replaces the more conventional way of hailing someone by using their name. Other examples: *The first violin has the flu,* ie the person in an orchestra who has this role (Panther & Radden 1999a:9). *He's sales. I'm IT. I'm Russian icons. I'm ceramics. I'm continuing education,* where a person is identified through the department they work for within an institution or company. In all these, use is being made of the metonymy SALIENT CHARACTERISTIC FOR PERSON.

In discourse and text, metonymy can create its own register and be used in structuring text (explored in more detail in the next chapter). In a radio review of a TV spy documentary, the reviewer says "I thought we'd see beads of sweat on upper lips at border crossings, that sort of thing, but we didn't", using metonymy over a longer stretch of language than just a clause (*Saturday Review*, BBC Radio 4, 5 June 2010). Similarly, a discussion on a radio news programme starts from an item which informs us that the 'trip hop' pop duo *Massive Attack* is dismayed that their music is favoured by the middle-classes as background music to dinner parties (*Today*, BBC Radio 4, 23 June 2010). The discussion is between a social observer and a music expert, and the feeling we have is that we are waiting for one of the contributors to give a metonymy which will 'nail' the paradox already flagged up in the news item. It inevitably comes. One of the contributors says "The dinner-party guests will be sitting there listening to Amy Winehouse [a British pop musician, now deceased] while tucking into the seafood linguini". This is extended in formulae often used in conversation of the types 'a cross between A and B', 'A meets B' and 'one part A, one part B', where a blend of two metonymic meanings helps the speaker achieve their communicative goals, for example in the following newspaper article reviews: "It's a cross between *Hair* and *Sunset Boulevard* for the under-thirties", "The end result is Jeremy Kyle meets *Gladiators* with *Big Brother* auditions thrown in" (Style Extra, *London Metro*, 3 June 2010, p.53) and "He has been described as one part Morrissey, one part Mahler" (Seven, *The Daily Telegraph*, 27 June 2010, p.8). The archetypical examination/essay question in education, "compare and contrast", requires metonymic thought for its execution. It asks the student to compare entities, ie look for relatedness between them, such as democracy and communism, China and India; it also asks them to contrast them, but to contrast is effectively looking for the absence of relatedness, thus both 'comparing' and 'contrasting' are metonymic. Lastly, an example of metonymy playing a role in structuring knowledge, Mendeleev's 'periodic table'. This is an arrangement of the chemical elements in a table on the basis of two types of relatedness, represented by two axes, vertically according to common chemical properties and horizontally according to the number of protons in the series.

The most discussed metonymy in the literature is surely *The ham sandwich is waiting for his check* (Lakoff & Johnson 1980:35), first mentioned in the context of polysemy and ostension by Nunberg as *The ham sandwich is sitting at table 20* (1979:149) and discussed extensively in different versions ever since. Here we have an extension of the metonymic principle of a part or attribute standing for the whole, to a feature peripherally associated with that person in that particular situation standing for the person as a whole. Other classic examples are: in a hospital context, *The appendectomy is in theatre* and, in a hotel context, *Room 44 hasn't had her dry cleaning yet.* Some scholars call them 'situational' metonymies, others 'extrinsic' metonymies (Croft & Cruse 2004:217), but because the ham sandwich example is so discussed, we could just as well call them 'ham-sandwich metonymies'. These metonymies are not novel any more than *Hey, You, Diana Ross!* or *Hey Smiler!* are novel, as they do not involve the exploration of a new conceptual association. An example in my data is the television programme *Question Time* on BBC TV, a political debate where a panel of speakers answers questions from the audience. When it is their turn to put their question, the audience member is identified by name. Audience members are also invited to comment on what is going on. To do so, they put up their hands, and if chosen are sometimes identified by what they are wearing and by their location in the hall, eg "Can we have the blue jumper in the back row", "The woman in the striped jacket first". Ruiz de Mendoza makes a distinction between 'source-in-target' and 'target-in-source' metonymies (Ruiz de Mendoza 2000), but neither of these really applies to ham-sandwich metonymies, as the target is not in the source, nor the source in the target; instead the source is in the *context*, and so the metonymic principle could be represented as SALIENT FEATURE IN THE CONTEXT FOR PERSON.

Triangle of Tropes

If we acknowledge that meaning making through metonymy and meaning making through metaphor are powerful resources in addition to 'literal' language, we see emerging what could be called a 'triangle of tropes', three resources available for expressing ideas, a literal, a metonymic and a metaphoric. This is different from Seto's 'cognitive triangle' of metaphor, metonymy and synecdoche (Nerlich et al 1999:367). Often, there will be 'room' in the lexicon for all three. The idea of one word having many meanings (polysemy) is of course familiar, though highly polysemous words in English are relatively rare. It seems to me that our conceptual system is particularly suited to one lexical item having a literal, a metonymic and a metaphoric meaning. There seems to be room in the lexicon for these to remain distinct and not cause misunderstandings. The lexeme *bubbly* has the literal meaning WITH BUBBLES; a metonymic meaning of CHAMPAGNE; and a metaphoric meaning VIVACIOUS, as in 'bubbly personality'. Here follow further examples: ***smooth*** means NOT ROUGH (literal), a FRUIT DRINK ie *smoothie* (metonymic), and DEBONAIR/COOL (metaphoric); ***flat*** means ON A LEVEL (literal), an APARTMENT (metonymic), and NOT LIVELY (metaphoric); ***green*** means the COLOUR (literal), ILL (metonymic), and ENVIRONMENTAL, as in *Green Party/green issues* (metaphoric); ***thick*** means NOT THIN (literal), MILKSHAKE ie *thickie* (metonymic), and STUPID (metaphoric); and ***brown*** means the COLOUR (literal), a CAKE ie *brownie* (metonymic), and PREVIOUSLY DEVELOPED, as in *brownfield site* (metaphoric).

It is noticeable that the metonymic sense of a lexeme often involves a change in the part of speech through zero derivation (conversion), as in *bubbly* (n) and *flat* (n), or nominalization through affixation, as in *smoothie, thickie* and *brownie*. I think it is also important to note here that it is inappropriate to assign a particular function individually to any of the three tropes. As discussed at the end of Chapter 3, the functions which can be assigned to metaphors are very varied, such as being real, evocative, powerful, vivid or compact (eg Ortony 1975), but can equally well be applied to characterize metonymic or literal expressions. The resources the triangle of tropes offers us are more fundamental than the assigning of individual functions to them would imply. Sometimes the three resources are used together in the same phrase. The undoubtedly offensive expression referring to the French, used in an episode (first aired 20 April 1995) of the TV animated series *The Simpsons*, "cheese-eating surrender monkeys", which makes the implication, no doubt unfounded, that the French put up too little resistance when the German army invaded in the Second World War, has each of these elements: *cheese-eating* is metonymic (as the French are cheese eaters); *surrender* is literal; and *monkeys* is metaphoric. The adaptation of this expression by the comic Graeme Garden on the BBC TV quiz show *QI* to characterize the Americans, *burger-eating invasion monkeys* (*QI*, BBC2 TV, Series 4, Episode 10, 24 November 2006), retains the three elements of the triangle. Another example: the boyfriend of the character Carrie in the TV series *Sex and the City* has three names (not two or four): his 'real' name, *John*; (*Mr*) *Big*, on account of his being tall; and *Crossword*, because he is hard to puzzle out. *John* is literal; *Big* is metonymic; *Crossword* is metaphoric.

Communicatively, the use of metonymic expressions as referents is not simply a matter of substitution, because metonymic choices give nuance; but neither is their use simply a matter of substitution in terms of morphosyntax, as I will explain. Although *bubbly* has the conventionalized meaning of CHAMPAGNE (and therefore has a place in the mental lexicon), you would not be readily understood if you were to say *bubbly cocktail* for 'champagne cocktail', *bubbly bottle* for 'champagne bottle', *bubbly breakfast* for 'champagne breakfast' or *bubbly flute* for 'champagne flute'. Neither would more metaphoric uses, such or *bubbly socialist* be understood. There are colligational and entailment restrictions in forming noun-noun compounds which do not permit this and which are not overridden by the metonymic source-target mapping(s), although *bottle of bubbly* and *cocktail made with bubbly* would be possible. Equally, to say you are going *to buy a small screen* to mean 'buy a television' is also not retrievable for similar reasons. Panther & Radden demonstrate this with the sentence "My husband is parked on the upper deck", where *husband* stands for 'car', but does not universally license substitutions of 'car' with *husband,* such as *My husband has a sun roof/Californian licence plate, husband radio* (car radio), *husband dealer* (car dealer), etc (Panther & Radden 1999a:10). In the next section I look at examples from personal and popular culture and recreational activities in order to demonstrate that here, too, metonymy plays a central role in a variety of phenomena.

TV QUIZ SHOWS

In this section, I look at the recreational role of metonymy by considering three UK TV quiz shows: *Who Wants To Be A Millionaire?*, *Eggheads* and *Only Connect.* In all three, metonymy plays a central role, the task of the contestants being to make choices or observe associations among metonymically-related items. In the ITV Show *Who Wants To Be A Millionaire?* contestants answer general knowledge questions by choosing from a set of four given answers, eg:

- Which gland is 'goitre' a disease of?
- A adrenal, B pituitary, C thyroid, D mammary

The given answers in this quiz are related metonymically. They have a common element. In the example above, the answers are all glands and can be referred to by adding the word *gland* for each, thus: *adrenal gland, pituitary gland, thyroid gland* and *mammary gland.* The contestant spends their 'thinking' time not so much finding the 'right' answer but exploring the metonymic relatedness of the four options until one emerges as the most appropriate. Processing an open question, where a choice of answers is not given, is more about memory and recall; where answers are given, it is more about comparing related items for matches and eliminating less probable options, based on features which emerge as salient through metonymic processing.

In the BBC2 quiz show *Eggheads*, there are two teams and for each question, three possible answers, eg:

Who is the most junior in the kitchen? — chef de partie; commis chef; chef de cuisine.
Which is a movie directed by Tarantino? — Death Proof; Bullet Proof; Shatter Proof.
What's the name of the edible paper used in macaroons? — cocoa paper; rice paper; sugar paper.
Which word relates to starting a computer? — bootstrap; bootlace; bootleg.

Here again the given answers are related metonymically, both in meaning and form, the common element, or 'overlap', in the questions above being *chef, proof, paper* and *boot*. The contestants are encouraged to speak their thoughts (rather like a Think Aloud Protocol), allowing the viewers an insight into how they come to their choices. Much of this commentary is a discussion of how the given options are related, and shows how the contestants arrive at a 'best fit', rather than recording the moment the 'right answer' is spotted.

The BBC4 TV quiz show *Only Connect* is based entirely on the ability to recognize different types of metonymic relations. It is so focussed on various aspects of the ability to analyze and process metonymically that the show could quite easily have the word 'metonymy' in the title. Even the team members introduce themselves by saying what 'connection' they have to the other members of their team, such as doing the same degree, attending the same college or working for the same company. In Round 1, CONNECTIONS, contestants are asked how four items they are given are related, eg ATM, HIV, UPC, PIN (answer: they all are abbreviations which are used tautologically, often being said in combination with the word which the last letter is an abbreviation of, eg PIN number). In Round 2, SEQUENCES, contestants are required to identify a sequence given to them item by item, scoring higher the earlier they recognize the sequence, eg *g, j, p, q* (answer: they are all letters with 'descenders', ie part of the letter goes below the line); *undo, copy, cut* and *paste* (answer: they are all key combinations in word-processing of the sort CTRL + key). In Round 3, CONNECTING WALL, sixteen seemingly-unrelated items are given in a grid, from which contestants are to find sets of related fours (Instructions: "There are four sets of four within these sixteen words. What are their associations?"), eg *cat, sleep, moon, cake* (answer: they can all be followed by 'walk' to give new words); *noble, heavy, base* and *scrap* (answer: they can all be followed by 'metal'); *Barry, Wren, Nash, Hawksmoor* (answer: they are all British architects). In Round 4, the MISSING VOWELS round, vowels are removed from expressions, titles or names and contestants are required to guess what they are against the clock, eg "These are all names of twins but without the vowels".

All four rounds rely both on the contestants' knowledge of the world and their ability to reason. To win, contestants have to be able to recall information from their long-term memories and reason metonymically. As far as what they actually do in the studio, it is the ability to draw on the single cognitive ability, to identify metonymic relations, which determines whether they win or lose. The components of general knowledge and competition between teams is enough to sustain a half-hour programme, but hidden here as well is the unconscious desire to share publicly a recognition that metonymic processing is central to our lives.

An informant told me one of his habits was to tune into a classical music station, BBC Radio 3, and try to guess the composer and the piece, and perhaps even the soloist, orchestra and conductor. The pieces are almost always announced at the end on this station. What he was doing was to look out for metonymic matches with pieces he already knew, characteristics of harmonies, melodic patterns and unique composer thumb-prints. The exploration of these metonymic associations was more important than the right answer, which could have been obtained easily by consulting a listing for the day or pressing the information button on the radio. The guessing process made listening more acute and presumably more enjoyable. Another informant told me of a game he plays with his CD collection with friends when they come round to dinner, which he calls "Beat the Intro!". For this, you try to identify a song from the instrumental lead-in before the voice begins—you try to 'beat' the introduction. This is also an activity around sound matching, a metonymic processing pursuit.

LOOKALIKES

The ability to recognize 'lookalikes', people who resemble others in how they look, speak, dress or behave (also 'deadringers'), is a phenomenon which has a special significance for us. Perhaps it is related to what at one time in our evolution was of survival value, an ability to distinguish friend from foe. Now, metonymic similarity around human characteristics seems to please us sometimes just for its own sake. There is great affection for lookalikes, impersonators, tribute acts and tribute bands in our cultures. One of the most popular tourist attractions in London is a waxwork museum, Madame Tussauds, where visitors can test the ingeniousness of the waxwork builders by getting up close to representations of world celebrities. Two household names in UK television, Rory Bremner and Jon Culshaw, are famous for their impersonations of famous people; while the artist Alison Jackson has gained notoriety for her photographs of lookalikes of celebrities, showing them in private moments, such as the Queen having breakfast in bed with her corgis, Tony Blair at a wild pool party and Kate Middleton preparing for her wedding day (Alison Jackson, *Private*, 2003; *Kate and Wills Up the Aisle: A Right Royal Fairy Tale*, 2011). This is an irreverent look at public figures but also a delight in the ability of someone unknown to 'pass off' as someone famous. In my data notebooks I noted a number of examples of metonymic processing around lookalikes. In one exchange, a parent and grandparent discussed whether Jessica, the young girl to whom they are related, looked more like her mother or her father. In another, an informant pointed out someone who had just got off a bus and remarked that he looked like "Mehta from IT", a work colleague. In a further exchange, two people discussed whether someone one of them saw that day in the doctor's waiting room was the UK comedian Jeremy Hardy:

Patient There was a guy in the doctor's waiting room today who looked like Jeremy Hardy.
Friend Perhaps it *was* Jeremy Hardy.
Patient He certainly spoke and moved around the way you'd expect him to.
Friend There's no reason why he shouldn't live round here.
Patient Or be ill like anyone else.
Friend Maybe it was him.

In another example, an informant described how he and his colleagues would pass time between classes at a language school in Spain assigning classic film roles to other members of the staff. They based their casting on personal characteristics such as weight, facial hair, mannerisms, voice quality and 'ditziness'. The same informant made me aware of the *Internet Movie Database* website IMDb, where in one section users post comments about physical resemblances, such as this observation about the actress Britt Ekland:

> She kinda reminds me of Duffy, especially when you look at pics of her in the 60s. Anyone else see it?
>
> (www.imdb.com, accessed 11 August 2010)

Another example, this time of physical resemblance between objects rather than people, is from a visit I made in 2010 to caves in Puglia, Italy, a region famous for caves with spectacular stalactites and stalagmites. Visitors are taken on a guided tour which lasts an hour. Approximately half of the commentary during this tour is about the history of discovering the caves, fatal accidents which occurred during the excavations, and scientific facts and figures; the other half is taken up with naming features, pointing out stalagmites and stalactites and giving them names, such as 'the Owl', 'the Ice Cream Cone', 'the Tower of Pisa', 'the Dancer's Foot', and 'the Mexican Landscape', while recurrent formations were also given names, such as 'the toilet brush motif' and 'broccoli'. The visitors nodded in recognition that what they were looking at really did resemble these things. It was clearly more interesting and worthwhile for the visitors to relate the forms in front of them to other more familiar forms than just looking at the features themselves. If we consider that in none of the examples above was there any transactional or practical purpose, nor that any action or decision was to ensue from this semiotic work around metonymy, we would be justified in concluding that the significance for the participants was a pleasure in exploring similarities of personal traits and resemblances of physical form purely for its own sake, that there is something positive and reassuring in the activity itself, and almost as if metonymic processing were experienced as 'play'.

HUMOUR

Humour takes many forms; it can be physical, like slapstick, come out of a particular situation or derive from word play, to name three. Physical humour, situational humour and word play all involve metonymic processing. They rely on a 'gap' set up between our expectations and the reality we are presented with, an incomplete 'match' of some sort. In this anecdote, intended to be humorous in the context of the broadcast, a fifteen-year-old pupil is talking to his career advisor:

Career advisor	What do you want to do for a career?
Student	I want to be an archbishop.

Career advisor How are you going to go about it?

Student Do A-levels, do 'theology' at university and then go on to theological college, and get an internship at a cathedral . . .

Career advisor What if you don't manage to become an archbishop? What will you do then?

Student Erm . . . I'll probably work for my dad in the papershop.

(*You and Yours*, BBC Radio 4, 18 March 2010)

The humour here comes from the idea that being an archbishop and working for your dad in a papershop are too dissimilar to be included in the same category. The student violates our expectations of metonymic processing. The language used here is nothing other than literal, in other words, there is no word play. Humour which does rely on word play, however, is exploiting the fact that signs are a fusion of meaning and form and that related forms can give rise to unrelated meanings, as is the case in this sketch by the British comedy duo Morecambe and Wise:

A scene in Sherwood Forest

Morecambe My name is Mud. [corrects himself] Hood. Robin Hood. I'm the swashbuckling type. But there's only one trouble.

Wise What's that?

Morecambe I swash when I should buckle and I buckle when I should swash.

Wise How did you fall in with the outlaws?

Morecambe I fell out with the inlaws.

(*Variety Fanfare*, broadcast on BBC Radio, July 1952)

The source of humour in this sketch is the similarity in sound between *mud* and *hood*, and therefore a pun between *My name is Hood* and the idiom *My name is mud*; around the compositionality of *swashbuckling*, *I swash when I should buckle* and *I buckle when I should swash*; and the altered meaning created by inverting *fall in with the outlaws* to give *fall out with the inlaws*, all humour reliant on recognizing metonymic relations between items. If there were no links through form, the sketch would not be funny, just random.

In the next example, from a sketch by the same comedy duo, the lack of physical similarity between the comedian and the character he is trying to represent is comic, because this too violates expectations of likeness, reinforced by the metonymic relation between *eight-stone weakling* and *seven-stone weakling*:

Morecambe Men! Are you worried about your physique? Would you want a big manly figure like me? You need not be an eight-stone weakling. You can be the same as I am: a seven-stone weakling.

Wise	And men, have you tried the new Hercules Hurry-Up system of muscular development?
Morecambe	Yes. You practise 12 hours a day with dumbbells, sleigh bells, cow bells and door bells.
Wise	And one day you will jump out of bed, look in the mirror, swell out your chest and say . . .
Morecambe	"Boy, am I a sucker".

(*Variety Fanfare*, broadcast on BBC Radio, July 1952)

But what is most striking in this sketch is the seemingly random list of compounds of *bell*: *dumbbells*, *sleigh bells*, *cow bells* and *door bells*. There is nothing else to the humour but the joy of exploring metonymic relations (as regards form) between different kinds of bells, allowing us to be sent off in different unrelated directions (as regards meaning), and inviting us to imagine exercises involving sleigh bells, cow bells and door bells.

The following jokes delight in phonic relatedness, syntactic ambiguity and phrase-level polysemy. The first is around *syphilis* and *chablis* and their interchangeability; the second relies on a disambiguation of two possible syntactic structures, *evening* modifying *primrose* versus *evening* as a salutation and *Primrose* as a vocative (name); in the third, two meanings of *being polite*, 'standing on ceremony' and 'not being rude' are invoked; while the fourth relies on the disambiguation of two meanings of *blind man*, 'not sighted' and 'a man who installs blinds'. The four jokes are:

> A nun goes in to see the Mother Superior: "I've come to inform you that there is a case of syphilis in the convent". The Mother Superior replies: "Oh good! I was getting tired of the chablis we've been having."
>
> A man goes into a health food shop and says "Evening Primrose oil". The man behind the counter answers "I'm Mr Vine to you, if you don't mind."
>
> A man has been invited to dinner with his boss and his boss's wife. She says "How many potatoes would you like?" He says "Just one". She says "You don't have to be polite, you know" He says "Ok, just one, you silly cow!"
>
> A man knocks on the door of the bathroom. A woman inside calls out: "You can't come in, I've got no clothes on". The man says: "Don't worry. It's the blind man". She says: "Ok, then come in". He goes in and says: "Nice figure! Now, where do you want the blinds?"

Two meanings sharing one word (punning) is also the source of humour in innuendo, as in the list of examples below from a round robin email, where *take off*, *open wide*, *tease* or *blow*, *back* or *front*, etc have innocent meanings as well as sexual meanings, but are related metonymically through form:

> Beware the double meaning when: the doctor says "Take off your clothes"; the dentist says "open wide"; the hairdresser says "Do you want it teased or

blown?"; the milkman says "Do you want it in the front or the back?"; the interior decorator says "Once it's in, you'll love it"; the banker says "if you take it out too soon, you'll lose interest"; the telephone guy says "Would you like it on the table or up against the wall?"

FORMAL METONYMY

In this section, I discuss 'formal metonymy', used here to mean the repetition of an element of form, either phonologically or graphologically, within a larger structural unit (and not in the sense that other scholars, such as Bierwiaczonek, use the term for initialisms (eg UN, NATO), cutbacks, clips and ellipses (Bierwiaczonek 2013)). Formal metonymy is often found in the lexicon, as in expressions such as *hocus pocus, hoi polloi, hoity toity, namby pamby, shilly shally, willy nilly* and *wishy washy*. It is also found in more recently-created expressions, such as *credit crunch, cultural cringe, happy slapping, lager lout* and *yummy mummy.* In many of these, the repetition of form is both phonic (sound repeated) and graphic (letters repeated)—the two types of formal metonymy. When there is an exact repetition of a form, such as *busy busy*, there is a metonymic relation between the repeated element and the lexical phrase as a whole. Rhythm, harmony and melodies set up metonymies by offering a frame of repetition into which different notes or words are inserted. Formal metonymy also includes more abstract, higher-level repetitions, such as consonant-vowel-consonant-vowel (CVCV) patterns.

Such is our appetite for metonymy, that when coining expressions we find it satisfying when formal metonymy is included, almost as if this 'clinches' the choice and signals it as appropriate and definitive. As noted above, models of cookers which have gas hobs and electric ovens are described by manufacturers as *dual fuel*; Lambeth Council in London calls the house-to-house collection of recycling *kerbside collection*; while the service of drinks and snacks on Southern Trains in the UK is referred to as a *seat-side service.* Many proverbs show formal metonymy, such as the rhymes in *A stitch in time saves nine* and *Pears for your heirs*, and the Italian expression *Traduttore, traditore* (translator, traitor), because formal metonymy adds persuasiveness to the saying. In data I collected, many in-family expressions (discussed in more detail in a later section) showed phonic metonymy, such as *rudey nudey* (in the nude and therefore rude), *weirdy beardy* (someone with a beard therefore weird) and *Wealth and Stealth* (the title one informant gave the spreadsheet summarizing his finances). Hong Kong parents like to give their children names which have a shared element, such as brothers called *Chi ho* and *Ki ho*. There is something very powerful about repeating a sound. Repetition with variation is prominent in children's verse and in fairy tales—*What big eyes/ears/paws/teeth you've got. All the better to see/hear/stroke/eat you with!*—which children, far from finding tedious, seem to enjoy for the ritual it introduces (Cook 2000:28). Cook recounts the various names he calls his son—*Toby the Boby, Turbot the Burbot*, etc—all phonologically related to his name, Toby, and including the repetition of sound segments (Cook 2000:165). As Cook points out, the repetition is "almost always only partial" and a "rhymed word is partly like, but partly unlike, its partner" (Cook 2000:29). This could almost be a definition of metonymy: like but unlike.

I now turn to a historical example I encountered in my reading in order to show that this phenomenon is not restricted to the modern era. The text below is the beginning of a letter by the composer W.A. Mozart to his cousin Bäsle, written in Mannheim in 1777. Theirs, at the time, was a relationship which was playful, flirtatious and scatological. We see here Mozart using a type of formal metonymy of his own invention, in which he adds words at the end of clauses which rhyme with the last word in the clause. I underline these pairs of words in the text below:

> Allerliebstes Bäsle Häsle! Ich habe dero mir so werthes schreiben richtig erhalten falten, und daraus ersehen drehen, das der H Vetter retter, die fr: Baaß has, und sie wie, recht wohl auf sind hind; wir sind auch gott lob und danck recht gesund hund. ich habe heut den Brief schief, von meinem Papa haha, auch richtig in meine Klauen bekommen strommen. Ich hoffe sie werden auch meinen Brief Trief, welchen ich ihnen aus Mannheim geschrieben, erhalten haben schaben. Desto besser, besser desto! [. . .] miehnnam ned ^{net}5 rebotco 7771.
>
> (W. Reich, *Mozarts Briefe*, 1948, pp.46–51)

The rhyming of *Bäsle*, his cousin's name, with *Häsle* (little hare) is followed by *erhlaten/falten* (received/folded), *ersehen/drehen* (see/turn round), *Vetter/retter* (his uncle's surname/saviour), *Baaß/has* (his aunt's surname/hare), *sie/wie* (you/how), *sind/hind* (are/behind), *gesund/hund* (healthy/dog), *Brief/schief* (letter/wrong), *Papa/haha* (father/ha ha), *bekommen/strommen* (received/strummed), *Brief/Trief* (letter/meet) and *haben/schaben* (have/scrape). Sometimes these rhyming words comment on what has gone before, eg the letter which has been received is folded and is turned around to be read properly; in other cases they do not, but instead make comic associations, like 'father/ha ha' or 'letter/wrong'; in yet other cases they seem to be there just for the joy of the repetition. Another of the expressions the cousins used in their private language, *spuni cuni*, appears later in the same letter, though it is unclear what exactly it might have meant to them—perhaps an English equivalent of something along the lines of *hanky panky*. Whatever it did mean to them, it is not by chance that this too involves formal metonymy.

Returning to more contemporary examples: a sketch by the British comedians Armstrong and Miller consists entirely of one character introducing himself using variants of his name, *Mick*, *Mike*, *Mickie*, *Mick the Nick*, etc, the humour deriving from the prolongation of the greeting and that the interaction does not get any further than this stage. Jokes where repetition with variation plays a role are common, appreciated by children and adults, such as 'Knock Knock' jokes:

Knock knock./Who's there?/Ice cream/Ice cream who?/Ice cream if you don't let me in!
Knock knock./Who's there?/B 4/B 4 who?/B 4 I freeze to death, please open this door!
Knock knock./Who's there?/Figs/Figs who?/Figs the doorbell, it's broken!

Formal metonymy is also involved in morphological reductions, 'clipping', such as short versions of names of people, place and shops, eg *Pret* for *Prêt à Manger* (a London sandwich shop chain), reflecting two basic principles of language in use, parsimony and metonymy. Radden gives *crude* for *crude oil* as an example and identifies morphological reduction as an instance of the PART OF A FORM FOR THE FULL FORM conceptual metonymy (Radden 2005:17). The mirroring of form can help to make a saying memorable, such this nugget of wisdom attributed to Winston Churchill: "The pessimist sees the difficulty in every opportunity; while the optimist sees the opportunity in every difficulty". Donald Rumsfeld, when US Defense Secretary, famously gave an exposition on 'knowns' and 'unknowns' at a press conference in 2002:

> As we know, there are known knowns. These are things we know that we know. There are known unknowns. That is to say, there are things that we know we don't know. But there are also unknown unknowns. There are things we don't know we don't know.
>
> (Donald Rumsfeld, widely reported and broadcasted)

The strength of this part of this speech comes from the truth it contains being made felt through the formal metonymies employed in saying it. The twelve occurrences of items containing 'know', ie *know, known, knowns, unknown, unknowns*, make the statement rhetorical, the formal metonymies flagging up to the listener that something significant is being said. There is a danger with rhetorical neatness of this sort that it can tip over into comedy. In fact, this speech was ridiculed by many at the time and even at the original press conference people can be heard sniggering. But, however individuals reacted at the time, Rumsfeld's use of formal metonymy certainly made this speech memorable, so much so that *Known and Unknown* became the title of his memoirs.

ALTERNATIVE NAMES

The need to have alternative names (ie a name other than the 'official' or given name for someone or something) is also strongly motivated by metonymy; so strongly, that for certain pairings, if one name is mentioned, it invariably evokes the other in the pair, such as: *Elvis Presley* and *The King*, *Margaret Thatcher* and *The Iron Lady*, *Princess Diana* and *The Queen of Hearts*, *Elizabeth I* and *Gloriana*, *Shakespeare* and *The Bard*, *John Prescott* and *Two Jags* (a former British politician), *Ireland* and *The Emerald Isle*, *Venice* and *La Serenissima*, the *Conservatives* and the *Tories*, *West Bromwich Albion* and *The Baggies* (a UK soccer team), *University* (one has attended) and *Alma Mater*; and terms such as *Brummies, Scousers, Paddies, Yanks*. The alternative name will usually have a more informal, familiar register. Individuals also have their own names for shops and department stores. In my data notebooks I collected a whole range of original expressions for British retail stores: *PJ's* (for *Peter Jones*); *Juan Louis*, *Johnny Lu Lu*, *Yonelle* (*John Lewis*); *Hallifucks* (*Halifax*); *Grotesquos*, *Toss-Co* (*Tesco*); *Shabby-tat*, *Shabby Twat* (*Habitat*); *W M* (*Morrisons*). These names reflect an irreverence but also an affection for these retail institutions: *Toss-Co*, suggests a company of 'tossers', while *Johnny Lu Lu* conveys the familiarity you would reserve for a close friend or family member.

The heading to an advertisement on the London Underground for a London restaurant booking service reads:

> Looking for a London Restaurant? We'll book it for you. Our New London Booking Service is here 118 118.
>
> (London Underground advertisement, June 2011)

Below this is a map, drawn in the style of Harry Beck's classic London Underground plan, but with formal metonymies relating to food replacing real station names: *Mornington Pheasant*, *Eggware Road*, *Puddington*, *Notting Hill Cake*, *Tortellini Court Road*, *Highbury and Biscuit Tin*, *Charing Croissant*, *Oxtail Circus*, *Piccalilli Circus*, *Greens Park*. The formal metonymies are entertaining but, as they all refer to food, also serve the functions of increasing the cohesiveness of the text and reminding the reader that the advertisement is concerned with a restaurant booking service. The American TV series *Sex and the City* has made its way into the collective unconscious to such a degree that the title has given rise to a whole host of names of businesses and organizations. This schema even 'sanctions' a large number of names containing "*in* the City" as this this sample from an internet search, accessed 8 May 2011, shows:

Secs in the City, a website for recruiting secretaries, PAs and office administrators;
Socks in the City, a podcast for knitters of socks;
Sweat in the City, a fitness site for women who want to "get fit and feel fabulous";
Decks in the City, a blog about rave music;
Vex in the City, a beauty blog;
X in the City, a lap-dancing chain;
Fresh in the City, a food, diet and lifestyle site;
Prospects in the City, an organization which gives young people insights into various careers;
Faith in the City, conference on religious architecture;
Classics in the City, classical music CD shop in Glasgow;
Pets in the City, a dog-care service;
Systems in the City, financial services;
Silence in the City, prayer and contemplation;

Pads in the City, a Birmingham letting agency;
Paws in the City, dog grooming;
Poetry in the City, promoting poetry to new audiences;
Christ in the City, a Christian event in Belfast.

The dozens of names thrown up by this search would surely not have come into existence without the huge success of the TV series. Being so popular, the name of the series entered the public consciousness and made available a syntactic/phonological frame which was then used to generate the names of numerous businesses, services and initiatives. It no doubt also generated a whole host of titles in other genres, such as newspaper headlines, names of TV and radio programmes and titles of undergraduate essays, the sheer number of variants showing just how powerful metonymy is as a tool for generating and extending meaning.

Another example of formal metonymy explored for its own sake is *Lost Consonants*, a feature which appeared in the UK *Guardian* newspaper from 1990 to 2005. It was devised by a collage artist, Graham Rawle, and shows how a single consonant missing from a sentence can completely change the meaning of that sentence. The effect is comic, for example "The hunter was an expert at tracing animals in the wild" instead of 'tracking'; "A bird in the hand is worth two in the bus" instead of 'bush' (http://en.wikipedia.org/wiki/Lost_Consonants, accessed 14 April 2011). Rawle illustrated these modified sentences with his ingenious collages. This again shows that formal metonymies are both easily understood and a source of entertainment. This, I would suggest, is because of the fundamental role metonymy plays in our lives; they would be neither easily understood nor entertaining if this were not so. Though a comment from an informant in my data notebooks about *Lost Consonants* suggests that ease of understanding can work against humour:

> It is sort of obvious that if you change a word by just a letter it can mean something completely different. I thought everybody knew that. I thought there was more to it than that. That's why I didn't get it.
>
> (Informant K, personal communication, 2011)

It is similarly the association between unrelated meanings via related form which is the source of amusement in bad translations. *Lost in Translation* started as a column in a UK newspaper and later gave rise to book publications. In them, we find amusing mistranslations which Charlie Croker collected together during his travels abroad, such as "Munich, Germany: In your room you will find a minibar which is filled with alcoholics", "Restaurant, France: Fish soup with rust and croutons" and "Guide to Buenos Aires: Several of the local beaches are very copular in the summer" (www.telegraph.co.uk/travel/arts-andculture/73840/Lost-in-translation.html, accessed 2 May 2011). The Translation-Studies scholar Robinson has also collected translation gaffes, such as "Ladies are requested not to have children in the bar", "Please leave your values at the front desk" and "Limpid red beet soup with cheesy dumplings in the form of a finger; roasted duck let loose; beef rashers beaten up in the country people's fashion" (Robinson 2003:101).

Parody also relies on metonymy, but on a more ambitious scale, involving a whole text or reference to a genre. The reader/viewer needs to be able to identify the original on which the parody is based for it to work. The illustration in Figure 5.1 (below) is based on the classic *Beatles* album cover *Sgt. Pepper's Lonely Hearts Club Band.* The original is recognizable in the parody by the layout, the colour scheme, how the group is arranged, the fact that it is a collage of images from other sources and the artefacts in the foreground. The faces in the foreground have been changed to those of personalities appearing on UK television, in particular the TV talent show *The X Factor* (*Times Higher Education*, 2 December 2010, p.48).

For someone who knows the album cover and follows the talent show, the metonymic links are easy to make. But even for someone who does not know the TV shows, the illustration would be recognized as a parody if they knew the album cover, because their metonymic processing of the illustration would tell them that changes had been made to the original, and they would infer that this had been done for a reason. This particular album cover has been a favourite for being parodied over the years. What perhaps lends itself to parody is the fact that it is a collage which makes substitutions easier.

IN-FAMILY EXPRESSIONS

The final category I want to consider in this section of cultural phenomena which centre around metonymic activity concerns 'in-family expressions'. An in-family expression is defined here as an expression unique to a close group of a few individuals, such as partners, colleagues, friends or near kin, while not being part of

Figure 5.1: Parody of *Sgt. Pepper* album cover

the repertoire of people outside the group and which is used on a regular basis over a long period of time. This original line of enquiry offers the potential for revealing processes by which new expressions come into existence in micro-communities. To investigate this area I collected data from five informants, who I am calling P, Q, T, U and W. I proceeded by first explaining what I meant by an 'in-family expression' and then asking in informal interviews:

- whether they had any expressions or sayings of this sort in their family or other close-knit group, and
- if so, where those expressions came from.

The data were collected informally over a period of three months in 2007 while socializing. I would start in this manner: "There is something I wanted to ask you for my research. Are there any expressions in your family or expressions you use with your partner or friends which no one else uses, expressions you have invented?" If what they then said was interesting, I would ask if I could write it down. I chose not to make audio recordings as I felt that this would inhibit the informants by making the process too formal. I continued asking about their expressions until I had all the information I could get. I also invited them to tell me of any expressions they thought of afterwards and to let me know (though none did). Of the five informants I interviewed, P provided a particularly rich source of in-family expressions, of which I report seven below, and came back to me after the first conversation to give more detailed accounts of the origins of her examples, while from W there was none I could report. In all, I collected and documented thirteen expressions:

***Burgess's* (Informant P)**

Burgess's is said when plates and cutlery are taken away more quickly than necessary after you have finished eating in a restaurant or at home. ORIGIN: The staff at Burgess's, a cafe in Newcastle-under-Lyme, would take plates and cutlery away the moment you stopped eating.

***It's only material things* (Informant P)**

Said when something of (especially sentimental) value gets broken and the owner needs consoling. ORIGIN: This was said by the informant's grand-mother to the informant's mother when a Wedgwood plate was accidentally broken. Rather than consoling this was felt to be unfeeling.

***Out of my bed!* (Informant P)**

The expression is used to tell you your behaviour is displeasing. ORIGIN: Two young children were having a Sunday lie-in with their mother, but they mis-behaved and were chased out of bed.

***Get off my land!* (Informant P)**

The expression is used when someone overreacts. ORIGIN: This was said by the informant's mother during an argument with a neighbour about a dog, when the neighbour's daughter stepped over the boundary line of their garden into the garden of the informant's family.

***Let us gather fresh coconuts!* (Informant P)**

Used when the family is about to leave for a trip or about to start a task which involves preparations. ORIGIN: The informant did not know the origin of this expression, but thought that perhaps it had come from a radio programme.

***It's just like Christmas!* (Informant P)**

Used when seeing an impressive spread of food. ORIGIN: The informant's grandfather would say this at Christmas but also any occasion where an impressive spread of food is offered.

***She's a beautiful dancer!* (Informant P)**

Used when someone on television is making an attempt to be glamorous or make an impressive go at something, but not really succeeding. ORIGIN: A catchphrase from a TV programme.

***Brown boots* (Informant Q)**

The expression is said when someone is lagging behind in a conversation or slow at getting the point. ORIGIN: Three friends are walking to a local pub one evening during the Second World War. One of them says something of little consequence about buying a pair of 'brown boots' early in the conversation. Other topics come and go. Much later on, one of the friends, who has said almost nothing during this time, in a serious-sounding voice, says "I used to have a pair of brown boots". They laugh.

***That'll do for Giles' lunch* (Informant Q)**

Said after a meal when there is food left over enough for a meal for one. ORIGIN: A female friend of the family would say this when there was food left over after dinner. Giles was the woman's young son.

***Raynes Park* (Informant T)**

Said when someone is being untruthful about their whereabouts when speaking on a mobile phone. ORIGIN: Someone on a train was overheard calling his wife from his mobile, saying he was at Raynes Park, a station on the suburban rail network in London, while actually somewhere else.

Comestibles **(Informant T)**

Used as an alternative to 'food' especially food which will go off, eg "Put the comestibles in the fridge". ORIGIN: *Breakfast Comestibles* was seen as part of the signage in a new supermarket. The informant found this amusing as it is not something anyone would ever say.

Dog food **(Informant T)**

Used to refer to TV adverts, as in "It's on a dog-food channel" (ie a channel with adverts) to contrast with BBC channels in the UK which show no advertising. ORIGIN: The actor Quentin Crisp famously said of the film about his life that it lasted forty minutes, or sixty minutes "with dog food".

Work **(Informant U)**

Used to refer to the puzzles of the kind you find in newspapers and magazines, such as Sudoku, number puzzles and crosswords. ORIGIN: A Canadian couple, friends of the informant, for their holidays would go on long-distance train journeys across North America. The most demanding thing they did on these journeys was to do puzzles in newspapers and magazines, which came to be called 'work': "Is there any work in that one?"

All the expressions above, where the origins are known, come from incidents of particular emotional significance for the participants. Their appearance can be traced back to a particular event, often in the distant past, which was memorable by being amusing or poignant in some way, and which had become part of the shared culture of the group. The expressions probably survived because the emotion associated with the incident is recalled when a matching situation is encountered. The recognition of matches/overlaps of this sort involves metonymic processing, relating what has just happened to a similar event stored in the (collective) memory. The original purpose for conducting this study was to identify the proportion of expressions, which had emerged uniquely among intimate groups, which was metaphoric. I found that although words are clearly being used metaphorically, eg *bed, coconuts, boots, dog food, work*, it is through metonymic associations that we connect emotionally to experiences which are important to us and share those memories by pointing out those associations.

AVOIDING COOPERATION

Above we saw how relatedness in form but unrelatedness in meaning, formal metonymy, can be a source of humour. I now want to illustrate how formal metonymy can also be used to avoid cooperative communication. Most linguists would associate the term 'cooperation' with Gricean pragmatics and the 'cooperative principle', the idea that speakers assume a common purpose of cooperation in their interactions (Grice 1975). This is the sense in which I am using it here. It has been observed that it is not the aim of all participants in all interactions to be cooperative. A classic example is 'adversarial court questioning', which Baker describes as "an example of a non-cooperative context in which one participant, the defendant, tries to be as uncooperative as possible" (Baker 1992:233). A defendant or witness in a courtroom who wishes to withhold information will use strategies in order to be economical with the truth, even if on the surface they appear to be 'playing the game' of cooperation. The expression "to be economical with the truth" also suggests flouting of the same Gricean maxim.

Formal metonymy can be used to avoid cooperation not just by withholding information but by making connections via related forms to meanings which are unrelated and not relevant to the context. Cockney rhyming slang, expressions such as *apples and pears*, *syrup of figs*, *plates of meat* (respectively meaning 'stairs', 'wig' and 'feet'), is thought to have evolved as a way of communicating in a private language so employers would not understand what their workers were saying to each other, as the 'slang' terms are rhymes which are unrelated in meaning to the words they rhyme with. Cooperation can also be avoided when one participant chooses deliberately to misunderstand the expression their interlocutor uses. In an exchange between two characters in a scene from a popular animated series *Creature Comforts*, a man tries to explain why he does not eat whelks or mussels. He says it is because it is "like eating slugs". The other character refuses to take on the idea. The misunderstanding lasts for four turns and revolves around whether you need to have eaten slugs in order to be able to say it is "like eating slugs" (*Creature Comforts*, DVD, 2004).

Another way to be uncooperative is to be literal, deliberately choosing to understand a conventional or novel metaphoric expression literally, or choosing to take another of the meanings of a polysemous word rather than the one intended. In a sketch from the TV series *A Bit of Fry and Laurie*, an irate parent is complaining to the headmaster of his son's school for his son being exposed to 'filthy talk' in his biology class. The headmaster uses literalness to deflect criticism:

Parent	You're here to provide a service. Call yourself a school?
Headmaster	Well, I don't actually call *myself* a school.

(*A Bit of Fry and Laurie*, BBC2, Episode 1.1, 13 January 1989)

In a dialogue from the film *Ali G, Aiii* (2000), Borat, a fictitious journalist from Kazakhstan, interviews an English policeman who believes he is a foreigner with little understanding of English customs. Borat refuses to accept the policeman's use of the expression *everything's cricket* to mean 'fair play'. The exchange from when the policeman first mentions cricket to the last time it is mentioned lasts for ten turns and includes: "No, it's just a saying", "I'm confusing you now", "Forget the cricket side of things", "It's just a saying", "Forget the cricket", "The cricket's purely a saying", "It's a saying". This dialogue is a satirical sketch from a film but such strategies can be observed in spontaneous interactions in real life as well. Avoiding cooperation through formal metonymy, 'acting dumb' one could perhaps characterize it as, is a strategy available to us all, but one which learners particularly can get away with, because learners can more easily disguise a deliberate act of un-cooperativeness as a mistake genuinely made.

Formal metonymy can have an entirely different function: it can be used for emphasis; in which case it no longer involves the avoidance of cooperation. The extract below from my data notebooks is from a conversation in which the speaker is thanking a friend for looking after her mother during a hospital visit:

> She was so glad you were there / reassured, you know, by your being there / because you are so calm and able // not Cain and Abel / calm and able [laugh] you just get on with it / without making a fuss / and she likes that / makes her feel safe
>
> (adapted)

Here the idea of being 'calm and able' is emphasized by contrasting it with 'phonic' metonymies, pairs of words which sound similar, "Cain and Abel", but which are unrelated in meaning. The language play of 'Cain and Abel' versus 'calm and able' allows the speaker to seem lighthearted and avoid being too serious, or embarrassing, when paying this compliment.

CONCLUSION

In this chapter, I have discussed the use to which metonymy can be put to give nuance, emphasis and spin, an essential tool in the language toolbox and one which, I argue, is the key to why language is so subtle, nuanced and fit for purpose. I have presented various data to demonstrate the central role played by metonymy in various popular cultural and recreational activities. I have discussed our fascination with recognizing similarities in people's appearance and spotting salient characteristics of behaviour, as well as pointing out the role metonymy plays in structuring jokes, in giving alternative names to people and things, in allowing us to index shared experience via in-family expressions and in both avoiding and promoting cooperation. I have introduced the idea of formal metonymy, partial phonic and graphic matches, and shown its relevance in social contexts. I have suggested that metonymy in many of our practices and cultural objects seems to be explored for its own sake, almost as an acknowledgement at an emotional level of the vital role it plays in the broader picture of our lives as a whole.

6 Metonymy and Metaphor in Discourse and Text

In Chapter 4, I developed a precise ontology of metonymy and used this to contrast metonymy with the ontology of metaphor developed in Chapter 3. In this chapter, I turn to the role metonymy and metaphor play in organizing longer stretches of language and their employment in making meaning at the level of the whole text. To do this, I extend ideas in this field to give a comprehensive framework for analyzing metonymy and metaphor at the level of the whole text. In the model I develop, four text-wide phenomena emerge: two are concerned with shifts in the way discourse is framed, either through narrowing the focus, Discourse Metonymy, or widening, Discourse Metaphor; while the second pair are concerned with setting up lexical networks either through metonymic links between items within the text, Textual Metonymy, or patterning within a text organized by metaphor, Textual Metaphor. I consider each in turn below but first I discuss the different ways 'discourse' and 'text' have been used in the academic literature, and how I will be using them. I briefly review work relevant in this context: Jakobson on metonymic and metaphoric 'poles' of communication (Jakobson 1956/1971), Lodge on metonymic and metaphoric 'modes' of writing (Lodge 1977), Semino on metaphor 'chains' and 'clusters' in discourse (Semino 2008), Al-Sharafi on textual metonymy (Al-Sharafi 2004) and Halliday & Hasan on cohesion (Halliday & Hasan 1976). In the last section, I introduce the idea of Text Metaphtonymy, metaphor and metonymy co-occurring at whole-text level.

DISCOURSE AND TEXT

Kress tells us that "The term *discourse* has been subject to cavalier usage" and as a result is 'under-lexicalized' (Kress 2010:114–115). The word 'text' has suffered a similar fate. The terms 'discourse' and 'text' are used widely in language studies and although 'discourse' tends to suggest spoken language and 'text' written language, they are often used interchangeably, their closeness in meaning reflected in the expressions 'spoken discourse' (eg Cameron 2001), 'spoken text' (eg Brown & Yule 1983), 'written text' (eg Coulthard 1994) and 'written discourse' (eg Hoey 2001). For these authors 'discourse' and 'text' are units of language where the emphasis is on 'real language', "language in use" (eg Brown & Yule 1983: xiii), language created for the purpose of communication in the 'real world'. Other scholars give even more emphasis to the social contexts in which language occurs. For Cook 'discourses' are "stretches of language, considered in their full textual, social and psychological context" (Cook 1989:ix), and, for Stillar, a 'discourse' is the relationship between language texts, social contexts and usage (Stillar:1998:14). For Beaugrande & Dressler, a 'text' is a 'communicative occurrence' in which 'seven standards of textuality'—'cohesion', 'coherence', 'intentionality', 'acceptability', 'informativity', 'situationality' and 'intertextuality'—must be met, and that "If any of these standards is not considered to have been satisfied, the text will not be communicative. Hence, non-communicative texts are treated as non-texts" (Beaugrande & Dressler 1981:3).

For other scholars, 'discourse' does not necessarily have to involve language at all. For Fairclough, discourse "*constitutes* the social. Three dimensions of the social are distinguished—knowledge, social relations, and social identity—and these correspond respectively to three major functions of language [. . .] Discourse is shaped by relations of power, and invested with ideologies" (Fairclough 1992:8). For Blommaert 'discourse' is "a general mode of semiosis" (Blommaert 2005:1), and comprises "all forms of meaningful semiotic human activity seen in connection with social, cultural, and historical patterns and developments of use" (Blommaert 2005:3). For O'Regan "Discourse is the universal mode of semiosis through which the material and the immaterial (social, cultural, historical, political, economic, religious, etc) are entered into a system of meaning relations. It is the means by which a world is acknowledged and brought within the realm of human experience and interpretation" (O'Regan 2006). For Block, "discursive activity means any semiotic behaviour on the part of an individual which counts as the expression of a subject position (or subjectivity)" (Block 2007:16); while for Kress discourse involves "canonical forms for interaction" (Kress 2010:46). Gee distinguishes between 'little "d"' and 'big "D" discourses', 'little "d" discourse' being "any instance of language-in-use or any stretch of spoken or written language (often called a "text" in the expanded sense where texts can be oral or written)" (Gee 2011:205), while 'big "D" discourse' is the enacting of "identities and activities not just through language, but by using language together with other 'stuff' that isn't language" (Gee 2011:201).

Given this diversity of definitions and approaches, what I want to do in the present context is to exploit the fact that two terms exist in order to use them to identify specific phenomena pertinent to the present study. I propose distinguishing between phenomena which allow the speaker/writer to change the 'frame' (or 'focus') of discourse by adopting distinct communicative 'voices' or 'registers', by referring to them as 'discourse' phenomena; and phenomena where metonymy and metaphor pattern lexical choices across text, by referring to them as 'textual' phenomena. Within these categories, I further distinguish whether metonymy or metaphor is involved, thus establishing a four-way differentiation between Discourse Metonymy, Discourse Metaphor, Textual Metonymy and Textual Metaphor. Before I consider these in turn, I briefly review the work of scholars who I feel have contributed to our understanding of figurative phenomena at text level.

Al-Sharafi, Halliday & Hasan, Jakobson, Lodge, and Semino

It is Jakobson's famous essay on aphasia from 1956 in which metonymy and metaphor are identified as fundamental processes in communication, metaphor involving similarity, set up through selection and substitution, and metonymy involving contiguity, set up through combination and contexture (Jakobson 1956/1971). Jakobson describes these as two distinct semantic lines, the 'metaphoric way' and the 'metonymic way':

> The development of a discourse may take place along two different semantic lines: one topic may lead to another either through their similarity or through their contiguity. The METAPHORIC way would be the most appropriate term for the first case and the METONYMIC way for the second, since they find their most condensed expression in metaphor and metonymy respectively.
>
> (Jakobson 1956/1971:90)

For Jakobson, language has a "twofold character" (1956/1971:72) and "in normal behaviour both processes [metonymy and metaphor] are continually operative" (p90); but he also sees metonymy and metaphor as offering 'polar' opposites (p83), different 'poles' (p90). This means that an author has a choice and can choose the metonymic pole over the metaphoric pole, or vice versa (p90). The consequence of this is that texts reflect these preferences such that some literature texts are inherently metonymic while others are inherently metaphoric. This, according to Jakobson, is achieved by the use of individual metonymies or metaphors in those texts. In the final pages of the essay, the idea is explored that whole genres reflect these preferences, artists favouring one pole over the other, for example, identifying cubist art and the films of Griffiths as metonymic, and surrealist art and the films of Eisenstein as metaphoric (p92).

Lodge takes up Jakobson's metaphor/metonymy distinction and develops it, devising his own typology of literary genres based on metaphoric and metonymic 'modes of writing' (Lodge 1977). For Lodge, reading Jakobson's 1956 essay provided a solution to his immediate problem of defining modernism but also a broader question of how to classify literary modes in general: "The distinction between metaphoric and metonymic types of discourse not only seemed a much more effective way of distinguishing between the language of modernist and antimodernist fiction than metaphor/simile; it suggested the possibility of an all-embracing typology of literary modes" (Lodge 1977:viii). Lodge marries realistic poetry/prose with the metonymic 'mode' and romantic poetry/prose with the metaphoric 'mode', identifying Philip Larkin, for example, as a 'metonymic' poet (Lodge 1977:214). Lodge takes this typology further, using it to map the history of modern English literature in terms of the metaphoric and metonymic modes, an oscillation in the practice of writing "between polarized clusters of attitudes and techniques: modernist, symbolist and mythopoeic, writerly and metaphoric on the one hand; antimodernist, realistic, readerly and metonymic on the other" (Lodge 1977:220).

Of particular significance to the present study is that Lodge recognizes that metonymic and metaphoric writing are not dependent on the presence of individual metaphors and metonymies in a text. He gives examples from literary texts: the opening of Forster's *A Passage to India* is "metonymic writing, not metaphoric, even though it contains a few metaphors and no metonymies; it is metonymic in structure, connecting topics on the basis of contiguity not similarity" (Lodge 1977:98–99); while Wilde's *The Ballad of Reading Gaol* is not metaphoric "in the quantitative dominance of actual metaphors (though the 'Ballad' is full of them) but in the way the discourse is generated and maintained by 'the projection of the principle of equivalence from the axis of selection into the axis of combination'" (Lodge 1977:104).

In the large body of writing on 'metaphor and discourse' which now exists, 'discoursc' is used predominately in the sense of the occurrence of metaphor in specific discourse domains, such as advertising, politics, conflict, science, and genres; and is used less in the sense I am concerned with in this chapter, namely, metaphor's organizational role at whole-text level. Examples of scholars who look at metaphor in discourse in the former sense include Steen, who develops a "checklist for metaphor analysis" (Steen 1999), Cameron, whose concern is to develop an "operational identification procedure for metaphor" (Cameron 1999), the Pragglejaz Group's word-level Metaphor Identification Procedure (MIP), which they describe as "a method for identifying metaphorically used words in discourse" (Pragglejaz Group 2007), further developed by Steen et al as MIPVU (Steen et al 2010), Cameron & Maslen's tool for "identifying linguistic metaphors in discourse data" (Cameron & Maslen 2010), and Semino who investigates "the forms and functions of metaphor in a variety of texts and genres on a range of different topics", such as politics, science, education, advertising and illness (Semino 2008:1).

Semino also offers a comprehensive overview of text phenomena involving metaphor (Semino 2008). She classifies the different ways in which "the patterning of metaphor in discourse" manifests itself using the headings 'repetition', 'recurrence', 'extension', 'clustering', 'combination and mixing' and 'literal-metaphorical oppositions' (Semino 2008:22–30). For my purposes, the first four of Semino's 'textual manifestations' of metaphor are the most significant, and can be glossed as: 'repetition', the same linguistic metaphor repeated at different points within a text; 'recurrence', the appearance of two or more metaphoric expressions from the same source domain at different points within a text; 'extension', a series of different metaphoric expressions from the same source domain occurring in close proximity; and 'clustering', an unusually high density of metaphoric expressions from different source domains in a particular section of text (Semino 2008:22–26). Semino makes a distinction between 'clusters' and 'chains' of linguistic metaphors: clusters draw from different source domains, while metaphors in chains derive from the same domain and arise "from a combination of repetition, recurrence and extension" (Semino 2008:226). Semino's 'chains' correspond closely to my concept of Textual Metaphor, and her idea of 'clusters' to my idea of Discourse Metaphor.

Al-Sharafi offers a detailed account of how figurative thought, especially metonymy, contributes to the cohesion and coherence of a text (Al-Sharafi 2004). He interprets all six of Halliday & Hasan's categories of cohesion in terms of metonymy, arguing that "metonymy ensures economy and compactness in text and thus shortens distances of interpretation" (Al-Sharafi 2004:115), and suggests that "metonymy accounts for the relations of lexical cohesion in a more satisfactory way than the term 'lexical cohesion' itself" (Al-Sharafi 2004:126). While accepting the assertion Al-Sharafi is making, in my framework I am focussing on the two categories of lexical cohesion only: 'reiteration', which corresponds to my concept of Textual Metonymy, and 'collocation', which corresponds to my concept of Textual Metaphor.

In Halliday & Hasan's system, 'collocation' is where words in a text are associated by virtue of being from the same domain of human activity (as opposed to the Firthian sense of associations between adjacent words, discussed in the context of the Mental Phraseicon in Chapter 2): the "co-occurrence of lexical items that are in some way or other typically associated with one another, because they tend to occur in similar environments: the specific kinds of co-occurrence relations are variable and complex, and would have to be interpreted in the light of a general semantic description of the English language" (Halliday & Hasan 1976:287–288). A text may draw from one, two or more different domains; an article on the finances of soccer, for example, would have lexis from the domains of 'finance' and the domain of 'soccer', the sense of the article being an exploration of the interaction between the two. Collocational links between lexical items in a text in Halliday & Hasan's sense concern literal meanings—their concern is not with figurative language, and their understanding of a "similar environment" is more a textual environment than a cognitive environment or 'domain'. Nonetheless, when lexical patterning across a text is generated by metaphor, and a number of lexical items in the text give mental access to a shared source domain, we have collocation of a kind compatible with both 'cohesion' in Halliday & Hasan's sense and Cognitive Metaphor Theory. Textual Metaphor is this sort of collocation, where the source domain of a conceptual metaphor structures a text by patterning its lexis.

I am now in a position to present the four phenomena—Discourse Metonymy, Discourse Metaphor, Textual Metonymy and Textual Metaphor—explaining each phenomenon through a variety of texts.

DISCOURSE METONYMY

Discourse Metonymy is a device for narrowing the focus of discourse by concentrating on a particular part of a frame or schema. The change of focus is a change of register in the Hallidayan sense (eg Halliday 1978). By focussing closer in on the subject matter, the discourse foregrounds certain features and evokes powerful physical images, thereby increasing the persuasiveness of the message; the content becomes more literal than literal, 'ultra real'. Discourse Metonymy allows an author to argue by *exemplification* and contrasts with Discourse Metaphor (discussed in the next section), which allows an author to argue by *comparison*. A public figure might argue by exemplification, using Discourse Metonymy (in bold), as in this extract from a radio interview (*Today*, BBC Radio 4, 11 January 2010):

> The earnings of lower-income workers are just not enough to live on. **One of my constituents receives £45 family allowance a week; she works full time, has a weekend job as well as helping out at a butcher's, but is still in debt.**

or by comparison, using Discourse Metaphor (in bold), as in this extract from the same interview:

> The only criterion for the Think Tank was that its members should have an IQ of over 140. **It is a bit like buying a computer, not loading any software and expecting it to do computations for you.**

Below I discuss a number of different texts to illustrate the use of Discourse Metonymy. They are: a travel guide to a French city, an email message, an interview with James Gooding, a magazine column on London hosting the 2012 Olympics, a Priministerial debate during the 2010 UK general election campaign, a self-help study guide for university students, promotional material for a health club and a speech given at a charity fundraising event.

The first text, a guide to the French city Lille, begins in the neutral register of 'default', what one might call 'literal discourse'. It then goes into Discourse Metonymy in the section (shown here in bold):

> The development in Lille which includes the Centre Euralille shopping mall [. . .] this huge business and leisure development is the key to the city's renaissance. Designed to serve more than ten times the population of Lille, **here you can shop for essentials or luxuries, attend some of Europe's most talked-about parties, enjoy concerts or even prepare a meal in a rented apartment**.
>
> (L. Phillips, *Essential Lille*, 2000, p.14)

The noticeable shift in register indicates to the reader that this part of the text, "here you can shop for essentials or luxuries, attend some of Europe's most talked-about parties, enjoy concerts or even prepare a meal in a rented apartment", is to be understood as a selective list of activities you can undertake and that they stand for the 'whole' of all possible activities. The effect is to give a vivid picture, which a phrase such as "retail and entertainment possibilities" would not achieve—though specifying a 'rented' apartment in the text does almost spoil the effect by making us think that this might actually be intended as literal!

In the next text, the author uses Discourse Metonymy in a personal email about a New Year party (Discourse Metonymy in bold):

> Dear Kate, I just wanted you to be party to the (breaking) news [. . .] which is basically that Steven is of the opinion that spending New Year with us (ie you two and me), **breaking open a bottle of bubbly and sharing a table in a local restaurant (or at home)**, would be far more agreeable than **flying to an unfamiliar destination, such as Prague, Budapest [. . .] and confronting the unpredictability of inclement weather, foreign folk, disease & etc**. I hope you can come to stay for New Year. All the best, Pete.
>
> (Informant D, personal communication, 2006)

The sections in bold employ Discourse Metonymy to contrast a party, "breaking open a bottle of bubbly and sharing a table in a local restaurant (or at home)", with a city break, "flying to an unfamiliar destination, such as Prague, Budapest [. . .] and confronting the unpredictability of inclement weather, foreign folk, disease & etc", while literal discourse is used for the rest of the message. The author's motivation here, we can imagine, is to persuade, entertain and give a sense of inclusion, conveyed through the use of distinct images.

The next text is an interview, *Ten Things You Need to Know about James Gooding*, which appeared in the London listings magazine, *Time Out* (*London Time Out*, August 20-September 4, 2003, p.14). In it, the interviewee, James Gooding, famous for having had a relationship with the Australian pop singer Kylie Minogue and selling his story to the press, uses Discourse Metonymy in two sections of the interview (the sections are presented as ten numbered paragraphs). These sections (shown in bold below) are 1) when describing how the art-collector Saatchi helped make art more accessible to young people: "I remember when I lived in New York, everyone wanted to be a documentary film-maker. Everyone traded in their bass guitars and bought their super-8 cameras and DVs, and started making little films" (paragraph 5); and 2) when arguing that contemporary art can be intimidating to the average person: "If I take my grandparents to see a Tracey Emin show and there's an unmade bed, they're going to ask, 'What's all that about?'" (paragraph 8).

> 5. THE BRIT ART MOVEMENT If Saatchi hadn't been so media savvy, I don't think it would have happened in quite the way it did. He made art more appealing to young people. **I remember when I lived in New York, everyone**

> **wanted to be a documentary film-maker. Everyone traded in their bass guitars and bought their super-8 cameras and DVs, and started making little films**. Now they either want to be artists or to study media. [. . .]
>
> 8. ART AND THE CITY It's not a high-brow art show, it's an accessible art show. A lot of contemporary art can be very intimidating. **If I take my grandparents to see a Tracey Emin show and there's an unmade bed, they're going to ask, "What's all that about?".** So this show is about talking to the artists and getting them to open the door a little bit.
>
> (Ten Things You Need to Know about James Gooding, *London Time Out*, August 20-September 4, 2003, p.14)

In both cases, Discourse Metonymy reinforces the argument with vivid examples, images which get us 'up close' to the matter in hand. In the interview, there are also less forceful instances of Discourse Metonymy, introduced by "My favourite artist from the show is . . ." and "The funniest thing was when . . .", as well as an instance of second-degree Discourse Metonymy (paragraph 8), where the focus is made even closer by reporting words which might actually have been said: "What's all that about?".

In the next text, a polemical (but also tongue-in-cheek) article by Robert Elms, *This Is the Capital, that Is the Way it Is*, Discourse Metonymy is used to argue that London, and only London, is suitable to host the 2012 Olympic Games. He characterizes Manchester, not a good candidate in his eyes, by its bars, gay scene and interesting buildings; while London is characterized by decades of pomp, circumstance and The Rolling Stones:

> Manchester is now trendy, has lots of bars by the canal, a good gay scene, a couple of interesting new buildings and even a Selfridges. But seen from afar those do not quite equal 2,000 years of pomp, circumstance and The Rolling Stones.
>
> (This Is the Capital, that Is the Way it Is, *London Time Out*, November 20–27, 2002, p.7)

It is important to note that individual linguistic metonymies are not necessarily involved in constructing Discourse Metonymy. In the metonymic passages in the texts considered above, the language is in fact literal. As was noted above in the context of the Gooding article, Discourse Metonymy is not just a device that is either present or absent; a speaker/author can create levels *within* the Discourse Metonymy register. Consider this example:

> In the seventies, those were the sort of jobs no one wanted to do. Like working in the sewers or kitchens. Imagine digging a grave in the snow.
>
> (*Today*, BBC Radio 4, 11 January 2010)

In this extract, "those were the jobs no one wanted to do" is literal; "like working in the sewers or kitchens" is what we might call 'Level 1 Discourse

Metonymy' (signalled by *like*), while "Imagine digging a grave in the snow" is 'Level 2 Discourse Metonymy' (signalled with *imagine*). Interestingly, the words signalling metonymy here, 'like' and 'imagine', are words just as likely to be used in other contexts to signal metaphor, eg "Being unemployed is a miserable existence. It is **like** being the spare wheel on a car. **Imagine** being a horse put out to pasture before your time".

The last example in this section is from the Priministerial debates shown on television during the campaign for the 2010 general election in the UK. These events attracted a huge amount of interest both from those professionally involved in politics and the general public. The reason for this, in large part, was that it was the first time an American-style debate had been organized in the UK, one which exposed the candidates to scrutiny and set them against each other on the same stage. As a result, the language and the body language used were studied with great interest by interested parties, journalists and commentators. What was notable for me in these exchanges was the use of Discourse Metonymy: all three candidates, but especially Cameron and Clegg, made frequent use of Discourse Metonymy as a rhetorical device. They did so by citing particular incidents to make their points, anecdotes from travelling around the country during the campaign (though these may well have been invented or embellished for the occasion). Here are some examples of how these stories were introduced:

> I went to Crosby the other day and I was talking to a woman there who had been burgled by someone who had just left prison. And he stole everything in her house; and as he left, he set fire to the sofa and her son died from the fumes. (Cameron)
>
> I went to a Hull police station the other day. They had five different police cars, and they were just about to buy a £73,000 Lexus. (Cameron)
>
> I was in a, err, factory in my own city where I'm an MP in Sheffield just a few weeks ago. And there was a great British company there, a manufacturing company, that produces great metal braces with these huge rollers, which apparently are sold to the American army. (Clegg)
>
> (*The First Election Debate*, ITV1, 15 April 2010, author's transcription)

A further metonymic device used rhetorically in the debate is 'formal metonymy', the repetition of form (discussed in Chapter 5). Cameron repeats the structure noun+er when he uses *crime fighters, not form-fillers* (noun+er, noun+er) as a way of concluding persuasively the section on the police already cited above:

> They had five different police cars, and they were just about to buy a £73,000 Lexus. There's money that could be saved to get the police on the frontline. The Metropolitan Police have 400 uniformed officer officers in their human

> resources department, when our police officers should be **crime fighters**, not **form-fillers**, and that's what needs to change.
>
> (ibid)

Clegg makes use of metonymy in yet another way in the debate, when summarizing his responses to questions from the audience:

> I know many of you think that all politicians are just the same; I hope I've tried to show you that that just isn't true. Whether it's on the questions from Alan on care, Jacqueline on crime, Helen on politics, Joel on schooling, Robert on, on the, on the deficit, I believe we can answer all of those questions . . .
>
> (ibid)

As well as these devices, both politicians also use the different 'levels' of metonymy within Discourse Metonymy mentioned above. In one of his anecdotes, Cameron moves from a general discussion to a particular incident, "I was in Plymouth recently, and a 40-year-old black man actually made the point to me" (Level 1 Discourse Metonymy) and then makes a further move within that incident to direct speech (Level 2 Discourse Metonymy); Clegg similarly identifies a situation, saying, "I was at a hospital, a paediatric hospital in Cardiff a few months ago, treating very sick prematurely-born babies" and then recreates an exchange within that story. After that he states the lesson to be drawn from the incident in a literal register. In the extracts below I have shown Level 1 Discourse Metonymy in *italics*; Level 2 Discourse Metonymy in ***bold italics***; and literal language as neither italics nor bold:

Cameron	*. . . I was in Plymouth recently, and a 40-year-old black man actually made the point to me; he said, "**I came here when I was six; I've served in the Royal Navy for 30 years; I'm incredibly proud of my country. But I'm so ashamed that we've had this out-of-control system with people abusing it so badly**".*
Clegg	*. . . I was at a hospital, a paediatric hospital in Cardiff a few months ago, treating very sick prematurely-born babies. I was being shown around and there were a large number of babies who needed to be treated. And I went into a ward and it was standing completely empty. It had the latest equipment, but it was standing completely empty. And I said to the ward sister "**What's going on? Why are there no babies here, being treated?**" She said "**New rules mean that we can't employ any doctors from outside the European Union with the skills needed**".* That's an example of where the rules are actually stopping good immigration which actually helps our public services to work properly. And that's what I want to see, not an arbitrary cap.

(ibid)

This was the first debate from that 2010 campaign. At the time, comments were made in the press that the device of using anecdotes was overused, and in the two subsequent debates the candidates incorporated Discourse Metonymy less in their presentations. This suggests that the journalists recognized Discourse Metonymy as a powerful rhetorical device which should be used sparingly.

Testimonies and Vox Pops

Another common use of Discourse Metonymy is in testimonies and vox pops, where a picture is built up from a series of individual contributions or 'mini-texts', giving a narrative which seems more 'real' and easier to identify with. Here the Discourse Metonymy register takes over the whole text or section of text. To stress the idea that testimonies are the contributions of individuals, they are often presented in different typefaces or handwriting to suggest different 'voices', and perhaps even in speech bubbles coming from cartoon heads or framed as if they were on notepads. A language school for example could be marketed through testimonies from past students such as: "Thanks to studying at the British School, I now work as an accountant with foreign clients"; "Learning English has meant that I can understand all the lyrics of my favourite songs which I couldn't do before"; "After finishing the course, I went to the US and now teach yoga to Hollywood stars" (invented examples). All these are metonymies which help construe a central message, the idea that the school can assist in realizing the ambitions of the students who attend it.

Below I discuss three examples of the use of testimonies: a study-skills guide on exam skills, promotional material for *Virgin Active* health clubs and after-dinner speeches at a fund-raising event for the charity *Terrence Higgins Trust*. The testimonies in the study guide come at the end of each unit and serve the purpose of reviewing the unit in a way which is more engaging and real than a formal summary. Here are four (the shortest) of the eight statements at the end of the unit on managing stress:

> I get on the bus and look out of the window: it makes me day-dream and I feel more relaxed when I get back.
>
> I put on my headphones, choose something really wild, and turn it up loud. I might even dance along if no-one else is in.
>
> I run a mile a day and that clears my system of worry and leaves me clear-headed.
>
> I don't think I have ever felt stressed. People keep asking me if I am but I don't know why. Maybe I seem stressed.
>
> (Cottrell 2007:170)

The publicity material for *Virgin Active* health clubs is a booklet, one page of which uses Discourse Metonymy to present client endorsements. Accompanied by Polaroid images of members in the gym, six handwritten contributions say positive things about the services offered by *Virgin Active* health clubs. One testimony starts "I love my club!", another reads "You are all so helpful on the gym floor. I get clear instructions on how to use equipment", and a third states "I wouldn't hesitate to recommend my gym or my personal trainer". Each contribution ends with the member's name and the branch of the gym they attend (possibly invented) to make the testimonies more immediate. Advertising for the musical *The Book of Mormon* takes this to an extreme, where stand-alone posters and advertisements consist solely of tweets, not just a page within a booklet, Discourse Metonymy becoming the register of the entire text.

The charity Terrence Higgins Trust holds a fundraising dinner each year at which the chief executive officer usually gives a speech. In 2008, the organizers departed from this format and, instead, four individuals gave personal testimonies. This was reported in the newsletter like this:

> We heard first from Neil. His tales of finding a boyfriend at first made us laugh and then silenced the room. He shared with us the issue of disclosing his HIV status to prospective boyfriends.
>
> And next Abigail and her heart wrenching story of the HIV diagnosis that has left her separated from her children in Zimbabwe.
>
> And then Marc, diagnosed with HIV 23 years ago . . .
>
> And finally we heard from Marc's mum, Jan, who was brought up in a traditional West Indian family in the 1960s and raised her children in a very similar set-up during the 1970s and 80s.
>
> (2008 Annual Report and Newsletter, Terrence Higgins Trust)

Hearing of the resourcefulness of these individuals in overcoming the difficulties they had encountered through contact with HIV will have had a strong impact on those present and would have made potential donors more likely to give generously. Discourse Metonymy makes the impression left by a text more real.

Individual testimonies are sometimes actively requested, by employers, for example, in a form of interviewing known as 'Competence Based Interviewing' (or 'Behavioural Interviewing'). In this, the candidate is asked to give specific examples of personal competencies elicited by questions of the following sort:

> "What achievements in your life are you most proud of?"
>
> "What in your life are you least proud of?"
>
> "Tell me about a time when you were in a difficult situation or a situation of conflict with a colleague, and how you set about resolving this situation".
>
> "Tell me about a time when you contributed proactively to the team in bringing about an improvement in working practices in the office".
>
> (Hazel Beale, personal communication, 2006)

In other words, the candidates are requested to present themselves using a register chosen by the interview panel. Discourse Metonymy allows candidates to present a series of vivid vignettes of their past work experience, elicited by questions such as those given above.

DISCOURSE METAPHOR

Discourse Metaphor is the companion to Discourse Metonymy and is its opposite in many respects. If Discourse Metonymy can be characterized as *more* 'real', Discourse Metaphor can be characterized as *less* real, in the sense that it leads to an increase in the sense of indeterminacy or fuzziness of meaning. Rather than involving a closer focus on the subject matter, the focus of Discourse Metonymy is broader; it allows speakers/authors to distance themselves from the subject matter, make connections outside the frame and draw comparisons with other domains. A physical comparison can be made to the human eye. When we focus on something close to us, such as the printed page, the muscles which control the focus of the lens of the eye are at their most tense and the lens itself is at its most round. If instead we are hill-walking, say, and looking into the distance, our eyes are at their most relaxed and the lens its most flat; we also become more aware of what is in our purview, our wider field of vision. Discourse Metonymy is like a close up, looking at detail; while Discourse Metaphor is like panning out, a panoramic view.

Discourse Metaphor is set up by clusters of metaphors occurring in the same section of text. (The term is used differently by other scholars.) In order to illustrate this I consider below three texts in which Discourse Metaphor plays an important role, the Gooding interview discussed above, a poem by Philip Larkin and *Silk Cut* cigarette packets. These examples demonstrate that the phenomenon of Discourse Metaphor is found in widely different genres. When discussing the interview with James Gooding above, our concern was with Discourse Metonymy, but the same text also offers an example of Discourse Metaphor. In the last section of the interview, Gooding talks about his relationship with the singer Kylie Minogue and in so doing employs a series of conventional metaphors, 'idioms', metaphoric expressions which have become incorporated into the language and therefore also reported in general dictionaries:

> It was hell at times, living inside that bubble. There were times when it really got to me, it really did upset me. But now it's all water off a duck's back. For the past six months, I've just kind of kept my head down and kept away from it all, and got on with my work.
>
> (*London Time Out*, August 20-September 4, 2003)

The effect of these expressions—*it was hell at times, living inside that bubble, it really got to me, it's all water off a duck's back, I've kept my head down, I kept away from it all*—appearing in close proximity increases the indeterminacy and ambiguity of this section of the interview. Semino identifies metaphor clusters as occurring, among other contexts, at significant points in discourse, such as when talking about sensitive issues (Semino 2008:25). This is the use Gooding is putting them to here; he uses a cluster of conventional metaphors to create an interpersonal buffer, a space between himself and the subject matter where he can talk about his stormy affair without loss of face or hurting anyone's feelings. The density of idioms in this passage is so great you wonder whether there was perhaps some editorial intervention in order to exaggerate the effect.

The poem *Toads Revisited* by Philip Larkin is also an example of a text which contains both Discourse Metonymy and Discourse Metaphor (Philip Larkin, *The Whitsun Weddings*, 1964, pp.18–19), which Lodge calls metonymic and metaphoric 'modes' of writing (Lodge 1977). Discourse Metonymy accounts for over two-thirds of the poem and is used in four separate sections, each describing a different theme: the park, the men you find in the park, what the men in the park do and the poet's office. The men in the park, for example, are characterized as "palsied old step-takers", "hare-eyed clerks with the jitters", "waxed-fleshed out-patients" and "characters in long coats". In the fifth stanza, Larkin introduces the metaphoric idea *WORK IS TOADS*, which is returned to in the last stanza with "Give me your arm, old toad" and which is both in the title of the poem, *Toads Revisited*, and the poem this is the sequel to, *Toads* (Philip Larkin, *The Less Deceived*, 1955, pp.32–33). In *Toads Revisited*, Larkin uses both the narrower focus of Discourse Metonymy and the wider focus of Discourse Metaphor (just like in the Gooding interview), one to give a vivid sense of life in the park, office, etc, the other to evoke oppressive but also reassuring aspects of work. Lodge gives further examples of poems in which Larkin employs both Discourse Metonymy and Discourse Metaphor—*The Whitsun Weddings* and *Church Going* (Lodge 1977:218).

The last example in this section is the packaging of the cigarette brand *Silk Cut*. This is the brand which characters in David Lodge's 1988 novel *Nice Work* famously discuss in terms of metonymy and metaphor. At discourse level, text compilers have three options when creating texts. Whether the text is spoken, written or multimodal, they have the choice of using Discourse Metaphor, the 'default setting' of literal discourse or Discourse Metonymy (and levels within it). The *Silk Cut* cigarette packets I have looked at show all three. On the front of the packets, Discourse Metaphor is used in the upper half, where the brand is stated, *Silk Cut–Purple*, expressed multimodally though colour; and literal discourse is used in the lower half, where general health warnings are given, "Smoking kills" and "Smoking seriously harms you and others around you"; while Discourse Metonymy is used on the back of the packet for more specific health warnings, such as "Smoking causes fatal lung cancer", "Smoking can damage the sperm and decreases fertility", "Stopping smoking reduces the risk of fatal heart and lung diseases", "Smoke contains benzene, nitrosamines, formaldehyde and hydrogen cyanide", "Smoking clogs the arteries and causes heart attacks and strokes" and "Smoking may reduce the blood flow and causes impotence". The specific health warnings are metonymic rather than literal because they are processed as particular instances of a more general message—that smoking is bad for you. If the reader was not meant to process them in this way, they would wonder why they were being given such specific information and given information which may not apply to them: for a woman, for example, that smoking can damage the sperm or cause impotence.

Why were these choices made? This is not hard to understand. The three modes of discourse are suited to different types of message. Discourse Metaphor communicates well what the cigarette companies want to communicate in order to promote the brand image, by taking the focus off smoking itself and connecting to other frames with positive connotations, in this case, luxury, royalty, smoothness, calm, etc, as embodied by purple; Literal Discourse is appropriate for the two mandatory health warnings cigarette companies can choose from, *Smoking kills* and *Smoking seriously harms you and others around you*; while Discourse Metonymy achieves the vivid and even shocking messages of the fourteen more specific warnings the manufacturers can choose from for the packet backs. From 2008 in the UK, visual metonymies were added to verbal metonymies: cigarette companies were required to include images representing smoking-related illnesses as well. It is notable that the focus of the "plain-packet debate" is to limit cigarette branding by removing the positive connotations achieved by metaphor—the colours and pictures the cigarette companies wish to use—and to replace them with larger type-faced and stark messages in the metonymic health warnings, a move towards Jakobson's 'metonymic pole'.

TEXTUAL METONYMY

I now turn to the other pair of figurative text phenomena I have identified, those which involve the patterning of lexis rather than the change of register, Textual Metonymy and Textual Metaphor. Textual Metonymy, in the sense I am using the term here (other scholars use the term differently), is the creation of chains of lexical items related in meaning through synonymy. Textual Metonymy differs from Discourse Metonymy in that it does not involve a change of register (focus or voice), but instead makes a contribution to textuality, 'mode' in the functional grammar sense (Halliday 1994). Textual Metonymy increases the overall cohesion of a text by creating 'metonymic chains' across text, or as Brdar-Szabó & Brdar call them, 'conceptual metonymic chains' (Brdar-Szabó & Brdar 2011:232)—a different sense from Reddy's 'chains of metonymies', where the function of metonymy is to elide and condense (Reddy 1993:187). Al-Sharafi uses the term 'textual metonymy' in a much broader sense (Al-Sharafi 2004), proposing that all six of Halliday & Hasan's categories of cohesion, the four grammatical categories, 'reference', 'substitution', 'ellipsis' and 'conjunction', and the two lexical categories, 'reiteration' and 'collocation', involve metonymic relations and make a contribution to textual metonymy (Al-Sharafi 2004:126). Al-Sharafi's proposal is sound, but for my purposes in this context it is the category of 'reiteration' which makes the most striking case for the role of metonymic processing in achieving textual cohesion.

In Halliday & Hasan's account of cohesion, 'reiteration' covers a whole range of sense relations: same word, superordinates/hyponyms, meronyms, synonyms and antonyms: "Reiteration is a form of lexical cohesion which involves the repetition of a lexical item, at one end of the scale; the use of a general word to refer back to a lexical item, at the other end of the scale; and a number of things in between—the use of a synonym, near-synonym, or superordinate" (Halliday & Hasan 1976:278). 'Same word' apart, these all involve part-whole relations; they all involve overlaps or partial matches in meaning between lexical items in the text. It could be argued that even 'same word' involves difference, as every time a word recurs it occurs in a different co-textual environment and therefore is making a slightly different contribution to the text as a whole. The function of reiteration for Halliday & Hasan is primarily one of co-reference, but it also serves another function: the progressive enrichment of the narrative or information structure of a text. I will demonstrate this below through a series six examples: a newspaper report of an accident, a text on soya, an extract from a self-help book on relationships, a text about the Himalayas, a newspaper article on soccer club transfers and another article about an accident.

In the first text, a newspaper report of a road accident, we learn that *Heelys* are a type of *wheeled shoe* and that *wheeled shoes* are a type of sneaker (*trainer*). These superordinate/hyponym relations between the words *Heelys*, *wheeled shoe* and *trainer* (bold in the text below) are not immediately evident, if not already known, without the context of the text. The organization of the text allows us to infer the relations between these words and construct a metonymic chain from them:

> HEELYS BOY HIT BY CAR FIGHTS FOR LIFE
>
> A boy of 12 is fighting for his life after he was struck by a car as he crossed a road, wearing a pair of **Heelys**. Jarred Twaits is said to have rolled under the vehicle's front wheels because of the **trainers**. The schoolboy, of Seaford, East Sussex, had brain surgery at King's College Hospital, London. Doctors last week warned the **wheeled shoes** could be a danger to children.
>
> (*London Metro*, 31 January 2007, p.19)

Reiteration, through the use of hyponym-superordinate relations, does two things in this text: it increases the cohesion of the text through co-reference, making it easier to process, but it also informs the reader (or confirms, if already known) that there exist sneakers with wheels and that *Heelys* is one brand of them.

This second text, an article from *New Scientist* on soya products, which I first met adapted in Salkie (1995:79), also informs but the relationship between the items is more complex. Here we have three types of reiteration: superordinate relations, *legume–soyabean, soya–tofu, soya–miso, soya–tonyu*; co-hyponyms, *tofu–miso–tonyu*; and synonyms, *tofu–beancurd, tonyu–soyamilk* (bold in the text below):

BRIGHTER FUTURE FOR THE HUMBLE SOYABEAN

Success with a new product and hopes for a new pest killer is generating excitement about one of Japan's staple foodstuffs, the **soyabean**. Japanese people consume the nutritious **legume** mainly as ***tofu*** (**bean curd**), or ***miso***, a thick brown salty paste used for flavouring. Several years ago, ***miso*** came under fire from researchers who claimed that it caused high blood-pressure, then Japan's number-one killer. Predictably, sales slumped. Now to the *miso* producers' rescue has come ***tonyu*****—soyamilk**. In fact, **soyamilk** is not new. The Chinese have drunk it, hot, for more than 2000 years. But many people find it unpleasant.

(*New Scientist*, 14 April 1983, p.77)

The result is a highly-structured text which is also highly informative, and typical of many scientific texts where knowledge is presented in terms of relationships and hierarchical organization. The italics (which are in the original) show that the author, by foregrounding these terms also considers them to be key to the meaning of the article. The proform, *it*, also contributes to the cohesion of the text, *miso—it; soyamilk—it—it*, by creating co-referential chains, though I have excluded them from my analysis simply for clarity and because lexical chains provide more powerful examples in the present context.

In the third text, an extract from a self-help book, the same dual function of Textual Metonymy, informing and structuring, is achieved through reiteration, but this time through the use of synonyms only; the nature of the 'informing' is also slightly different. The expressions used for Andrew's coldness towards Gwen in this text, *turn a deaf ear*, *the deep freeze*, *unavailable*, (not) *ready to interact*, *pull back*, *wall out* (bold in the text below), are different ways of saying the same thing, and therefore are co-referring, but they also progressively enrich the message, so that at the end of the text we have a fuller impression of what being in a relationship with Andrew was like for Gwen:

Andrew handled his sensitivity and reactivity somewhat differently. Andrew's style was **to turn a deaf ear** to Gwen. She referred to this as "**the deep freeze**". He was civil, even polite, but completely **unavailable**. Gwen had learned it was best to leave Andrew alone until he was **ready to interact**. Trying to talk with him when he **pulled back** was like cornering a fox, which will bite when trapped. It was hard for Gwen when Andrew **walled her out**.

(D. Schnarch, *Resurrecting Sex: Resolving Sexual Problems and Rejuvenating your Relationship*, 2002, p.142)

Although some of these terms are metaphoric, eg *turn a deaf ear*, *deep freeze*, *pull back*, *wall out*, it is nonetheless a metonymic chain we are dealing with at the whole-text level, as the realities the terms are referring to in this context are closely related, even if various domains are employed to express them. Textual Metonymy can also be a stylistic choice, as the avoidance of same-word repetition contributes to what is sometimes called 'elegant variation'.

In the fourth text, about the Himalayas, we see this phenomenon again; a series of synonyms, *mountain range*, *barrier*, *high and desolate passes*, *frontiers* and *mountain wall* (in bold in the text below) co-refer to one entity, the Himalayas, but also progressively enhance our understanding of these mountains and the influence they have had:

> The ancient civilization of India grew up in a sharply demarcated sub-continent bounded on the north by the world's largest **mountain range**—the chain of the **Himalayas**, which, with its extension to east and west, divides India from the rest of Asia and the world. The **barrier**, however, was at no time an insuperable one, and at all periods both settlers and traders have found their way over the **high and desolate passes** into India, while Indians have carried their commerce and culture beyond her **frontiers** by the same route. India's isolation has never been complete, and the effect of the **mountain wall** in developing her unique civilization has often been overrated.
>
> (Leech et al 1982:194)

In the fifth text, a newspaper article about the transfer of soccer players between clubs, a further function of Textual Metonymy is added to informing, enriching and entertaining as identified above, namely that of inclusion and exclusion. *(The) Baggies*, *West Brom*, *Albion* and *The Midlanders* (in bold in the text below) are all names for the same club, *West Bromwich Albion*. This information is needed in order to understand the article, and, unlike the *Heelys* text, it cannot be readily inferred from the text:

> BAGGIES IN A HURRY TO MAKE DOUBLE SWOOP
>
> **West Brom** yesterday revealed they had renewed their interest in Leicester midfielder Lee Marshall after agreeing a fee for Ipswich defender Hermann Hreidarsson.
>
> **The Baggies** are keen to wrap up both deals ahead of their opening Premiership game against Manchester United on Saturday. **Albion** managing director Brendon Batson said: 'We have had further talks with Leicester and Marshall's agent, which are ongoing. We want to try to conclude a deal as soon as possible.' **The Midlanders** have agreed a fee for Hreidarsson which beats the club-record £2.1 million they paid Bristol Rovers for Jason Roberts two years ago. Batson added: 'We've been focusing on several players and Hermann Hreidarsson is one of them. We've agreed a fee with Ipswich and have been given permission to talk to the player.' Ipswich boss George Burley said: 'Our financial situation is well known. Relegation from the Premiership means we must sell and the club have reluctantly accepted this offer.'
>
> (*London Metro*, 13 August 2002, p.47)

An insider would enjoy the use of the familiar names for this club when reading this article and feel a sense of inclusion and allegiance with West Bromwich Albion, set up through Textual Metonymy; an outsider would not. Ipswich Town Football Club also has nicknames, such as *The Blues* and *Tractor Boys*, but the author does not use them, to avoid showing any allegiance towards the Ipswich team, perhaps, as it is less well known.

The last text I consider in this section, the report of an accident a man has with a power tool, also uses a chain of metonymically-related expressions, but this time Textual Metonymy is there to entertain rather than in service of any other discourse function; Textual Metonymy amuses the reader by displaying a repertoire of euphemistic terms for the male genitals, *family jewels*, *manhood*, *lower region*, *private parts*, *old man*, *privates*, *tackle*, *everything* (in bold in the text below), rather than enriching the meaning of the text or structuring the text:

> SAW CLOSE! BARRY NEARLY CUTS OFF **FAMILY JEWELS**
>
> Builder Barry Moran was left in agony when his circular saw went haywire—and sliced into his **MANHOOD**. Married Barry, 38, left the whirring saw on the ground after cutting up a door. But the safety guard failed and the powerful blade propelled the tool across the deck—and up horrified Barry's left trouser leg. He said "It ripped right up the leg and into my **lower region**. I didn't realise what had happened at first—then I looked down and saw my **private parts**. Someone called an ambulance and a doctor put 20 stitches in my **old man**. The pain was terrible. A few more millimetres and my **privates** would have been cut off. The doctors said I was very lucky not to bleed to death—but I'm just relieved my **tackle** is still intact." *Barry of Westcliff-on-Sea, Essex, has only just started walking again.* He said: "Now I'm only hoping that when the stitches come out **everything** is going to work." Wife Mikki, 30, echoed his fears saying: "That was the first thing I thought when I heard."
>
> (*The Sun*, London, 26 July 2001, p.19)

As with the self-help text discussed above, while at the surface level of the text many of the terms are metaphoric, such as *family jewels*, *tackle*, at the textual level, we are concerned with metonymy, not metaphor. Textual Metonymy is a whole-text phenomenon and by operating at this level, it does not rely on individual metonymies to set it up. Textual Metonymy involves reiteration through metonymic chains—part-whole overlaps and partial matches between items—and can be set up by using individual metonymies, individual metaphors or literal language.

TEXTUAL METAPHOR

I am using the term Textual Metaphor to indicate the phenomenon where a single metaphoric idea systematically organizes a whole text or section of text. In Textual Metaphor, conceptual metaphor patterns lexical choice in a text or section of text to the extent that it has a dominant presence in the text and a role in structuring it. Which conceptual metaphor is involved will depend on the subject matter and on the speaker/author. Certain topics are difficult to discuss without using certain conceptual metaphors and the conventional language they give rise to; other topics invite authors to choose metaphoric ideas which are novel, making the language they use in constructing the text novel too, in which case, the association between the source and target domains may need to be spelled out. Below I look at seven examples of Textual Metaphor involving both conventional and novel metaphoric expressions: a report of the collapse of the investment bank Lehman Brothers, a card promoting the UK British National Party, an article on the UK soccer First Division, an advertisement for traincards, a promotion for a UK bank, a poem by Philip Larkin and the editor's introduction to a collection of essays in cognitive linguistics.

In the first text, concerning the 2008 financial collapse of the investment bank Lehman Brothers, the conceptual metaphor BAD IS DOWN plays an important role in patterning lexical choices in the text. In the extract below (a little less than the first tenth of the article) the words relating to the domain DOWN are: *dive*, *collapse*, *plunged*, *down*, *slumped* (in bold):

> WORLD SHARES **DIVE** AFTER LEHMAN BROTHERS **COLLAPSE**
>
> LONDON (AFP)—Global stock markets **plunged** Monday as the dramatic **collapse** of [. . .] Lehman Brothers sparked sharp losses across the financial sector [. . .]. With European bourses **down** between three and four percent, Wall Street **slumped** after a bankruptcy filing by Lehman Brothers.
>
> (AFP, 5 September 2008)

When we consider the text as a whole, the complete list of lexical items which relate to the source domain DOWN is: *dive*, *collapse* (x2), *plunged*, *down* (x5), *tumbled* (x4), *fell* (x4), *slumped*, *low* (x2), *shed*, *under*. They are all terms which form part of the conventional language used in discussing and reporting financial events of this sort and are found scattered throughout the text, rather than clustered in a particular section. Other metaphors play an important role, too, also creating conventional expressions, such as those around LOSS, but there is a sense that the financial crisis is being spoken about predominantly in terms of BAD IS DOWN (and therefore also LESS IS DOWN from which it derives).

The next text is structured using a less familiar metaphoric idea, *CRIMINALS ARE VERMIN*. The text appeared on either side of a credit card-sized card distributed to London homes in 2008. The source domain, VERMIN, is represented on the front of the card by *rat*, *cage*, *feed*, reinforced by a picture of a rat (Figure 6.1 below); while the target domain, CRIMINALS, is represented on the reverse of the card by *judicial and prison policy*, *criminal*, *crimewave* (Figure 6.2).

Figure 6.1 Front of BNP card

> Of course not! Only a lunatic would do such a thing. Yet such 'lunacy' just about sums up successive Tory and Labour government judicial and prison policy, giving the green light to the criminal and facilitating the ever growing crimewave.

Figure 6.2 Reverse of BNP card

The two domains are separated out, words relating to VERMIN appearing in the text on the front of the card and words relating to CRIMINALS appearing on the back. The systematic metaphor *CRIMINALS ARE VERMIN* is not explicitly stated anywhere on the card, but we are aided in inferring it from the stark distribution of source- and target-domain terms on opposite sides of the card. This contrasts with the scattered distribution of terms used in the Lehman text.

In the next text, an article on the 2001/2002 soccer season in the UK entitled *First Division Predictions and Fixtures*, the author also makes use of an unfamiliar metaphoric idea *TEAMS ARE INGREDIENTS* or even *SOCCER IS FOOD*. This article came out before the soccer season had got underway when there was little factual to say about the championship. The piece entertains the reader by speculating on what might happen and the potential of each team, using food metaphors. The metaphoric expressions in this extract which derive from *SOCCER IS FOOD* are in bold in the text below:

FIRST DIVISION PREDICTIONS AND FIXTURES

1 WATFORD. A more open division this year, without the likes of Fulham and Blackburn getting in the way. It's like a big **mixed salad**—lots of fresh **ingredients**, hopefully a **tasty** whole. But Gianluca Vialli's Hornets could be the **shaved parmesan** that finds itself on top when the **dish** is finished.

2 MANCHESTER CITY. The **tuna** in the mix—hard to ignore but tends to be a bit **flaky**. Have changed divisions every season for the last four—let's hope Keegan hasn't **bitten off more than he can chew**.

3 PRESTON NORTH END. In David Moyes Preston boast one of the best young **bakers** in the Nationwide **cookery class**. Will once again bring the best out of available **ingredients** to prove that last year's success was not a fluke. [. . .]

5 COVENTRY CITY. Of the three relegated sides Coventry could find themselves a bit lost, particularly as the season starts. In **salad** terminology, they're **marshmallow**—completely out of place.

6 BRADFORD CITY. **A bit of lemon juice to keep our salad sharp**. Bradford felt the squeeze last season but have returned full of **zest** and their **acid bite** will be frequently felt this year. [. . .]

10 WEST BROMWICH ALBION. Will lose **freshness** after last season's surprise success and might end up looking a bit **limp**. The **lettuce** in our top-10 **salad**—a vital part of the First Division mix, but a bit **tasteless** when you think about it.

(*Weekend Guardian* supplement, 11 August 2001)

Talking about soccer in terms of food is not an immediately familiar metaphoric concept; therefore, in order for readers to fall in with structuring of the article, the journalist feels it necessary to state the metaphor explicitly in the first few lines, "[the First Division] is like a big mixed salad". The source domain FOOD is represented in the remainder of the text by *ingredients*, *tasty*, *shaved parmesan*, *dish*, *tuna*, *flaky*, *bitten off more than he can chew*, *bakers*, *cookery class*, *ingredients*, *salad*, *marshmallow*, *a bit of lemon juice to keep our salad sharp*, *zest*, *acid bite*, *freshness*, *limp*, *lettuce*, *salad* and *tasteless*. By half way through the article, the author has dropped the food analogy but picks it up again when he comes to Norwich City, the reason for this being that one of the owners of the team at the time was a celebrity chef, which perhaps serves as a trigger to reopen the FOOD 'mental space': "Inevitable, really, that the club that boasts Delia Smith on its board should be more sous-chef than soufflé—destined never to rise."

The metaphoric idea in the next text, an advertisement for advertising on traincards, is also not a familiar one; the source domain is ROCK MUSIC, the target domain is RAIL TRAVEL. The source domain is set up by the lexical items *fans*, *gig*, *audience*, *rock star*, *audience* (in bold in the text below) and a picture of a guitarist wearing a suit and tie:

2.5 MILLION **FANS** AT EVERY **GIG**

With over 2.5 million passengers spending an average of 3.5 hours per week on the train, Travelcards are the most cost effective way of hitting the

> commuter rail **audience**. To find out the **rock star** potential of Traincards call 020 [. . .]. Traincards: Focussing on the rail **audience**.
>
> (Traincard poster, National Rail, 2010)

The two domains appear in close proximity in *commuter rail audience*, *rail audience* and *the rock star potential of Traincards*, as well as the image on the poster of a commuter performing with a guitar.

The fifth text is an advertisement for a preferential banking service which is also based on the interplay between conceptual domains, in this case BANKING and HOTEL LUXURY. The text being:

> WELCOME TO CLUB CLASS BANKING . . .
>
> How does a king size current account with freshly laundered sheets and goose down pillows feel? You know the beds you just never want to leave? Comfortable, soft, perfectly made? How would you like a bank account along the same lines? [. . .]
>
> (London Underground, 2009)

The source domain, HOTEL LUXURY, is represented by the lexical items *king size*, *freshly laundered sheets*, *goose down pillows*, *beds you never want to leave*, *comfortable*, *soft* and *perfectly made* [beds]; and, later in the text, *upgrade*. A row of images shows beds, pillows, a breakfast tray, feet in bed, a torso in bed and a maid. As in the previous text, there is the close juxtaposition of the two domains within phrases: *king size current account*, *club class banking*.

The next text is another poem by Philip Larkin, *Water* (Philip Larkin, *The Whitsun Weddings*, 1964, p.20). We saw how Larkin used Discourse Metonymy and Discourse Metaphor in the poem *Toads Revisited*; here, he uses Textual Metaphor as a frame to structure the entire poem. The poem is about RELIGION but explored in terms of WATER and starts:

> If I were called in
> To construct a religion
> I should make use of water

thus explicitly stating the metaphoric idea *RELIGION IS WATER*. The lexical items *water*, *fording*, *dry*, *sousing*, *drench* and *glass of water* (perhaps also *any-angled light*), used in the poem derive from the source domain, WATER; while *religion*, *going to church* (perhaps also *different clothes*), *litany*, *devout*, *in the east* and *congregate* derive from the target domain, RELIGION. Here again there is often a close interface between source and target domain in phrases such as *devout drench*.

The final text I have chosen to illustrate Textual Metaphor is the introduction to a collection of essays, *Cognitive Linguistics: Basic Readings*, written by Dirk Geeraerts, the editor (2006). Geeraerts employs the metaphoric idea *AN ACADEMIC GUIDE IS A TRAVEL GUIDE* at the beginning of the piece (source domain language is in bold):

> A **Rough Guide** to Cognitive Linguistics
>
> When you move through the following chapters of this volume, **you get to see a top twelve of sights that you should not miss** [. . .] Still, to give you a firm reference point for **your tour** you may need some initiation to what Cognitive Linguistics is about. That's what the present chapter is for: it provides you with **a roadmap and travel book** to Cognitive Linguistics. [. . .] It's only **a rough guide**, to be sure: it gives you the minimal amount of background that you need to figure out the steps to be taken and to make sure that **you are not recognized as a total foreigner** or a naive apprentice, but it does not pretend to supply more than that. [. . .] To understand what you may expect to find in **this brief travel guide**, we need to introduce one of the characteristic ideas of Cognitive Linguistics first. [. . .]
>
> (Geeraerts 2006:1)

Geeraerts returns to the TRAVEL GUIDE metaphor at different points through the piece, particularly at the beginning of each new section, and makes use of it in headings of sections, such as "What is so special about this place?", "What does the tour include?", "Where do you go next?". Much of the language in these sections is polysemous, applying equally to source and target domain. The last section, twenty-four pages into the book, begins (source domain language is in bold):

> So now you know your way around in Cognitive Linguistics. **You can walk the walk and talk the talk**, and there's no way that you'd be exposed as a novice. But **why would you be coming back**? What would be a good reason to **become a permanent resident**? An obvious but relatively superficial motivation would be **the diversity of the panorama**: there's a lot to be found in **the Cognitive Linguistics archipelago**, and the framework is not so strict as to stifle creativity. **It's a lively, colorful, varied environment, and you're likely to find some corner of special significance to you, where you can do your thing and meet people with similar interests**.
>
> (Geeraerts 2006:25)

The choice of the GUIDED TOUR metaphor in this text may or may not be a knowing nod to Lakoff's discussion of it in his classic essay on the "contemporary theory" of metaphor in which he identifies 'the guided tour', 'the heroic battle' and 'the heroic quest' as "three common academic discourse forms" (Lakoff 1993:243). Lakoff suggests the guided-tour metaphor is a version of a more primary metaphor THOUGHT IS MOTION and that his own essay belongs to the 'guided tour' category of academic writing, "where I, the author, am the tour guide who is assumed to be thoroughly familiar with the terrain and the terrain surveyed is taken as objectively real" (Lakoff 1993:243–244).

I may have given the impression that there is a high concentration of language relating to the TRAVEL GUIDE domain in Geeraerts' text. In a sense this is so: it is high for a text, though the actual number of words is in fact relatively small; only 270 words (3.5% of the total word count) of the whole twenty-seven-page introduction derive from the TRAVEL GUIDE domain. In order to test whether this deliberate and large-scale use of Textual Metaphor was successful or not, I conducted an informal experiment with a group of MA applied linguistics students at a London university. I asked them first to identify if there was any systematic metaphor which was organizing a large amount of language in the text. This they were able to do readily, and they were also able to identify TRAVEL GUIDE as the source domain. I then asked them their opinion of the text, whether they thought it was good, clever, appropriate, inappropriate, or how else they would describe it.

In their reporting, some of the students found the text too 'clever', even a bit contrived; some felt the travel-guide metaphor had been extended too far, in spite of it having only a relatively minimal presence in terms of number of words as a percentage of the text. I thought this reaction was interesting, as it shows that the metonymic processing involved in interpreting novel metaphoric ideas is an activity we embark upon with a sense of parsimony. Textual Metaphor is used for two purposes in this text: to make the prospect of embarking on a new field of study exciting by construing it in terms of travel (though as the students' reactions show, an author has to be careful not to overuse this device); the other is to give the text cohesion by making links across large stretches of text, in this case, making links between pages 1, 2, 6, 20, 22 and 25 of the book. It is significant that the travel guide language appears mainly at the beginning of sections, as this is where metaphor is most useful in framing the topic and where cohesion is most needed. It is then abandoned in each section as the author goes more deeply into the subject matter at hand and says what he has come to say.

TEXT METAPHTONYMY

In this section, I return to 'metaphtonymy', the term coined by Goossens to refer to the co-occurrence of metaphor and metonymy in language (discussed in Chapter 4), but here project the concept to the macro level of the whole text. This I am calling Text Metaphtonymy. The two of Goossens' categories I am going to consider are 'metonymy within metaphor' and 'metaphor within metonymy' (Goossens 1990). Both involve a scalar difference, the notion of a smaller unit contained 'within' a larger unit. It has been noted a number of times in this chapter that figurative text phenomena do not necessarily involve figurative language in their construction; if figurative principles apply on a macro scale, these will not necessarily involve linguistic metonymy or metaphor at the surface level of text. Thus, Discourse Metonymy does not necessarily involve linguistic metonymies, and may indeed contain metaphors, as Lodge observes (Lodge 1977:98–99). Metonymy and metaphor can, however, easily occur together at different levels of scale, thus giving Text Metaphtonymy of the kinds 'metonymy within metaphor' (ie linguistic metonymy within either Discourse Metaphor or Textual Metaphor) and 'metaphor within metonymy' (ie linguistic metaphor within either Discourse Metonymy or Textual Metonymy), as I will demonstrate now, using texts already used in this chapter.

Firstly, Discourse Metonymy. In Larkin's poem *Toads Revisited*, as discussed above, there are a number of sections in which Discourse Metonymy is adopted to evoke different situations, such as the park, the office, etc. Within the section of 'the men you meet in the park', we find individuals described as "hare-eyed clerks" and "waxed-fleshed out-patients". The elements *hare* and *wax* in *hare-eyed* and *waxed-fleshed* are both used metaphorically, and so we have metaphor within metonymy, that is, linguistic metaphor occurring within the organizing principle of Discourse Metonymy, and so an example of Text Metaphtonymy.

Discourse Metaphor was illustrated above with the Gooding interview, where the interviewee uses a cluster of conventional metaphors when talking of matters of the heart. In this case, the global and local levels of the text are *not* independent, as it is the clustering of linguistic metaphors which creates the effect of Discourse Metaphor. There could also have been linguistic metonymies in this section of text, but there is not. Metonymy, however, is present in this text in another sense, for the ability to use metaphoric ideas relies on the ability to process metonymically. The term *bubble* in "living inside that bubble" and *duck* in "water off a duck's back", if processed as novel utterances, need to be selected metonymically before they are projected metaphorically (as discussed in Chapter 3). Thus we have an example of 'metonymy within metaphor', metonymy on the micro sub-word feature level and metaphor on the macro Discourse Metaphor level.

One of the examples to illustrate Textual Metonymy was an extract from a self-help book about relationships in which a metonymic chain was used to describe Gwen's sense of isolation. In this extract, these terms appear: *freezing*, *pulling back* and *walling out*. The context is a passage constructed using Textual Metonymy, but the use of 'freeze', 'pull' and 'wall out' in these individual expressions is metaphoric. Thus, we have a 'metaphor within metonymy' type of Text Metaphtonymy. Similarly, in the *Saw Close* text, we have a metonymic chain of synonymous terms for the male genitals and many of these are metaphoric, eg *family jewels*, *old man*, *privates* and *tackle*. Again, these are linguistic metaphors on the surface of text occurring in the larger picture of a metonymic text phenomenon, Textual Metonymy.

Finally, Textual Metaphor. One of the examples used to illustrate this was an HSBC private banking text. This text is organized using an over-branching metaphor, which could be framed as BANKING IS HOTEL LUXURY. Within this text we find a three-item metonymic list, "freshly laundered sheets", "goose down pillows" and "beds you never want to leave", a use of Discourse Metonymy. So, here too we have figurative thought operating at two levels of organization in text, but, in this case, it is of the type (Discourse) Metonymy within (Textual) Metaphor.

CONCLUSION

In this chapter, I have given a brief review of the writing on how metonymic and metaphoric thought are used to organize whole texts. I then presented four phenomena in my own framework for the analysis of metonymy and metaphor operating at the level of the whole text: Discourse Metonymy, Discourse Metaphor, Textual Metonymy and Textual Metaphor. I showed through sample texts how metonymy and metaphor operate to change register, Discourse Metonymy and Discourse Metaphor, and pattern lexis across text, Textual Metonymy and Textual Metaphor. I showed metonymic processing plays a role at the level of the whole text in interpreting 'metonymic chains' (Textual Metonymy) and 'metonymic lists' (Discourse Metonymy), and through a variety of texts that figurative text phenomena are not limited to a few text types or contexts (and certainly not restricted to literature). I also introduced the idea of Text Metaphtonymy, the co-occurrence of metaphor and metonymy at the whole-text level.

The implications of the findings in this chapter for language users in general and language professionals in particular are these. We are all text analysts in the sense that we all engage with the processing of language at the level of text in our dealings with others. It follows then that all language users need to have an awareness of how meaning is constructed at *all* levels of the language hierarchy, from phoneme to whole text, whatever they do in their lives. The figurative text phenomena described above will be constantly encountered, by all language users, not only wordsmiths, journalists and editors. We all need to develop an awareness of these phenomena in order to create, manipulate and replicate them. This chapter adds further weight to the argument that the role of metonymy in communication is under-acknowledged; it adds detail to the picture of metonymy as a device operating at every level of communication and constantly drawn upon as a vital resource in the choices made by all speakers and authors. In the next two chapters, I explore the role of metonymy in two specific areas of applied linguistics: in Chapter 7, I look at language learning and teaching and in Chapter 8, translation.

7 Metonymy and Language Learners

This chapter looks at the importance of metonymy and metonymic processing for one particular category of applied linguist, the language learner. I argue that metonymy plays an important role in interactions between learners and their interlocutors; that those interactions depend for their success on the ability of the participants to process metonymically; and that learners and their interlocutors—who may be native speakers or themselves learners—are constantly using aspects of their 'metonymic competence' in production and comprehension. I discuss the importance that recognizing near equivalents and partial matches has for learner communication and language learning. I also discuss the role acoustic and graphic relatedness ('formal metonymy') has in learner communication and reframe the idea of 'speech errors' in terms of metonymy theory.

FIGURATIVE LANGUAGE AND LANGUAGE LEARNING

Published teaching materials for English, if concerned with figurative language at all, have tended to focus on metaphor rather than metonymy, conventional metaphor rather than novel metaphor, and low- rather than high-frequency items. This is regrettable, as it robs the learner of exposure to the whole range of phenomena which lie between literal language and one-off colourful idioms, the very area which offers speakers expressive scope from within the resources of their existing knowledge. The purpose of this section is to review the teaching of figurative language, firstly, as reflected in teaching materials, and then, as reflected in scholarship on teaching.

A standard coursebook in English language teaching presents non-literality as rare, colourful and tricky to master, and therefore probably dispensable or, at best, at the margins of what 'should' be taught. This has been the experience of Littlemore & Low (2006b): "Even now, there are few commercial second-language courses which teach metaphor as anything other than the basis of colourful idiomatic phrases" (Littlemore & Low 2006b:268). A traditional coursebook typically included one or two, usually quite obscure, idioms per unit/chapter (on a par with *raining cats and dogs* and *kick the bucket*), without giving any practice or much of an indication of how they are actually used. Idioms do receive special attention when they are the topic of separate practice books, which typically offer multiple-choice or gap-fill exercises in which the students choose the correct idiom from a short list (eg Allsop & Woods 1990, Thomas 1996, Watcyn-Jones 2002). Here too, the idioms considered are often uncommon expressions with specific functions, but presented as if they could simply be interchanged with equivalent literal expressions, the sort of expressions which Moon notes are unlikely to appear in even larger corpora (Moon 1998:83).

It has been my observation that students have a keen interest in idioms because they see their mastery as an indicator of gaining a high level of competence, as well as enjoying them for the unexpected insights into a different culture they often reveal. Idioms also bring them in contact with colourful language of the sort they will have encountered and enjoyed in their first language. Cornell confirms that native speakers have an advantage when it comes to idioms: "There can be few areas where there is such a contrast between the uncertainty of the learner and the confident instinct and experience of the native speaker" (Cornell 1999:15). In expressions such as *to look daggers*, *to be at sixes and sevens*, *to jump out of your skin* and *to get knotted* learners are quick to detect an element in language which is entertaining and playful. But little of the fun and delight around 'outlandish' idioms is exploited in teaching materials, and their flamboyance and oddness is rarely exploited for practical ends. Idioms are perceived as weird and wonderful, indicators of cultural differences, but little more. In one conversation I had with a learner, he related how he had been intrigued by the non-equivalence of certain idioms between French and English as reported in his dictionary when learning French at school. He observed that *One swallow doesn't make a summer* in English became . . . *doesn't make a spring* (*ne fait pas le printemps*) in French, and *to have other fish to fry* became . . . *to have other cats to whip* (*autres chats à fouetter*). More modern textbooks integrate idiomaticity more successfully into the main linguistic work of the course. This has been motivated by two independent areas of linguistic research, phraseology theory and metaphor theory.

Phraseology theory treats idioms as phrases which have 'added value' (usually added specificity of meaning) by virtue of being processed as whole phrases, as if they were 'long words'. These 'lexical phrases' include metaphorically-derived phrases, but also a whole range of other expressions which show different degrees of lexical and syntactic fixity, and therefore availability for patterning. Phraseology scholars recognize within the spectrum of lexical phrases gradients of transparency, normality, flexibility and frequency, and the existence of 'aberrant' grammar, as in *to go great guns*, *to do the dirty on someone*. These approaches grew out of an interest in collocation hand-in-hand with a wish to examine real data, made possible through developments in corpus linguistics, especially database building (Sinclair 1991). The influence all this has had on pedagogy can be seen in new approaches to English language teaching, such as Lewis' 'lexical approach', which moves the focus away from grammar and more towards lexis, characterizing language as grammar-in-lexis rather than lexis-in-grammar (Lewis 1993); and in coursebooks, such those by Dellar & Walkley, where recognizing the centrality of lexis in language description gets students closer to an English which is 'natural' and 'real', reflected in the titles: *Innovations Upper Intermediate—A Course in Natural English* (Dellar & Walkley 2004) and *Outcomes Pre-intermediate—Real English for the Real World* (Dellar & Walkley 2010).

Another way in which idiomaticity has been integrated into teaching is through metaphor theory, where metaphoricity is the focus, presenting idioms as evidence of cognitive patterning with conceptual metaphors as their origin. Materials writers influenced by metaphor theory offer students a more systematic, and therefore more economical (in terms of study time), way of learning new expressions. In the *Collins Cobuild English Guide* on metaphor, Deignan embraces both the phraseological and metaphoric approaches by organizing expressions under keywords (which activate source domains for metaphors) as well as broad categories, such as 'sport', 'farm animals', 'wind and storms', 'unhealthy plants' and 'routes' (Deignan 1995); while Wright organizes idioms by keywords, such as *all*, *way*, *know*, *point*, *life*, *line*; topic, eg 'family', 'holidays', 'dreams', 'health'; and the conceptual metaphor they derive from, eg BUSINESS IS WAR, LIFE IS A JOURNEY, PEOPLE ARE LIQUIDS (Wright 1999). The aim, according to the promotion blurb on the cover, is to make things easier for the learner: "Idioms Organiser is the first practice book which sorts idioms into different categories so that students find them easier to understand and learn" (Wright 1999). The *Phrasal Verb Organiser* from the same publisher is also influenced by conceptual metaphor theory. It presents phrasal verbs by particle rather than the root verb, for example, verbs with UP—*put up*, *break up*, *bring up*, *dream up*, *hush up*, *use up*, etc—are considered together, in order to make learning more systematic and develop an instinct for understanding phrasal verbs when they are first encountered (Flower 1993). Modern EFL dictionaries also offer students material which takes on the developments in linguistics. *Macmillan English Dictionary for Advanced Learners* (2002) offers a series of language awareness essays on subjects such as pragmatics and phraseology, among which is one on metaphor. Also, scattered through the Macmillan dictionary are 'metaphor boxes', which present metaphoric expressions by source domain, eg changes in quantities and amounts are like movements UP and DOWN (p1153); and an organization is a like a BODY (p1001).

When we turn to the scholarship on teaching figurative language, we find surprise that developments in linguistics have not been taken up more enthusiastically. As early as 1988, Low notes that discourse and pragmatics research had had an influence on the language teaching literature and teaching materials in a way which Metaphor Studies had not, and that "few of the results have filtered down to the 'shop floor' of language teaching methodology and courses" (Low 1988:125). There is certainly quite a body of literature both on how figurative language might be taught (eg Lazar 1996) as well as empirical studies showing the efficacy of different methods of teaching, reviewed for the period before 1990 by Low (1988) and for the next decade by Cameron & Low (1999a, 1999b). Nonetheless, there is still a sense that English language teaching had not kept up with developments, that the Metaphor Studies 'revolution' had had little impact on language teaching: "The study of metaphor has exploded in the last decades, but little of the impact of that explosion has so far reached applied linguistics" (Cameron & Low 1999a:77), and "There has to date been very little research into metaphor in second language acquisition, and very little into teaching control over metaphor. [. . .] Hopefully the next ten years will see an explosion of applied linguistic research" (Cameron & Low 1999a:91). What the next ten years did see was an exploration of non-literal language and its significance for language learning in a much wider sense. We have Littlemore and Low principally to thank for this. They have written extensively, both as single authors and together, introducing a number of useful terms which reflect their interest in the learning mind as a nexus of processing and cognitive skills: 'metaphoric competence' (Littlemore 2001a, 2006b, 2010), 'metaphoric intelligence' (Littlemore 2001b, 2002) and 'figurative thinking' (Littlemore & Low 2006a).

'Metaphoric competence' includes both the ability to produce and comprehend language and depends on the individual's speed and fluency to do so (Littlemore 2001a). Its usefulness, particularly in the context of learners in an academic environment, such as when reading academic texts, writing assignments and attending lectures, is explored by Littlemore (2001a) and Littlemore & Low (2006b). Littlemore compares 'metaphoric competence' in a speaker's first and second languages (Littlemore 2010). In another exploration of metaphoric competence, Littlemore extends the range of Gardner's list of eight intelligences, in the context of the theory of 'multiple intelligences', to include a ninth, 'metaphoric intelligence' (Littlemore 2001b, 2002). Littlemore & Low also investigate the advantages of encouraging 'figurative thinking' in learners (Littlemore & Low 2006a). Holme also discusses 'metaphoric competence' and advocates adopting the use of conceptual metaphor in teaching lexis, arguing that this permits a more systematic approach and a greater awareness of networks within the target language (Holme 2004).

Although the research cited above demonstrates a move away from teaching low-frequency conventional metaphors to a wider awareness of figurative language, and thus helps to offer a systematic framework for learning and remembering language items, I feel an even more useful strategy would be to expose students to high-frequency conventional metonymies, such as *head for the door*, *bums on seats*, *small screen*, *pay with plastic*. Furthermore, the ability to understand and create novel metonymies would also be of great utility in the toolbox of any learner. I suggest that developing a wider awareness of metonymy in thought and of conventional and novel linguistic metonymies, for which we could collectively coin the term 'metonymic competence' to parallel Littlemore & Low's term 'metaphoric competence', would be a profitable use of classroom time. An approach to teaching figurative language which focusses more on strategies for creating common types of novel metonymies than low-frequency conventional metaphors would contribute more to a learner's overall communicative competence. This competence would include both the ability to notice close-relatedness as well as to create language involving close-relatedness, and thereby expand the speaker's receptive skills and expressivity in real time during speech events. Low observes that "it is commonly accepted that young children demonstrate a preference for thinking metonymically before they think metaphorically [. . .] and this has recently been found to be the case for young L2 learners" (Low 2008:223), suggesting that the learning I am advocating would be more easily within the grasp of the learner than other abilities. Metaphor is different from metonymy. It is perhaps harder for learners to know how they can take awareness of metaphor further; it is perhaps easier to encourage learners to develop skills around metonymy and use part-whole productively.

The next section moves from the learner as a student in a teaching context to the learner as a language user in the real world, and looks at the role which skills involving metonymy, 'metonymic processing', play in making interactions between learners and their interlocutors successful.

METONYMY AND LEARNER COMMUNICATION

Metonymy plays an important role in all communication but plays a particularly significant role in learner communication. It is an essential feature of learner-learner and learner-native speaker interaction. Without the ability to use metonymy to process language, the interactions learners have with other learners and native speakers would have little or no success. In this section, I look at four aspects of the active manipulation of metonymic relatedness when processing language, metonymic processing, which I consider to be of particular significance. The first is the processing work which interlocutors do in order to compensate for the differences between what they expect to hear and what they actually hear, discussed under the heading 'Accommodation'. The second is the modified version of speech/writing which interlocutors produce in order to make their speech/writing easier for learners to understand, discussed under 'Foreigner Talk'. The third is the learner's use of metonymy to move away from a fixed one-to-one attitude towards language and explore instead the more flexible, nuanced, creative and expressive zone of near-fit equivalents and blended signs, discussed under 'Extending the Lexicon'. The fourth is the way similarity in form between words in different languages can scaffold the learning of new lexis, discussed under 'Formal Metonymy'.

Accommodation

If we were to imagine someone on a trip to Hungary who does not have much Hungarian, who on their arrival in Budapest takes a taxi from the airport to the hotel with a driver who does not have much English, the interaction this imagined person has with the taxi driver during the journey would probably involve a lot of effortful processing. It would be hard work on a number of levels due to the differences in the varieties of the language/s they are using in order to interact. There would be differences in phonology, morphology, syntax, semantics, pragmatics, discourse and genre, as well as at the level of cognitive frames, conceptual metaphors and social/cultural practices. The people learners speak to, their interlocutors, need to be able to compensate for the unexpectedness of what they hear; they need to do processing work in order to understand the speaker's intentions. Metonymic processing is employed to notice differences between what is heard and the patterns we store in our long-term memories as part of our competence knowledge of the language. The cognitive process is a form of 'compensation', analogous to the compensation translators carry out to reduce 'loss' when translating (explored in Chapter 8). Learner utterances are experienced as 'shifts' from an ideal norm. 'Shift' is also a term used in Translation Studies, referring to the use of near equivalents when an exact equivalent is unavailable. The process of understanding learner utterances can be seen as translation in the wide sense of the word, an example of what Jakobson calls 'intralingual translation' (Jakobson 1959/2004).

If we were to look at how a typical intermediate Italian speaker might pronounce the English sentence *What are you doing?* and compare it to the performance of the same utterance by a typical Southern Standard British English (SSBE) native speaker, we would notice a number of differences. The two most significant are the differences in stress patterns and the positioning of the vowels and diphthongs. The Italian speaker would probably use a syllable-timed version of English (as Italian is syllable timed), each syllable being given almost equal time and equal stress; while the SSBE version would be stress timed (fewer stresses and with stresses falling 'on the pulse'). The two versions are also different in terms of the positioning of the vowels/diphthongs and the placing of the consonants, but not so different that the Italian speaker would not be understood by the SSBE speaker. The metonymic processing, noticing relatedness, which the SSBE speaker carries out is vital for sustaining communication. It involves what Holme refers to as 'inadvertent metaphor': "These sentences are incorrect because the categories that they deal with have been grasped in a way that does not match the conventions of English" (Holme 2004:196). Inadvertent metaphor is analogous to inadvertent humour, such as making puns without intending to. The unwanted un-literality learners present us with (and all speakers to some extent do so) has to be processed as metonyms or metaphors by their interlocutors, whether intended or not. Metonymic processing involves 'shifts' at the level of phonology, syntax, semantics, pragmatics, discourse, genre, frames and social practices; but if the metonymic shifts are too great, and the metonymic links are stretched too far, then even with the best will in the world on the part of the interlocutor, relatedness can no longer be recognized and communication breaks down.

In order to illustrate metonymic shifts which are challenging to process, without the challenge being so great they cause communication breakdown, I wish now to present data from a recording I made of informant Zara (anonymized). These data were collected as part of a pilot study to investigate whether advanced learners use figurative language differently in their first and second languages, but the strategies Zara uses stand out as relevant to the present topic. Zara was born in Germany to Greek parents, studied English at school and university in Germany, and took an MA in Shakespeare Studies at a UK university. For the study, I asked her to talk on two topics, 'The New York street map' and 'Social change over the last ten years', first in German and then in English. The time spent on each language was approximately half an hour. I was present but did not interact with her during the recordings in order not to influence her performance. This is an extract from Zara's monologue in English on social change:

> English has become more simple // they are not really full decorative embellished sentences / well structured sentences // they are short sentences / just swift to send them away / even in staccato language // and I think it has becomes more / because of the Americanisms / in our language / in English
>
> (Zara 2006)

Seeing this passage written, one could be forgiven for thinking that it has little coherent sense—what are *full decorative embellished sentences*; what does it mean to *send a sentence away*; what is 'staccato' language?—but if one hears the recording, the impression one gets is of speech which is completely intelligible. We have quite a clear idea of what Zara wants to say and how she positions herself, in fact the passage is very expressive and delivered with great fluency. Why she used this strategy may be to do with her level of competence in English (the recording of her speaking in German show these characteristics to a lesser degree), or her own individual relationship to English; equally it could reflect her history or rhetorical styles from her Greek heritage.

Later in the same interview, Zara communicates her worries about young people vis-à-vis digitalization, and does so with the same effectiveness, though many words are extended beyond their typical use, such as *cope* and *method*:

> these children / they know how to cope with the computer / but they don't know how / how to cope with other methods / with other things / everyday life // they are so much into this / electronic things
>
> (Zara 2006)

The sense I have here is of a speaker not confident enough to 'nail down' what she wants to say with precise words, but able to offer a cluster of adequate approximations, such as *other methods/ other things/ everyday life*. By doing so, she creates an effect which is far from second best, her solutions being perhaps more expressive and richer in meaning than the single-word solutions she might have come up with given more time. This leads me to the view that learner utterances are neither definitively 'correct' nor 'incorrect' but somewhere in between, neither 'good' nor 'bad' but attempts at meaning making 'on the fly', taking place in real time and under pressure in a social context, which are for the most part successful utterances, but occasionally not. When not, they lead to misunderstandings or communication breakdowns, metonymic processing on the part of the interlocutor being unable to retrieve the speaker's meaning. But this is no different really from any speech event, whatever the competence of the speaker or whether the speaker is a native speaker or not.

A scale of processing effort could be envisaged with native-native speaker interaction requiring the least effort, native speakers of different dialects of the same language interacting with each other requiring more effort, learner-native speaker interactions still more and learner-learner interactions the most. But this is surely simplistic as the picture is complex and involves a whole set of variables. Learners are not necessarily harder to understand than native speakers. Many Britons from the south of England find broad local accents from Newcastle (Geordie) and Glasgow (Glaswegian) hard to understand, and vice versa, and would perhaps find learners whose native language is a romance language easier to understand. As a Londoner, I have a lot of practice accommodating to learner English of various kinds in service encounters in the capital but have less contact with speakers of regional accents such as Geordie or Glaswegian, and therefore am less familiar with them. As they are bi-directional, the success of interactions involving learners is as much a matter of the learner's ability to articulate their wishes as it is the interlocutor's ability to accommodate their own utterances to the needs of the learner—the topic of the next section.

Foreigner Talk

Another skill involving metonymic processing which the interlocutors of learners have in their repertoire is 'foreigner talk'. This is not an ideal term, particularly from a World Englishes perspective, but it is one which is used frequently in the literature (eg Jenkins 2000, Ellis 2008) and therefore is useful in identifying the phenomenon. It is a term from the Creolist Charles Ferguson and refers to the modified form of a language which proficient speakers use when speaking to learners, characterized by "less syntactic complexity, fewer pronouns, the use of higher frequency vocabulary, more clearly articulated pronunciation [. . .], slower speech rate, more questions [. . .], as well as the tendency to speak more loudly and to repeat" (Jenkins 2000:177). Being able to accommodate to learners in this way is part of a speaker's metonymic competence. The relationship between foreigner talk and unaccommodated talk is metonymic, as is the relationship between 'baby talk' (also called 'caretaker talk', 'Child Directed Speech', 'motherese' and 'parentese') and the language the adult uses in other contexts.

A Creole and its 'superstrate', such as French in the Caribbean Creoles of Martinique, St Lucia, Dominica, Haiti and Guadeloupe, and a Creole and its 'substrate' language, are also metonymically related; as are Creoles and the decreolized forms which derive from them. Most Caribbean speakers have the ability to switch from the Creole through the decreolized form to Caribbean French (a skill similar to the ability to change from adult to foreigner talk), for example, *dapré mwen imach* (Creole), *dapré mwen i pati* (decreolized) and *a man avis il est parti* (Standard Caribbean French), meaning "I think he has left" (Gournet 2010). Language varieties, such as the Indian, Australian, West African, British and American varieties of English, and registers (eg formal/informal or politically correct/politically incorrect), sociolects and idiolects are related metonymically, so are intra-national varieties of languages, such as standard and vernacular Arabic, Swiss and High German, Katharevousa and Demotic Greek, Bokmål and Nynorsk Norwegian. All relationships between languages are metonymic and it is the job of the translator to explore the metonymic relations between distinct languages as manifest in text, when carrying out their work—the subject of Chapter 8.

Extending the Lexicon

Meaning making is partial; language has a loose fit around reality. Meaning can be 'got at' in various ways (as discussed in Chapter 5). As a result, only a part needs to be referred to in order to communicate the whole, the listener supplying what is not encoded. Metonymy theory characterizes meaning as 'emergent' rather than 'determined', and a model of communication which is more flexible than determinist, one in which fixed one-to-one correspondence between words and things is not the main emphasis. The upside of this for learners is the flexibility it offers, metonymy allowing them to exploit information they already have in the mental lexicon. I presented data from my informant Zara earlier in this chapter and now present other extracts from the same recording. Here we have speech which is creative, expressive and, as the recording testifies, fluent, in which the speaker cleverly exploits the restricted resources available to her. She requires her interlocutor to use metonymic associations in reaching her communicative goals. In the extract below, *in speed*, *speedful*, *character*(s), *outer looking*, *react yourself* (in bold below) are either expressions she has invented or words used in ways which depart from their core meaning:

> the world has becoming more and more **in speed** / more **speedful** // and more superficial // because no inner **characters** are more admired / but more superficial things / the **outer looking** / how you look / how you **react yourself** / how you cope by not being a **character**
>
> (Zara 2006)

Another meaning-making strategy Zara uses is to give two or three words/expressions where one would do. Often one *will* do but she is perhaps not confident enough to know which one to choose, and so leaves it to the interlocutor to make the choice. In the extracts below she gives us *discern* and *tell*, *start* and *begin*, *quarrel* and *argument*, *certificate*, *dissertation* and *thesis*, *computer* and *laptop*:

> . . . in Germany they don't wear uniforms so that is a problem for them you can **discern or tell** which children are poor and which children are rich by their clothes and they **start begin** to have **quarrel an argument** together and is not really nice . . .
>
> . . . we had a computer at university and there I could type **my certificate my dissertation my thesis** I could even borrow **a computer a laptop** that time I could take it with me.
>
> (Zara, 2006)

We have a sense here that Zara is using the guise of her limited confidence in the learnt language to display her knowledge. There is a sense of bravura in her speech, even one of 'showing off' a bit, something which learners are often inclined to do because, by operating in a learnt language, they are more aware they are 'performing'. As was the case in the examples given in the section on accommodation, the solutions Zara comes up with cannot be classified as 'correct' or 'incorrect', but belong instead somewhere in between, and are probably best judged in terms of 'adequacy'. Adequate solutions are solutions which involve metonymic processing both in their creation on the part of the speaker but also in their interpretation on the part of the interlocutor.

Littlemore observes that adult learners use metaphoric extension to fill gaps, like children do, and gives an example from one of her informants of this type of 'lexical innovation', where the invented word *unjunktion* stands for 'street cleaning' in the sense of removing 'junk' (Littlemore 2001b:4). Littlemore also gives examples of metaphoric extension helping in vocabulary learning: *cup* extended beyond the core meaning of 'drinking vessel' to a sports prize and part of a bra, an acorn and a hip joint (Littlemore 2001a:459); and *eye* used in connection with a potato, a needle and a hurricane (Littlemore 2001a:485). Low argues that "metaphor makes it possible to talk about X at all" (Low 1988:127), and observes that there is "considerable evidence that learners try to overcome gaps in their knowledge of a second language by exploiting what they *do* know how to say, and that this can involve the creation of metaphor [. . .], that is to say, what they do not yet know is treated as if it were part of the reduced inventory, or stock, of the second language that they do know" (Low 1988:135). Littlemore suggests that the inclination to use figurative language to increase language competence, and the ability to do so, varies from student to student, and characterizes those who produce a lot of figurative language as 'metaphorical thinkers'; that "By using such strategies, metaphorically intelligent language learners are able to use their language resources in order to express a wider variety of concepts. They are therefore able to increase both their fluency and overall communicative effectiveness" (Littlemore 2001b:4).

Most of Low and Littlemore's examples are metaphoric, but there is a huge area of flexibility and expressivity which learners exploit intuitively which is more metonymic than metaphoric. I would suggest that it would pay dividends to direct our attention to the metonymic end of figurative language. These more subtle matchings of similarities are less noticed perhaps for the very reason that they are subtle, but it is this subtlety which gives metonymic shifts such power and universal applicability; and after all metonymy is doing the work behind Littlemore's examples of metaphor: the characteristics of *cup* which get transferred to objects other than drinking vessels are related metonymically, similarly, the characteristics of *eye* which get transferred. Metonymy, even more than metaphor, offers a huge resource of potential flexibility and creativity to the user. The flexibility which metonymic processing affords the learner is illustrated in this overheard conversation from my data notebooks, in which a gardener, a learner, is talking to a gardening enthusiast, a native speaker, about work he had done that morning:

Gardener:	We had seven or eight boxes of them. Is it sowing or planting? Because it is not really a seed and not really a plant.
Enthusiast:	A seedling?
Gardener:	More like a broadbean.
Enthusiast:	I suppose it's more like a seed.
Gardener:	So, anyway, I sowed them.
Enthusiast:	You put them in the ground.
Gardener:	Yes.

(Data Notebooks, 2009)

In this extract, the two participants are exploring the boundaries between categories on two continua: *seed/bean/seedling/plant* and *to sow/plant/put in the ground*. The learner knows you 'sow' a seed but 'plant' a plant, and wants a word suitable for the in-between category *seedling*. The discussion, led by the learner, is metalinguistic, that is to say, talk about language rather than talk itself, and explicitly explores relatedness between the categories *seed*, *plant*, *seedling*, *bean*, *sowing*, *planting* and *putting in the ground*. The purpose of this exploration is to add to the learner's knowledge of the language ahead of any other, such as advancing transactional goals, constructing narrative, establishing intimacy or serving a phatic role. It is communication "mixed with pedagogy", forcing the interlocutor "to adopt the subject position of teacher" (Block 2007:166). The learner is using the interaction for his own learning purposes; he is using his interlocutor as an expert to gain knowledge. The native speaker cooperates in this but seeks to resolve the questions the learner poses with immediate solutions, such as *A seedling?*, *I suppose it's more like a seed* and *You put them in the ground*, in order to move the dialogue on to a narrative with shared goals rather than one which is sided to the goals of the learner. It is metonymic processing which enables both participants to engage in this discussion and establish which words they are assigning to which categories, work which they do collaboratively.

Formal Metonymy

In Chapter 5, I discussed the role played by formal metonymy—the recognition of similarities in form but not necessarily meaning—in various aspects of everyday communication. I cited its use in closing off episodes in discourse, in humour, in expressions such as *dual fuel* or *kerb-side collection*, in in-family expressions and in avoiding cooperation. Here, I look at the significant role formal metonymy can play in learning lexis, the guiding principle being that new words which sound or look similar to words you already know are easier to learn. I realize this may seem an obvious claim, but am devoting a section to it as I feel the role that 'relatedness in form' plays in language learning has been seriously underplayed, as I hope to demonstrate below.

If we consider European languages in general and imagine native English speakers encountering them for the first time, relatedness in form can be a powerful handle, a good way in. From this viewpoint, for some lexical items the unfamiliar words seem to have no association at all; for others there are associations. In Czech, for example, for an English speaker, there does not seem to be any clue to help us know which of *dnes*, *včera* and *zitra* mean TODAY, YESTERDAY and TOMORROW, while it is clear which of *sekunda* and *minuta* means SECOND and which means MINUTE. Similarly, if you are not familiar with Polish, Finnish and Spanish, it is hard to tell the words for BREAKFAST and LUNCH apart; they are *śniadanie* and *obiad* (Polish), *aamiainen* and *lounas* (Finnish), and *desayuno* and *almuerzo* (Spanish). The words for YES and NO in Dutch are *ja* and *nee*, in Norwegian *ja* and *nei* and Swedish *ja* and *nej*. For all three we can be fairly certain which is which without being told, while it is less clear in Finnish, where the two words are *kyllä* and *ei*. Words for PUSH and PULL (signs on doors, for example) are *tam* and *sem* in Czech, *spingere* and *tirare* in Italian, and *tolni* and *húzni* in Hungarian. All are hard to guess at, while *drag* and *skjut* in Swedish have overtones of DRAG and SHUT, which help us guess they might mean PULL and PUSH respectively.

Continuing this line of argument: it is clear which months are referred to with *avril*, *mai* and *juin* in French, *April*, *Mai* and *Juni* in German, *április*, *május* and *június* in Hungarian, but not so with *huhtikuu*, *toukokuu* and *kesäkuu* in Finnish; which of *água fria* and *água quente* is hot water and which is cold in Portuguese is less clear, while whether *completo* in Italian or *fullt* in Norwegian mean a hotel has vacancies, or not, is easier to arrive at. The words for 'dialling code', *kod*, and 'email address', *adres email*, in Polish seem obvious, so do *tarifas* (charges) in Portuguese and *linka* (telephone extension) in Czech. The words for LIFT is *hiss* in Swedish, *hissi* in Finnish and *winda* in Polish, which seem to have no phonological or graphological relation to English words, though there is perhaps a suggestion of a 'hissing' sound of a lift arriving or the idea of lift 'winding' its way to your floor?

The resonances set up by formal metonymies between languages exist even more strongly between varieties of the same language. If we compare American and British English, we find there are words which are the same, words which are similar and words which are completely different between the two varieties. Examples of words which are the same in standard American and British English are too numerous to be worth citing. Some words are fairly transparent in their meaning, such as *windshield* versus *windscreen*; some words give strong clues, such as *gas* versus *petrol*, *school* versus *university*, *candy* versus *sweets* and *elevator* versus *lift*; while others give no clue at all, such as *socket* versus *point*, *faucet* versus *tap* and *eggplant* versus *aubergine* (examples from Kövecses 2000 and McCreary 2002). Even noun-noun compounds where both elements are different, such as *stick shift* versus *gear lever*, *pull-off* versus *lay-by* and *Denver boot* versus *wheel clamp*, provide enough partial matching not to make their unrelatedness a problem.

The under-acknowledged role of formal metonymy in language learning perhaps explains the 'magic point' which some learners report reaching where they seem to be learning lexis at an incredibly fast rate without really knowing why. To my mind, this may in part be thanks to the associations laid down by words between cognate languages which are related in form and meaning. For example, for a British English speaker encountering American English for the first time, it is not hard for them to learn that *ill* in British English is *sick* in American English, both because *sick* exists in British English and because there is a network of formal metonymies available to them where 'sick' means 'ill' in British English, in expressions such as *throw a sickie*, *sick note*, *be off sick*, *sick leave*.

Words which look as if they should be related but are not ('false friends') are often cited as traps which language students can fall into, and indeed they can be the cause of errors and misunderstandings, but they also contain elements which aid memory once the traps are identified. In Italian, the word *fattoria* means 'farm' not 'factory', *parente* means 'relative' rather than 'parent', *vernice* 'paint' rather than 'varnish'; but 'farm' and 'factory' have in common that they are places of production, 'parents' and 'relatives' are to do with family relations, and 'paints' and 'varnishes' are both applied to surfaces to protect them; and so the true meaning of false friends, although shifted, still belongs to the same domain.

MA translation programmes offered by a London university offer their students the opportunity of studying a 'cognate' language, that is, a language which is related to the main language/s they are taking. In recent years, students taking French, Italian, Portuguese and Spanish have been offered Romanian (as it is a Romance language). The students who take these classes are trained to read certain types of text, 'institutional' and 'technical', with a view to translating those texts. The skills they are developing are very specific; they are not learning to listen, speak or write, and they are working within a very narrow field and range of registers and text genres. Their progress over the year is startling, such that by the end of the year they are able to translate confidently and quickly from Romanian to English. A lot of this progress has to do, no doubt, with the fact that hundreds of metonymic clues—morphological, syntactic, lexical, pragmatic and discourse clues—are picked up on by the student, consciously and unconsciously. This was clearly the intention of the organizers of the programme; they anticipated that relatedness would aid their students in learning a language they had never encountered before, and that metonymic processing would enable them to build on knowledge that they already had. This indeed proved to be the case.

SPEECH ERRORS AND METONYMIC MONITORING IN THE SPEECH PROCESS

The figurative language which learners produce without intending to, but which their interlocutors are obliged to process as non-literal, was described in the previous section as 'inadvertent metaphor' and identified as a feature of learner speech. For Holme inadvertent metaphor is a substitute for precision: "Sentence 86 ('A coat is an object we support to disturb the wind') is finally an inadvertent metaphor and shows metaphor-making as a substitute for precise lexical knowledge" (Holme 2004:196)—though many educators would simply call them errors. The notion of error and what exactly constitutes an error was considered above in connection with Zara's style of performance, where it was suggested that there is no clear-cut divide between 'correct' and 'incorrect' when discussing learner speech (or any speech, for that matter). The pressures of time and the pressures of performing socially dictate that speaking is a matter of mobilizing the resources the speaker has to hand 'on the fly'. Speaking is more akin to improvisation than mechanical encoding, involving split-second decisions, which once made cannot be gone back on. Utterances are the best you can come up with in the time rather than perfect solutions cast for posterity. Metonymy theory helps replace a 'deficit model' of errors with one which is less deterministic, where errors are neither avoidable nor necessarily undesirable.

Learner errors have been characterized above as metonymic variation in terms of phonology, morphology, syntax, semantics, pragmatics, discourse, genre and schemata. Errors require the interlocutor to accommodate to the learner when they hear, for example: *I find myself boring myself* instead of *I find I get bored, I cannot support it* instead of *I can't stand it, Prices have gone through the carpet* instead of *Prices have gone through the floor*. I am now going to consider another type of error, 'speech errors' or 'slips', which are a consequence of the process of speech production itself. These are different from 'inadvertent metaphor' as speakers are usually immediately aware they have made them and usually self-correct. They also differ from inadvertent metaphor in that they are extremely rare, an exceptional rather than a prominent feature of speech. In order to understand them better, I offer a survey of the psycholinguistic models proposed by Fromkin, Garrett, Levelt and Dell. I then use data I have collected to identify the principal categories of speech errors, which I interpret in terms of metonymic processing. What emerges is that metonymic processing plays a vital role in all speech, whether it is error-free or self-corrected and whether it is the speech of learners or native speakers. I conclude that it is the very rarity of speech errors which reveals that monitoring for metonymy is an activity which is constantly in operation.

Our ability as speakers to respond with speed, accuracy and fluency to the unpredictable speech of others has prompted a number of different investigative approaches: marvelling at speech as a physiological phenomenon, measuring it quantitatively, hypothesizing the essential stages of speech production, devising models based on these hypotheses and using empirical data to peek into the 'black box' of the speaking mind. Speech is certainly an awe-inspiring phenomenon: English involves the finely-tuned co-ordination of 100 respiratory, laryngeal and supralaryngeal muscles to produce the forty-plus phonemes and gestures relating to stress, intonation and coarticulation needed to produce connected speech in English (Levelt 1989:413), an activity "neurologically and psychologically far more complicated than negotiating a flight of stairs" (Scovel 1998:27). The average native adult speaker of English selects from an active vocabulary of over 30,000 words and speaks at an average articulatory rate of two words (five syllables or fifteen speech sounds) a second with an extraordinarily low error rate of one slip per 1,000 (Scovel 1989:199). The psycholinguistic models I now consider are in general agreement on a number of points, the differences between them being more differences of detail than fundamental divergences. They all model speech as a process which goes from abstract thought to articulated speech in three main stages: 1) an abstract preverbal form of the message goes to 2) an outline/detailed planning stage and finally to 3) an 'articulatory plan', which the speech organs execute.

In more detail: Fromkin's Utterance Generator Model from 1971 has six stages: 1) the generation of an abstract message; 2) the representation of syntactic and semantic information in an abstract form; 3) the addition of stress and intonation contours; 4) the selection from the lexicon of word stems and their phonological representation; 5) phonological completion (attaching affixes); 6) the expression of phonemes by the articulators, using 'distinctive feature' information. (Fromkin & Ratner 1993:328–330). Garrett's 1975 model also has six stages: 1) the creation of an abstract message; 2) the creation of an abstract representation of the message as 'lexical formatives' and 'grammatical relations'; 3) a functional level representation (F) where lexical formatives are given phrasal roles; 4) a positional level representation (P) where grammatical relations select positional frames; 5) a sound level representation in which phonetic detail is specified; 6) the transmission of instructions to the articulators (Fromkin & Ratner 1993:331–333). While Levelt's 1989 model has five: 1) the 'conceptualizer' generates a preverbal message using macro- and microplanning; 2) the 'formulator' translates the message into a more concrete form, using (a) the 'grammatical encoder', which creates surface structure by retrieving lemmas from the lexicon, and (b) the 'phonological encoder', which uses the surface structure and lexeme information to encode a 'phonological plan'; 3) the 'phonological plan' is then *reduced* to a 'phonetic plan' ('internal speech') to achieve coarticulation phenomena typical of connected speech (such as 'assimilation', 'elision', weak forms) and loaded into the 'articulatory buffer'; 4) the 'articulator' executes the phonetic plan as 'overt speech'; 5) the 'speech comprehension system' feeds back the speaker's internal and overt speech to the conceptual system to monitor it (Levelt 1989:27–28).

Dell's 1986 'spreading activation model' attempts to explain why some speech errors seem to be both semantic and phonological and why unwanted items enter the articulatory buffer from the working memory (Dell 1986). It is a connectionist model and gives an insight into how the mental lexicon is organized. When the word *swim* is activated, its activation spreads to other items, related semantically, eg *drown, sink,* and phonologically, eg *swimmer, swimming, swims* (Dell 1986:290). For Dell, connections between items are networks rather than lines, and connections are two way rather than one way. Extraneous sensory data and pre-conscious thoughts occasionally intrude into the language system and become expressed as speech.

The most significant difference between these models, and one which is of particular significance in the present context, is the last stage of Levelt's model, the 'speech comprehension system'. This is a 'feedback loop' which allows the speaker to 'proofread' what they say; it "presumes that people don't just communicate with others, they communicate with themselves; they don't just listen to others, they listen to themselves" (Scovel 1998:48). The listening they do employs metonymy in order to monitor content, syntax, word choice and phonological form for slips, so, if needed, 'spontaneous self-repair' can be carried out (Levelt 1989:497). Feedback loops are common in all biological systems, for example, for regulating breathing rate, blood sugar and temperature. The 'speech comprehension system' is a feedback loop which monitors for metonymy. It compares every utterance with what 'should' have been uttered. If metonymy is detected, in other words, if an imperfect match is detected (one in which certain elements are different), a message is sent to the formulator/articulator to recast the utterance. Thus, the 'speech comprehension system' not only plays a role in the rare cases when slips are made, but is constantly active during all speech, ready to detect metonymy and initiate compensation for metonymy with self-correction. Metonymy and metonymic monitoring emerge as essential features of all language production, and, though not evident, metonymic monitoring is present also throughout all uncorrected speech.

An Empirical Study of Speech Errors

The purpose of this study is to demonstrate the variety of speech errors in naturally-occurring speech and use this as a form of proof that metonymic monitoring of various kinds is an essential stage of the speech production process. Fromkin and Garrett relied heavily on their corpora when developing their models. Wishing to follow in this tradition, I carried out my own empirical study on speech errors or slips, though on a much smaller scale, by noting down slips I encountered over a period of three weeks in 2008. About half the speech was from BBC Radio and TV, not an ideal source perhaps, for though broadcasting includes much spontaneous speech, much of it is scripted or mentally rehearsed; in addition, broadcasters are experienced performers, not typical speakers. The other half however was from conversations I was party to, which did present examples that were both spontaneous and typical. Early on when collecting data, I would often forget to listen out for slips, showing how instinctive it is to ignore slips and prioritize meaning, a form of metonymic processing. I chose to study predominately native-speaker English rather than learner English, because I wanted to examine the slips of what could be considered a target language community, where the effortful metonymic processing discussed above is at a minimum. There were about 100 items in the data I collected, a much smaller body of data than the corpora of Fromkin or Garrett, but nonetheless large enough to give a representative glimpse into the speaking mind. The slips involved various units of language—word, morpheme and phoneme—and various operations—adding, deleting, swapping, repeating and blending. Many misselections go unnoticed because the speaker does not repair, making it hard to judge whether you are dealing with an error or not. I only noted instances where the speaker made a repair.

Psycholinguists make a distinction between 'selection' errors and 'assemblage' errors, a distinction which was reflected in my data. Aitchison suggests that selection errors are more 'slips of the brain' than 'slips of the tongue', because they occur early on in the speech process, in the 'outline planning' stage, reflecting problems of 'lexical access'; while assemblage errors are true 'slips of the tongue', occurring later in the speech process, during 'detailed planning' (Aitchison 2008: 241). I identified four types of *selection error* in my data: 'phonological errors', 'semantic errors', 'shared-element errors' and 'blends', corresponding closely to Aitchison's (2008:241–244). I identified three types of *assemblage error*: 'affix errors', 'swapped phonemes' and 'inappropriately-inserted phonemes', similar to Fromkin & Ratner's categories of 'anticipation', 'perseveration' and 'exchange' (Fromkin & Ratner 1993:315). Below is a selection from data I collected, presented under seven headings: phonological errors, semantic errors, shared-element errors, blends, affix errors, swapped phonemes and inappropriately-inserted phonemes.

Phonological Errors

Here, the slip and the target word are related phonologically, often through the initial segment. This type of error, popularly known as a 'malapropism', was by far the most frequent in my data. Though basically phonological, many of the examples had a semantic motivation in the context in which they occurred: the pan which was surprisingly light was also hot; the woman who was wearing a belt was also wearing boots: *I've just had an* ***amazing*** *e-mail from a listener in Kent* for "amusing"; *the divorce money came* ***true*** for "through"; *I thought it would be* ***hotter*** for "heavier"; ***boot*** for "belt"; ***discovered*** for "discussed"; ***present*** for "pressing"; ***play*** *close attention* for "pay"; ***chicken*** for "chimney", ***send it*** for "said it"; *what do you want to do* ***to do*** for "today".

Semantic Errors

Here the slip and the target word are related semantically, not only in the sense of semantic relations, such as synonymy, antonymy, meronymy, but also by being related in the context of the utterance: *I think it is going to stay* ***open*** (for *empty*);

He *bores me* (for *I bore him*); *Oh,* **Ron, David, Steve** *could you get me . . .* The speaker has three goes at getting the right name, more members of the set of 'family members and close friends' being activated than necessary.

Shared-Element Errors

Here the slip contains part of the target word. There is a match with one of its elements, for example: *social* ***prototype*** for *stereotype* (shared element = *type*); *empty the* ***dishwasher*** for *washing machine* (shared element = *wash*); ***short-circuit*** *television* for *closed-circuit* (shared element = *circuit*); ***grandstand*** for *bandstand* (shared element = *stand*). Spreading activation 'lights up' words which are related both phonologically and semantically.

Blends

Blends arise when two words, usually similar in meaning, are activated simultaneously, both contributing an element to form a novel word: ***sfield*** from *field* and *sphere*; ***Borderstones*** instead of *Borders* or *Waterstones* (names of bookstores); ***YouBook*** from *YouTube* and *Facebook*; *she's concentrating on* ***motherhead*** for *motherhood*; ***idiotic-sy*** from *idiotic* and *idiocy*. I also noted instances of blends of lexical phrases, eg ***on the line*** from *on line* and *on the web.*

Affix Errors

The speech errors in this category are more functional than lexical. They involve the incorrect insertion of inflectional or derivational affixes and arise at the level of the syntactic frame: ***privates teacherly*** for *teaches privately*; *that* ***what's*** *happens*; ***what*** *coming up*; *remember to* ***giver*** *it some water*; *have you* ***speaken*** *to him*; ***I'm going to a film with Ritzy*** for *I'm going to a film at the Ritzy with Julie*, etc.

Swapped Phonemes

Here phonemes are either swapped, eg ***gline wassies*** for *wine glasses* or ***cub hap*** for *hub cap*, or rotated, eg ***boup, soul and rutter*** for *soup, roll and butter.* These slips, popularly called 'spoonerisms', though spoonerisms usually make sense, seem to be driven by ease of articulation not necessarily the case for fictional spoonerisms. My data suggest it is easier to start with a plosive than an approximant or a fricative. With ***boup, soul and rutter***, the sequence is more rotated than swapped, as if the sequence s-r-b has been moved on one place in order to start with the plosive (but b-s-r not b-r-s).

Inappropriately-Inserted Phonemes

In these slips, the wrong phoneme is inserted, eg *ho**n**e-owners* for *home-owners*; *Hea**s**row* rather than *Heathrow*. These examples are probably driven by 'lazy' articulation rather than deficient planning. Slips at the level of the phoneme arise late on in speech production, after the 'phonological plan' is in place. In *ho**n**e-owners*, which occurred twice in my data, closure using the tongue is easier to achieve than closure with the lips; in *Hea**s**row*, it is easier to drop the gesture of tongue grooving than perform it. We are unlikely to hear *twitter and bisted* for *bitter and twisted*, because it is harder to say.

What is significant about both selection errors and assemblage errors (malapropisms and spoonerisms) is that they "rarely cross clause boundaries, and are predominantly phrase internal" (Garrett 1988:75), giving further confirmation that the clause is the basic unit of speech (Field 2003:35). All the examples I have given above were repaired by the speaker, showing how vigilantly we subconsciously monitor our speech and how quickly we make repairs. Speech in every sense of the word is 'performance'; it reveals thought bit by bit in real time, driven by the speaker's desire to communicate. It is carried out quickly because the process from intention to articulation is highly automatized: "we can only produce speech at this rate because we do not pay conscious attention to the process" (Field 2004:18). It is carried out fluently because clauses are incremental (cascaded) and planned ahead of time—phonologically one clause ahead and syntactically two clauses ahead, according to Garrett (Whitney 1998:282). It is carried out accurately because the mind is selective in what it allows in the working memory/syntactic buffer/articulatory buffer, and because at each stage a feedback loop monitors for metonymy, prompting self-correction where necessary.

The speech errors described above are uncommon but frequent enough for us to regard them as a characteristic of all talk. We are constantly compensating for errors by using metonymic monitoring to such an extent that they are a feature of native-speaker and learner speech. Compensating for errors in learner speech is just an extension of the automatized processes associated with the speech production. Slips are telltale indicators of how speech is produced and of the stages the mind goes through when going from intention to articulation. Levelt's 'speech compensation system' is a proof-reading loop which allows the speaker to respond to slips with metonymic processing. Levelt suggests this monitoring is carried out by the same function of the brain which attends to the speech of others: "A speaker can attend to his own speech in just the same way as he can attend to the speech of others; the same devices for understanding language are involved" (Levelt 1989:469).

CONCLUSION

In this chapter I discussed four areas in which metonymic processing can benefit the learner when performing as a language user. They were: when interlocutors accommodate learner talk by processing shifts from the expected; when interlocutors accommodate to learners by adopting a less complicated register, foreigner talk; when learners use metonymic processing to overcome gaps in the lexicon when producing speech; and when learners use formal metonymic features to scaffold their acquisition of new lexis. The role of metonymic processing in monitoring speech was also explored. What I have shown here is that the distinct and unrelated phenomena discussed above, when reframed in this way, show that metonymic processing, essential to speech in general, is also important in the specific area of learner competence. The ability to manage small changes based on near equivalents gives the learner greater flexibility, more choices and choices which are more finely differentiated, a greater range of expression and more creativity in their performance. These findings also have implications in a language learning context, potentially influencing how learners are taught, what they are taught, how language teachers are trained, how material writers approach their work and what sort of language awareness input learners are given on taught courses. The next chapter looks at another category of applied linguists, the translator, and demonstrates that here too metonymy is at the heart of what they do.

8 Metonymy and Translation

This chapter continues to explore the role of metonymy in the social world by turning to another applied linguistics context: translation. A Metonymic Theory of Translation is presented in which translation is defined in terms of metonymy. This is situated in the context of some of the main approaches to defining translation in the Translation Studies literature: translation as equivalence, translation as action, translation as intercultural communication and translation as ideology. The literature on metaphor in translation (MiT) and shift theory are discussed, as are psycholinguistic approaches and the methodologies used to investigate translation as a mental process. This metonymic approach to translation is applied to various examples of translation tasks carried out by participating subjects. The involvement of metonymic processing is shown to be significant in both the 'interlingual' transfer stage of translation, going from source text to first draft, and the 'intralingual' revision stage, going from first draft to final version.

TRANSLATION STUDIES AND TRANSLATION LOYALTIES

There are parallels between the rise of Translation Studies and the rise of Metaphor Studies. Both have seen exponential growth over a similar period and have advanced along similar trajectories. The passage from Bassnett below describes the rise of Translation Studies, but if it were rewritten by replacing all the occurrences of the word 'translation' with the word 'metaphor', it could equally well describe Metaphor Studies:

> The 1980s was a decade of consolidation for the fledgling discipline known as Translation [Metaphor] Studies. Having emerged onto the world stage in the late 1970s, the subject began to be taken seriously, and was no longer seen as an unscientific field of enquiry of secondary importance. Throughout the 1980s interest in the theory and practice of translation [metaphor] grew steadily. Then, in the 1990s, Translation [Metaphor] Studies finally came into its own, for this proved to be the decade of its global expansion. Once perceived as marginal, translation [metaphor] began to be seen as a

> fundamental act of human exchange. Today, interest in the field has never been stronger and the study of translation [metaphor] is taking place [. . .] all over the world.
>
> (Bassnett 2002:1, words in square brackets added by the author)

Translation Studies is the academic discipline which has grown up around the practice of translation and interpreting, and is now a mature discipline in its own right, testified by volumes, such as Baker & Saldanha (2009), Millán & Bartrina (2013), Munday (2012) and Venuti (2012), and glossaries of terms, such as Munday (2009), Palumbo (2009) and Shuttleworth & Cowie (1997). The discipline is sufficiently well established for scholars to have mapped its ascent in different ways. Pym, for example, overviews Translation Studies in terms of dominant 'paradigms'—natural equivalence, directional equivalence, purpose, description, uncertainty, localization and culture (Pym 2010); while Snell-Hornby reviews its history in terms of cultural, interdisciplinary, empirical and globalization 'turns' (Snell-Hornby 2006).

In this section, I offer my own overview of the Translation Studies literature, framed in terms of 'loyalties'. I have chosen the term 'loyalty', because being 'loyal' (or 'faithful') to the source text is for many people, lay and professional, the starting point for thinking about translation. I then extend this idea to consider three other priorities: loyalty to the target-text reader, loyalty to the source culture and loyalty to the translator themselves. In so doing, I demonstrate that the Metonymic Theory of Translation I present in this chapter offers a new paradigm, one which has not been explored before. What is also apparent in any overview is that Translation Studies is, at root, concerned with the question of what translation is and, by implication, what constitutes a good translation. Translation is a complex cognitive activity, which takes place in a complex interpersonal, social and cultural setting, and often within exacting commercial constraints, the mind of the translator providing the bridge (or interface) between languages, texts and cultures. What each Translation Studies scholar does is to shed light on a particular aspect of translation, each scholar taking an original 'slice' through the subject to reveal a partial truth and contributing to our understanding of the phenomenon as a whole. It is not that we need to choose one theory over another; theories are compatible, even though they are often presented as competing.

First Loyalty: Equivalence

The definitions of translation to be found in Translation Studies are many and varied, but one idea which has dominated in the history of translation theory is that of 'equivalence'. This sees translation as an attempt to create a new text in the target language which is an equivalent, or mirror image, of the source text. The traditions of Cicero and Horace, through Dryden and Jerome, to the writings of Jakobson, Nida, Newmark and House all work from this premise. The classic 'literal versus free' debate is in essence a debate within the equivalence paradigm, a literal approach focussing on form (words) and a free approach focussing on function (meaning). Literal versus free expresses the paradox all translators confront, the wish to produce a translation which is both faithful to the original and fluent enough not to sound like a translation. The historic authors who engaged in this debate unanimously recommend giving less attention to form and more attention to meaning. Cicero recommends 'sense-for-sense' translation, which he describes as translating 'like an orator', *ut orator*, rather than 'like an interpreter', *ut interpres* (Cicero 46BCE); Horace recommends "nec verbum verbo", the avoidance of 'word-for-word' translation (Horace 20BCE/1989); Jerome claims that in translating from the Greek he renders "not word-for-word but sense-for-sense" (Jerome 395/2004); and Dryden, in the introduction to his translation of Ovid's *Epistles*, identifies "turning an author word by word, or line by line, from one language into another" ('metaphrase'), as being as confining and unnatural as "dancing on ropes with fetter'd legs" (Dryden 1680/2004).

When we come to twentieth-century authors, the term 'equivalence' acquires a semi-technical status. Jakobson recognizes it as "the cardinal problem of language and the pivotal concern of linguistics" as well as being ever present between languages (Jakobson 1959/2004:139). Nida suggests that it is only by aiming for 'dynamic equivalence' rather than 'formal equivalence' that 'the principle of equivalent effect' can be achieved: "a translation which attempts to produce a dynamic rather than a formal equivalence is based on 'the principle of equivalent effect'" and that "[i]n such a translation one is not so concerned with matching the receptor-language message with the source-language message, but with the dynamic relationship, that the relationship between receptor and message should be substantially the same as that which existed between the original receptors and the message" (Nida 1964:159). Pym makes a distinction between 'natural' and 'directional' equivalence, translations which reflect natural meaning-making norms of the language, which can be back-translated, and translations which result from motivated choices on the part of the translator, which cannot (Pym 2010).

The discourse-analysis approaches of the early 1990s, such as Hatim & Mason (1990), Bell (1991) and Baker (1992), are equivalence theories, too, but with added insights gained from the developments in discourse analysis in the 1980s. They recognize that there are many text-level features which contribute to their construction of text. Baker shows her commitment to the notion of equivalence in her chapter headings, *Equivalence at Word Level*, *Equivalence above Word Level*, *Grammatical Equivalence*, *Textual Equivalence: Thematic and Information Structures*, *Textual Equivalence: Cohesion* and *Pragmatic Equivalence*, while at the same time acknowledging that she adopts the term 'equivalence' more "for the sake of convenience [. . .] than because it has any theoretical status" (Baker 1992:5–6).

Second Loyalty: The Target Text Reader

Equivalence theories assume that loyalty to the source text is the overriding concern of the translator, but other loyalties are also desirable and possible. 'Action theories' move the focus of loyalty to the target-text reader. Reiss & Vermeer's

'Skopos Theory' (Reiss & Vermeer 1984), Holz-Mänttäri's 'Translational Action Theory' (Holz-Mänttäri 1984) and Nord's 'Integrated Text-Analysis Approach' (Nord 1991) emphasize the importance of the translator's brief/commission and entertain the possibility of the final text being different, even radically different, from the original in both form and content—for example, a spoken TV interview may become a written press release, or a four-page medical text for doctors may become a one-page non-technical illustrated pamphlet for patients. Pym calls them 'purpose-based' theories within the 'purpose' paradigm (Pym 2010). In skopos theory, the first rule is that the 'translatum' (translation) should be determined by its 'skopos' (purpose), and the fifth rule, the 'fidelity rule', that there should be 'intertextual coherence' between the source text and target text (Reiss & Vermeer 1984). Thus equivalence, while still important, is demoted to last place on the list of priorities, while considerations of purpose are promoted to the first place.

Third Loyalty: Translating Culture

The third focus in Translation Studies I consider is culture and, particularly, loyalty to the source culture. A translator has the choice either to keep any exoticisms of the source culture intact or smooth them over by expressing them in terms of the target culture. For the German romantic Schleiermacher the choice is between 'verfremdende Übersetzung' and 'einbürgernde Übersetzung', usually translated as 'alienating translation' and 'naturalizing translation'. Schleiermacher offers us an image of the translator as cultural mediator between writer and reader in this famous quotation: "Either the translator leaves the writer in peace, as much as possible, and moves the reader towards the writer; or leaves the reader in peace, as much as possible, and brings the writer towards the reader" (author's own translation). At the same time he recognizes that, as a general rule, alienation is the more appropriate approach for the translation of literature and naturalization more suited to the translation of business texts (Schleiermacher 1813/2004). Venuti rediscovered Schleiermacher's dyad in terms of 'foreignizing' and 'domesticating' (Venuti 1995). Kwiecinski expands this to four 'procedures' for translating culture: 'exoticising procedures', 'rich explicatory procedures', 'recognised exoticisation' and 'assimilative procedures' (Katan 2009:79–81); while Katan gives translation a wider cultural context, seeing translation as "intercultural communication" and the translator as a "cultural mediator" (Katan 2009:88).

The Fourth Loyalty: Loyalty to the Translator

A fourth focus in this overview is loyalty to the translator themselves and discussions around the extent to which a translator is/can be faithful to their own ideologies. Critical movements which promote feminism, gay rights, anti-racism, anti-classism, anti-colonialism, anti-globalization, environmental issues, and so forth, question ideological assumptions behind certain social practices of the status quo. Translators are obliged to make decisions in their work as to whether they wish to promote or subvert the ideologies naturalized in the texts they translate. The translator is faced with the choice of either being a neutral observer, simply exchanging signs in one language for signs in another, or carrying out their occupation as politically-engaged individuals, ready to question the assumptions of society. This plays itself out even in seemingly banal choices: the decision to translate the pronoun, when referring back to "the operator" in an instruction manual with *he*, *she*, *s/he* or *they*, involves political choices. Work in this field includes Niranjana (1992) on colonialism, Simon (1996) on gender and Venuti on the translator's 'visibility' (Venuti 1995).

DEFINING TRANSLATION IN TERMS OF METONYMY

The foci of loyalty discussed above—translation as equivalence, translation as action, translation as intercultural communication and translation as ideological engagement—provide us with different ways of viewing the complex phenomenon of translation and different ways of defining it. The definition of translation I wish to explore is an approach not found in the Translation Studies literature: translation as metonymy. I have made the case earlier in this volume that metonymy and metonymic processing are fundamental to language and communication. It is a small step therefore to suggest that the special case of translation also involves metonymy in a fundamental way. The Metonymic Theory of Translation proposed here, stated simply, maintains that the relationship between a source text and a target text is neither literal, as terms in different languages very rarely correspond exactly, nor metaphoric, as a translation is seldom a metaphoric version of the original text; instead, the relationship between the two is all about metonymic relations, close relatedness across the whole spectrum of linguistic features, from individual words to whole texts and genres, and that carrying out translation is overwhelmingly concerned with managing these correspondences through metonymic processing.

Quine, writing on the 'indeterminacy of translation', notes that "systematic indeterminacy" is involved in "the enterprise of translation" (Quine 1960:ix) and queries why this has not been investigated with more vigour: "Indeterminacy has been observed with a single language, so it is ironic that the interlinguistic case is less noticed, for it is just here that the semantic indeterminacy makes clear empirical sense" (Quine 1960:79). Quine was writing in 1960. More recently, Bell also recognizes that partial correspondences are a central feature of both monolingual communication and translation: "Perhaps the most significant message [. . .] for translation is the recognition that the essential characteristic of the lexical systems of languages is not precise boundary-marking but fuzziness and that it is the inherent fuzziness of language which presents the most formidable obstacle to the translator" (Bell 1991:102). Metonymic relations are involved when producing any text, whether a 'spontaneous' text or a translation; but, in the case of translation there is a further layer of the involvement of metonymy, as the comparison with an existing text and another language system is at the heart of the process. If we accept the notion that translation is metonymic, we can consider choices based on metonymy as more significant than the loyalties discussed above, that all four foci discussed above rely on the exploration of metonymic relations between elements of the source language and target language for their realization, and that metonymic processing is the mechanism which makes it possible for those loyalties to be expressed.

One area of Translation Studies where we would expect to find a discussion of metonymy is in relation to translating figurative language, but in fact we find very little; if discussed at all, the concern is almost exclusively with the translation of idioms. Scholars in this area tend to see idioms as deviant and to be dealt with in isolation, characterized as problematic, occasional interruptions to the otherwise relatively effortless flow of literal translation. Scholars offer self-help-style lists of how to deal with them when they do occur. Broeck (1981:77) suggests three strategies: using the same metaphoric image (sensu stricto), using a different metaphoric image (substitution) and using a non-metaphoric alternative (paraphrase). Baker adds a fourth strategy to Broeck's list, namely, to leave the expression out entirely, which she calls 'omission' (Baker 1992: 63–81); but while viewing metaphoric language as problematic, she concedes that 'opaque idioms' "can actually be a blessing in disguise" because they are more readily recognized by the translator than more transparent idioms, and therefore are less likely to be mistranslated (Baker 1992:65–66). Newmark's solutions are: to translate the source metaphor with the same image in the target language, with the same image plus a literal gloss or explication, with the same image expressed as a simile, with a different image, with a literal translation, and through deletion (Newmark 1988:87–91). Dagut adds the possibility of going from a literal to a metaphoric expression, thereby giving non-literal language an enabling role by offering other options, rather than seeing it only as a problem to be solved (Dagut 1976).

A far more adventurous and fruitful approach to metaphor in translation has been that of Schäffner, who takes on board the developments in Conceptual Metaphor Theory and applies them to a database of professionally-produced translations (Schäffner 2004). In a comparative study across European Union documents, she identifies systematic metaphors, such as EUROPE IS A HOUSE, and records when language representing these metaphoric ideas is retained and when it is replaced (Schäffner 2004). This is a departure from the rest of the literature on metaphor and translation, as it looks at metaphor occurring at the level of whole text/genre rather than isolated within individual phrases/clauses, having a systematic role in meaning making in multilingual communities such as the European Union, and having a positive and enabling function in solving problems for the translator rather than just creating them. Schäffner & Shuttleworth have made a useful contribution in their work on Metaphor in Translation (MiT) by moving the focus from product to process: "Most of the work conducted on MiT within translation studies has been text-based, and thus product-oriented. The text shows us the result of very complex cognitive processes, which moreover occurred in specific socio-cultural, historical, and institutional contexts" (Schäffner & Shuttleworth 2013:97). The processes we should turn our attention to, I believe, are those involving metonymy in translation rather than metaphor.

The Metonymic Theory of Translation I am proposing here sees figurative language as enabling translation in a fundamental sense. Rather than concentrating on the extreme end of figurativeness, such as Baker's 'opaque idioms' (Baker 1992:68) or Newmark's 'stock metaphors' (Newmark 1985:303–311), it looks at the middle-ground of closely-related shifted meanings, which exist not only between source text and first draft but also between first draft and final version. It is suggested that translators, in carrying out their professional duties, spend most of their time and energies exploring the metonymic relations between and within language systems. The practical reality of the translator's work consists of assembling words, phrases and clauses in the target language which have metonymic correspondences with units of language from the source text. Jakobson distinguishes between 'interlingual' translation and 'intralingual' translation, which he glosses as 'translation proper' and 'rewording' (Jakobson 1959/2004). The two phases of written translation can be seen in these terms, writing a first draft as translation proper and revising the first draft to achieve a final version as rewording; and in both, the exploration of metonymic relations is involved. In spoken translation (interpreting) there is only really time for the first phase, translation proper. Translation is a process whereby metonymic relations are explored not just in one dimension, but across a whole web of relations across text. In the next section I look in more detail at the different types of metonymic relations which exist between units of text and to do so explore the concepts of 'loss', 'gain' and 'shift'.

LOSS, GAIN AND SHIFT

If we accept 'translatability' as a given, that translation is possible at all—and surely it is—we have then to acknowledge that it will inevitably involve 'loss', linguistic and cultural. While in the popular mind the first association with translation is 'loss', as in "loss in translation" and "lost in translation", a professional translator will usually have a more positive association, acknowledging that every translation, however bad, involves some degree of 'gain', as it has the potential of allowing communication between two parties who would not otherwise be able to communicate. There is also a sense among translators and critics that a translation can improve on an original. Gabriel García Márquez famously credited the translator Gregory Rabassa with having produced a version of his classic novel *100 Years of Solitude* which was better than the original (Rabassa 2005). The solution to loss is 'compensation' and translators have a myriad of techniques for achieving it. These all involve metonymic relations of some kind but are referred to in Translation Studies as 'shifts', a term first adopted by Catford. In the rest of this section, I discuss the contributions to translation shift theories of Catford, Leuven-Zwart, Vinay & Darbelnet and Hervey & Higgins to demonstrate that translation shifts are in fact metonymic shifts.

For Catford, "translation is a process of substituting a text in one language for a text in another" and "a central task of translation theory is that of defining the nature and conditions of translation equivalence" (Catford 1965). This is achieved at word level through 'formal equivalence', resorting to 'textual equivalence' when formal equivalents are not available. Textual equivalence involves compensation through the use of solutions which are near-fits rather than exact equivalents. These can be either 'level shifts', where grammatical meaning is expressed by lexis (or lexis by grammar), or 'category shifts', where a different grammatical structure, part of speech, rank or idiom is used (Catford 1965:73–80). From his data, Catford calculated that shifts were necessary in as many as 65% of the instances of *the*, when comparing English and French versions of the same text (Catford 1965:82). I would argue that even the remaining percentage, the straightforward, literal, one-for-one 'formal correspondences', are also shifts. They are shifts because categories do not correspond exactly between languages (even items such as the definite article), because words take on slightly different meanings depending on the context set up by the other words around them, and because meaning making is by nature partial, relying on part of a semantic frame giving access to the whole frame, as was demonstrated in the discussion of FLOATING RIB, RIB CAGE, MOBILE PHONE and ANSWERING MACHINE in Chapter 4.

The degree of departure in meaning of items in the target text from items in the source text is the criterion used by Vinay & Darbelnet in their classification of seven 'procedures' (Vinay & Darbelnet 1958/1995), work prompted by observing the wording of English and French road signs when driving from New York to Montreal. Translations are of two types, 'direct' and 'oblique', oblique translations being turned to only when direct strategies give unsatisfactory results. The direct translation strategies go from the least intervention, 'borrowing', where a source language word is introduced unchanged into the target text; through 'calque', where the lexis or structure reflects the source language, eg *compliments de la saison!* or *science-fiction* (in French); to 'literal' word-for-word translation. The oblique strategies are: 'transposition', involving a change in the part of speech, eg *No smoking* versus *Défense de fumer*; 'modulation', using a near equivalent, eg *The time* ***when*** *. . .* versus *Le moment* ***où*** *. . .*, *It is* ***not difficult*** *to . . .* versus *Il est* ***facile*** *de . . .*, *No vacancies* versus *Complet*; 'equivalence' (in their use of the term), changing the concept or image, eg *Too many cooks spoil the broth* versus *Deux patrons font chavirer la barque* ("Two skippers make the boat capsize"); and 'adaptation', making changes in order to achieve cultural compatibility, eg the film title *The Wanderer* translated to *Le Grand Meaulnes* (Vinay & Darbelnet 1958/1995:30–42). The procedure which involves the most extreme shift in Vinay & Darbelnet's scheme, adaptation, goes beyond substitution of small units of text and can involve choices which have implications across a whole work, such as the choice of Neapolitan dialect to represent the Irish accent or transferring the setting of Shakespeare to the 1920s. The unit of translation is sometimes the whole text, what Hatim calls 'genre shift' (Hatim 2009:46–47), a large-scale metonymic shift.

In Leuven-Zwart's version of shift theory, developed to compare translations in Dutch of Latin American literature with their originals, three types of shift are identified, 'modulation', 'modification' and 'mutation'. She takes as her unit of meaning the 'transeme', basically a clause, and examines the extent to which there is a meaning shift between the source and target text, modification representing more of a shift than modulation but less than mutation (Leuven-Zwart 1989, 1990). While Hervey & Higgins identify four types of shift: 'compensation in kind', which includes various types of linguistic strategy used to achieve equivalence, such as those discussed above; 'compensation by merging', where two or more linguistic elements of the original become a single element in the target text; 'compensation by splitting', where one linguistic element of the original becomes two elements in the target text; and 'compensation in place', where the location of the meaning of a particular unit is moved to another part of the text (Hervey & Higgins 1992). These can all be seen as metonymic shifts.

Common to all these approaches is the idea of spectra with small shifts at one end and greater, more dramatic shifts at the other. In my Metonymic Theory of Translation we can describe the two ends of the spectra as 'weak' and 'strong' metonymic translation. A strong metonymic translation might involve a significant reduction of the original text, such as when "Hello Ladies and Gentlemen, it's wonderful to see so many of you have braved the elements and made it to the first day of our conference on healthcare in a snowbound Canterbury" is reduced to a single word "Bonjour!"; or a cultural shift, such as in Gilbert Adair's *A Void* (a translation of Georges Perec's *La Disparition*), where a joke about the Paris Metro on page 98 becomes a joke about London buses on page 210, the key element, 'difficulty of getting around a busy capital', being drawn on in both cases (David Hornsby, personal communication, 2010).

TRANSLATION AS A PSYCHOLINGUISTIC PROCESS

Another approach scholars have taken in investigating translation has been to see it as a mental process rather than a product. They have attempted to understand what goes on in the translator's mind, translation being defined as a psycholinguistic process. Many attempts have been made to model the process, to understand the sequence of events and identify the cognitive resources a translator calls upon. What has intrigued scholars in this area above all is the idea of a non-verbal intermediate stage, when the message is no longer encoded in the source language but not yet re-encoded in the target language. For psycholinguists, the idea that in the human mind one can go from a preverbal thought to a message encoded in language (or another semiotic system) is not surprising. Levelt's speaking model, discussed in the previous chapter, uses empirical evidence to identify the stages involved in doing just that, going from 'intention to articulation' (Levelt

1989). Nor is the reverse surprising, going from a linguistically-encoded message to a thought (or indeed operating with thoughts at all); but in translation, perhaps because two languages are involved, this abstract, language-free stage has acquired an almost mythical status, described variously as a 'pre-linguistic' phase, 'déverbalisation' (Lederer 1987:15), a 'semantic representation' (Bell 1991), the 'third code' and 'tertium comparationis'.

My simple (but hopefully demystifying) analysis of what is involved is as follows. Translation involves the encoding of ideas, just like speaking and writing, but translation is communication of a different type, as it also involves an initial decoding stage, which proceeds just like listening and reading. Furthermore, the decoding and encoding stages occur in different code systems (languages) and take place in the privacy of the translator's mind rather than between two people. What is more, if the translation event is complete, there is a further encoding stage before translation, the production of the source text by the text producer, and a decoding stage after translation, the consumption of the target text by a text recipient. Thus, 'normal' communication can be represented as a V (Figure 8.1) and translation/interpreting as a W (Figure 8.2), where the part that the translator/interpreter plays, without the text producer and text recipient, is an inverted V (Figure 8.3).

Interest in translation as a process has produced models by Wilss, Levý, Krings, Bell, Kiraly and PACTE Group, among others. I review these here to demonstrate that this literature can be interpreted in terms of metonymic theory. Wilss sees translation in terms of problem solving, decisions being made by reference to two different knowledge systems: knowing things, or 'declarative knowledge', and knowing how to do things, or 'procedural knowledge' (Wilss 1998:58). Wilss identifies six phases in the process of solving problems: 1) identifying the problem; 2) clarifying the nature of the problem; 3) searching and retrieving

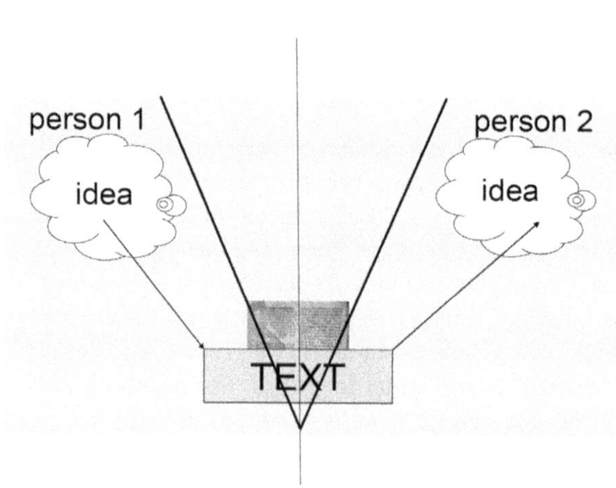

Figure 8.1: 'Normal' communication

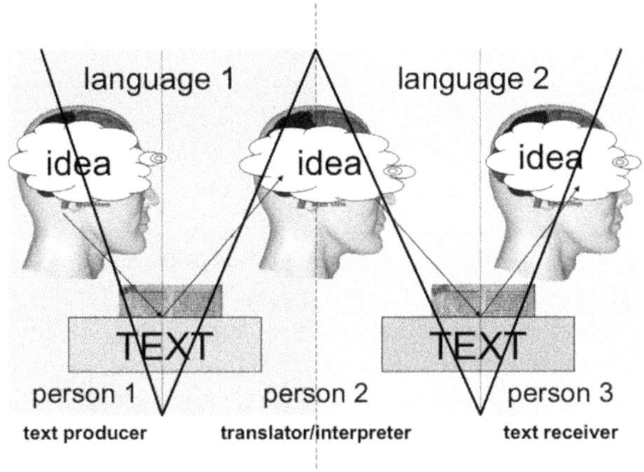

Figure 8.2: Translation and interpreting

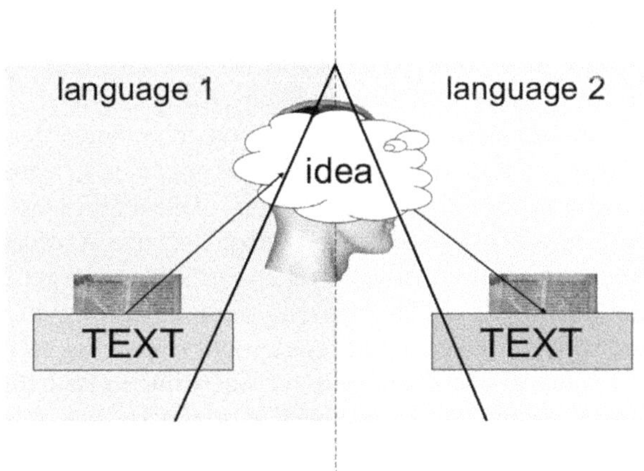

Figure 8.3: Translation and interpreting—the translator's role

information relevant to solving the problem; 4) adopting a problem-solving strategy; 5) choosing one solution among many; and 6) evaluating the success of the solution (Hurtado Albir & Alves 2009:60). Decisions are made at both 'macro-' and 'micro-' contextual levels, the more local the problems (the smaller the scale), the less likely it is that translators will have infallible rules for solving them: "The more unique a translation problem the less practicable the general problem-solving procedures and the less like a game of chess or an algorithmically organized flowchart the whole activity becomes" (Wilss 1998: 58). Taking his ideas from 'game theory', where behaviour is modelled in terms of choice, Levý holds that the translator while translating is constantly presented with a number of alternative solutions or 'paradigms', and that within each paradigm the choices are unequal, some more suitable than others, otherwise the translator would be left in a dilemma as to which to choose (Levý 1967/2000). Choosing one word over another has been seen by Cronin to be a bit like choosing to play one card rather than another in a card game, and that it is "the 'ludic' (play) quality of translation and its unpredictability, which makes translation motivating for professionals" (Cronin 1998:92–93).

Krings also sees translation in terms of problem solving. Examining data from German native-speaker learners of French, he draws up a flow diagram to represent the decision-making processes involved (Krings 1986:269). For each word/phrase in the source text, the student first decides whether there is a translation problem or not. If there is no problem, they simply translate and go on to the next word/phrase. If there is a problem, it will be either a 'comprehension' or a 'retrieval' problem, comprehension problems being resolved using comprehension strategies and retrieval problems using retrieval strategies. If there are 'competing equivalents' in the target language, 'decision-making strategies' are adopted in order to decide which to choose; if there is no adequate equivalent, 'reduction strategies' are adopted, which include "dispensing with markedness", "dispensing with metaphor" and "dispensing with specific semantic features" (Krings 1986). This is summarized in Krings' diagram in Figure 8.4.

Bell compares translation to reading. They have in common that they both involve decoding but the ends to which the decoding is put differ: in reading, processing activity is simply in order to understand the message of the original text; in translation, it is in order to end up with a derived text in another language. A reader's reactions to a text, such as curiosity, pleasure, disapproval or puzzlement, are personal reactions; while a translator's reactions are less personal and motivated by the exigencies of the task, such as noticing indicators of register and responding to features of the text which signal potential encoding problems. According to Bell, this makes reading 'sender-oriented' and the reading involved in translating 'receiver-oriented' (Bell 1998:186–187). Bell sees the clause as the default 'unit of meaning' in translation. The restricted capabilities of the short-term (working) memory limit the amount of language which can be manipulated at any one time. For Bell, top-down concept-driven and bottom-up data-driven processes are both involved in translation with an interactive process linking the two (Bell 1991:235). There is a balance between 'whole text' *top-down* and 'local' *bottom-up* processes, *micro* (bottom-up) and *macro* (top-down) processes working together (Bell 1998). Empirical research suggests that professional translators use more top-down 'sense-oriented' strategies, with a focus on "function rather than form", while non-professionals tend to use bottom-up 'sign-oriented' strategies with a focus on "form rather than function" (Bell 1998:189). In Bell's model, syntactic, semantic and pragmatic *analyzers* look after decoding the source-language message, while the pragmatic, semantic and syntactic *synthesizers* look after encoding into the target language. Between the two is a pre-linguistic 'semantic representation', depicted as a cloud to show its non-verbal status. Bell presents his model as a flow diagram, reproduced in Figure 8.5.

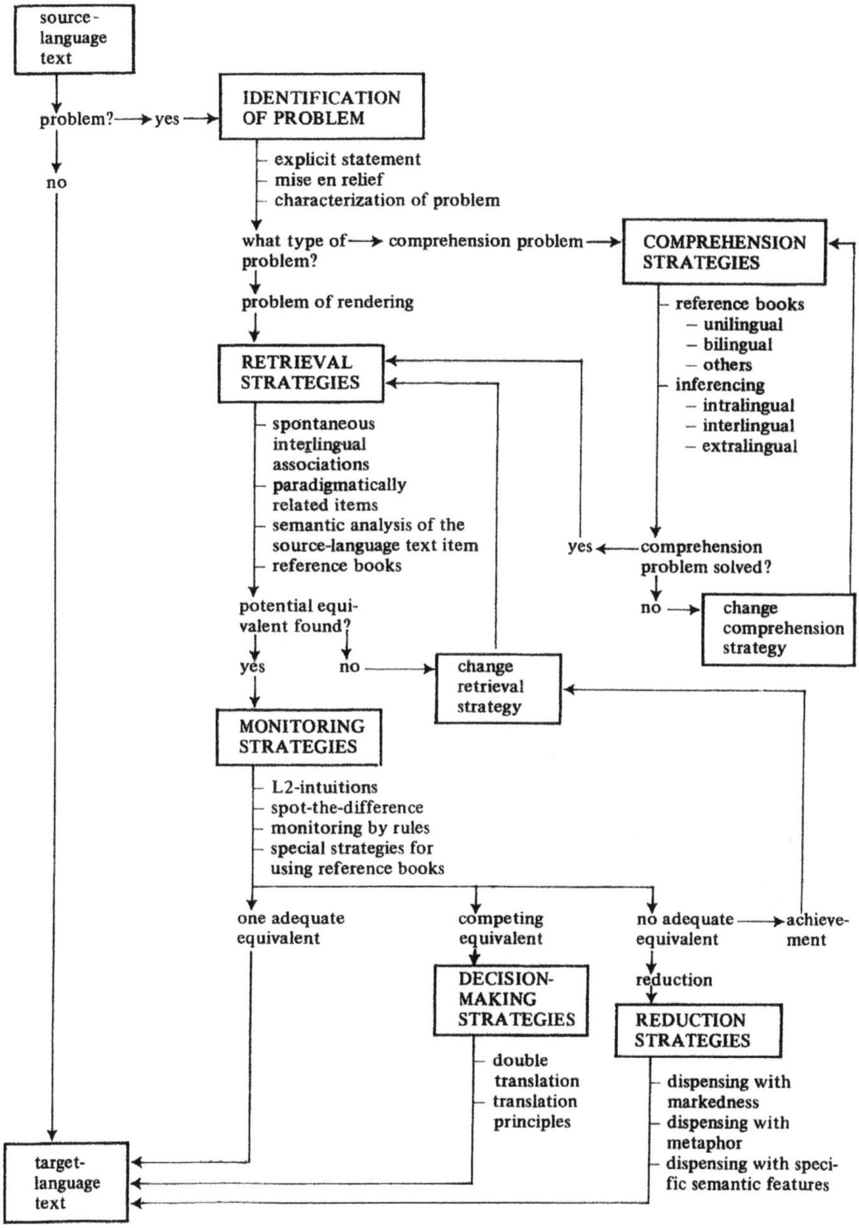

Figure 8.4: Krings' model (1986:269)

The clause is the default unit of translation for Bell, but he acknowledges that other units play a role and that clauses overlap and cascade (Bell 1991). Many scholars recognize that the unit of translation can vary, for Newmark, for example: "all lengths of language can, at different moments and also simultaneously,

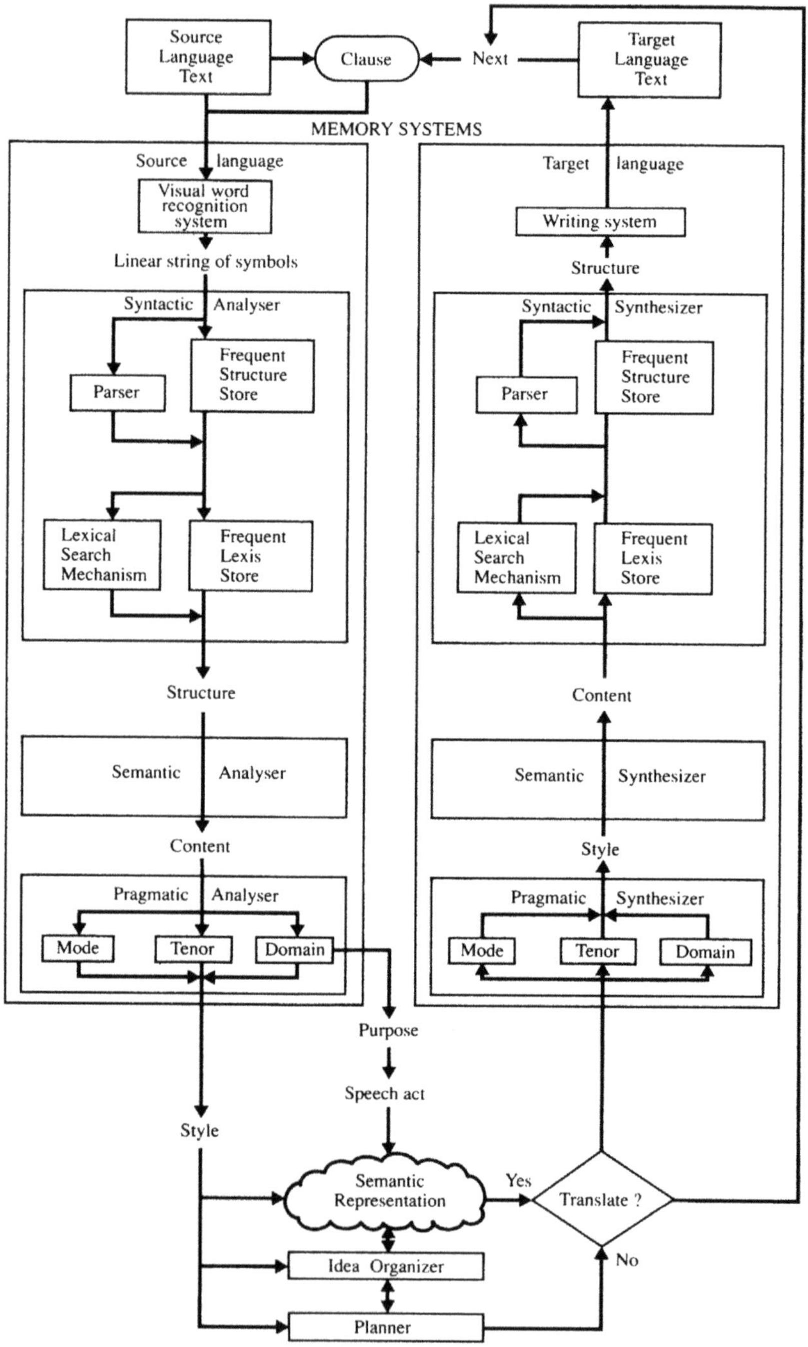

Figure 8.5: Bell's model (1991:59)

be used as units of translation in the course of the translation activity; [. . .] further I have tried to show that, operatively, most translation is done at the level of the smaller units (words and clauses), leaving the larger units to 'work' (*jouer*) automatically, until a difficulty occurs and until revision starts" (Newmark 1988:66–67). Hatim & Munday give a full spectrum of possible units of translation: "Translation theorists have proposed various units, from individual word and group to clause and sentence and even higher levels such as text and intertextual levels" (Hatim & Munday 2004:25). For Malmkjaer the translator may work at several levels at once: "It needs to be stressed that momentary attention to units of fairly fixed sizes during translating and during comparison of source and target texts does not preclude the translator or analyst from considering the text as a whole" (Malmkjaer 1998:288). This provides an answer to the question of whether translators operate 'top down' or 'bottom up'; we can infer they do both, and probably simultaneously.

In Kiraly's model, three modules—an 'intuitive workspace', a 'controlled processing centre' and 'information sources'—interact with each other in the translation process (Kiraly 1995:101). Much of this work involves just the intuitive or subconscious 'workspace', where inputs from various sources, including the source text, interact, without involving much conscious control (Kiraly 1995:101–102). It is only when problems occur that automatic processing gives over to the more conscious work of the 'controlled processing centre' (Kiraly 1995:102). The approach of the PACTE Group has been to explore the concept of 'translation competence' by breaking it down into six translation subcompetencies: the 'bilingual', 'extralinguistic', 'strategic', 'instrumental', 'knowledge about translation' and 'psycho-physiological' subcompetencies (PACTE Group 2005:610–611). It is the 'strategic subcompetence' which is of most interest in the present context, as it is here that problem solving takes place; deficiencies are compensated for, problems identified and procedures applied to solve them (PACTE Group 2005:610).

What emerges from this review of psycholinguistic models of translation is a picture in which many shared principles come together. There is agreement that: 1) translation is an activity which involves a series of stages and that the stages come in a specific sequence; 2) the process does not occur in isolation but that each event connects to other events at many points; 3) translation involves knowledge about language/culture as well as procedural knowledge; 4) translation is an activity where the recognition, analysis and solving of problems play an important role; and 5) translation is an activity in which informed choices are made by reference to information stored in the long-term memory. It is this picture of translation as a process in which the mind is constantly acting on units of language (of various lengths), referring to stores of knowledge about each language, comparing items, consulting knowledge stores and carrying out high-level cognitive operations which I use in characterizing translation in my own studies. These are all aspects of metonymic competence which come into play at different moments while the translator is going about their work. Before I consider these studies, I first discuss the methods commonly used for investigating translation as a psycholinguistic process in order to show why I have chosen to conduct my studies in the way I have.

PSYCHOLINGUISTIC METHODS FOR INVESTIGATING TRANSLATION

The methods commonly used for investigating translating as a psycholinguistic process, 'Think Aloud Protocols', 'introspection' and 'retrospection', reflect those used more broadly in psychology and the social sciences for investigating mental processes. A Think Aloud Protocol (TAP) requires the translator to provide a running account of what they are thinking and doing, to express in words as best they can the mental and physical activities they are carrying out while translating: "TAPs will typically involve the 'subjects' verbalizing everything that comes into their minds and all the actions they perform as they work on the creation of a TT" (Shuttleworth & Cowie 1997:171). The term Think Aloud Protocol is used to refer to the technique but strictly the 'protocol' is the written transcript. Here is an example of the beginning of a TAP protocol from Bernardini:

> ok now let's see *lieti eventi* maybe 'great news' but probably I'm putting 'great news' because I want to start writing something ehm and this means that I could well go back to it [pause=think 8.30 secs] ehm now again I could put 'two new planets discovered outside the Solar System' rather boring though is it? not not particularly attractive as a title [pause=think 24.50] maybe I'll change 'news' to 'discoveries' [pause=type 4.54] [pause=think 4.24] no I think I'll put 'two new planets discovered' so I'll go back to 'great news' and then 'two new planets discovered outside the Solar System' have to spell it properly . . .
>
> (Bernardini 1999:20–21)

The TAP technique has been criticized on a number of counts. It is hard to deliver a protocol without at the same time giving an interpretation, a running account can easily become a running commentary; and however cooperative the subject wants to be, what they say they are thinking is not necessarily an exact account of what is going on in their mind. Also, much mental activity is either not available for inspection by the conscious mind or not expressible in words, and in any event giving a fluent protocol is a skill which only comes with practice and training: "Subjects involved in such experiments need special training to enable them to verbalize freely instead of analysing and commenting on their thought processes" (Jääskeläinen 1998:268). In spite of these criticisms, TAP is generally thought to be a direct, reliable source of rich data which give insights into how translators make choices, how they deal with equivalence at problematic points in a translation and how they come up with creative solutions. Research using TAPs can help reveal, for example, whether professionals translate more quickly and more automatically than trainee translators or whether they use longer units of translation. The technique has helped show that translation is not a single invariable process but one which has many forms: "the findings of TAP studies have so far offered indisputable evidence to support the view that there is no single monolithic translation process. The nature of the process varies considerably depending on several factors, including type of text, type of task and type of translator" (Jääskeläinen 1998:268).

Another commonly-used technique, introspection (or 'immediate retrospection'), involves subjects commenting on their performance immediately after carrying out a task. Fraser used introspection, in conjunction with TAPs, but was concerned that underlying processes might not always be revealed in this way, as experienced subjects use "language processing strategies of which they have long ceased to be aware because long practice has resulted in automatization" (Fraser 1996:77). In retrospection the subject reflects on a task they have carried out at some distance in time from the event and can take the form of interviews, questionnaires or reflections delivered by email. TAPs, introspection and retrospection can all be supported by data from tracking software. *Translog*, for example, keeps a log of the keystrokes, so that a protocol can be built up of exactly which keys are pressed and in what order. This allows researchers to examine a translator's performance in real time, and see how solutions are arrived at, where hesitations occur and where deletions/corrections are made (Jakobsen & Schou 1999). *Proxy* software also records keyboard activity and *Camtasia* records screen shots (Hurtado Albir & Alves 2009).

In the studies I have undertaken, presented in the next section, it is *retrospection* I have chosen to use, used in conjunction with source text, first draft and final version evidence provided by the translator. I made this choice for a number of reasons. First, I wanted to avoid being intrusive during the translation process. Another consideration was that as the editing stage of translation is a retrospective activity, a retrospective tool of enquiry seemed well suited for investigating it. Finally, I anticipated that the retrospective comments of the translators would complement well the data I had of the translation event itself, as the translator and I could refer to the source text and different versions of the translation in the interviews.

STUDIES INVESTIGATING THE TRANSLATION PROCESS

In this section, I examine translation in terms of the Metonymic Theory of Translation outlined earlier in this chapter. I look at four examples. The first is a task based on instructions for a kitchen appliance. The second is a translation of an article from the French newspaper *Le Figaro* by a trainee translator, studying for his MA at a London university. The third and fourth are taken from the work of a professional freelance translator living in Germany, translating the publicity material for a food store and a website for a marketing company.

Study 1: Translating the Instructions for a Handheld Food Mixer

The source text for this study is the Italian section of an instruction leaflet for a handheld food mixer. It starts (errors in the original have been left uncorrected):

> Inserire la spina nella presa di corrente. Insere le spirali frullatrici (impasto di farina ecc.) oppure quelle impastatrici (impasto tipo panificacione, ecc.). Mettere sempre la frusta con la corona dentata nell'aperture contrassegnata con corona dentata (1). Mattere gli ingredienti da lavorare in un recipiente adatto (scodella di miscela o bicchiere di miscela). Immergere le fruste nel recipinete ed avviare l' apparecchio. Avviare sulla posizion 1 (per evitare spruzzi), poi passare sul 2 (2). Il TurboMix si avvia sull'1 o sul 2, e si passa poi al 3 (3).

A translator with the brief of translating this text (into English or another language) immediately encounters two difficulties in this first paragraph: 1) how to distinguish between the two different types of beater supplied with the mixer (Figure 8.6); and 2) how to describe the distinctive shape which allows the user to tell the beaters apart (Figure 8.7).

The translator can get information on both these points from the text and from the illustrations which accompany the text. Which in practice is the most useful of these depends on the quality of the text and the quality of the illustrations, the translator's own repertoire of competencies, and the resources available to them, such as glossaries, parallel text in the target language, and so on. They may also have been supplied with the appliance itself or even have contact with the company's technical department. If the translator starts from the illustrations, they

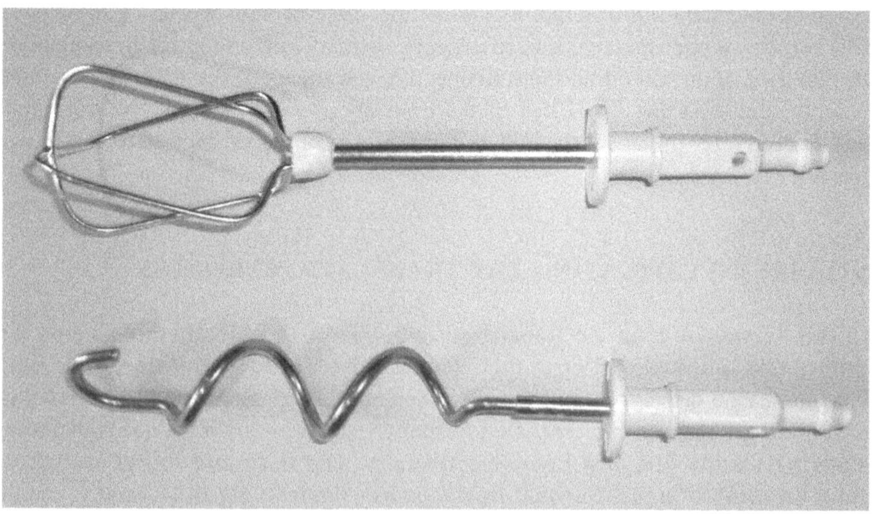

Figure 8.6: The beaters

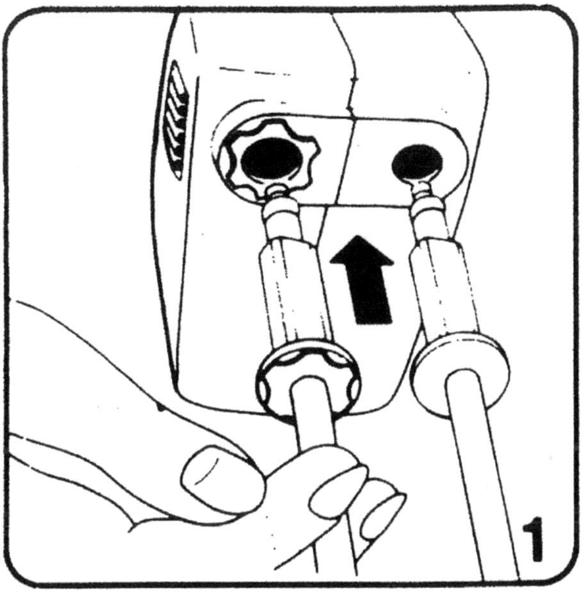

Figure 8.7: Inserting the beaters

will be carrying out what Jakobson calls 'intersemiotic' translation, that is, in this case, going from image to words; if they start from the Italian text, they are carrying out 'interlingual' translation, translation from Italian to English (Jakobson 1959/2004). Whatever source of information the translator has at their disposal (let us imagine they have all of them), metonymic processing offers solutions to both of the problems identified above.

Metonymy allows access to the meaning of the whole by highlighting a single aspect or part. Here, to distinguish between the different types of beater, the writer can choose to refer to the SHAPE or the ACTION IT PERFORMS or the TYPE OF MIXTURE it is used on. The shape can be described as 'spiral' (or 'hooked') versus 'cage-shaped' (or 'box-shaped'); the action can be described as 'whisking' (or 'whipping' or 'beating') versus 'kneading'; and the type of mixture can be described as 'batter' (or 'pancake mix') versus 'dough'. All these offer potential solutions and there are certainly others to choose from as well. The distinctive pattern which identifies the right beater and the hole in the body of the appliance which it goes into also present translation problems which can also be solved using metonymy. It can be described as 'crown-shaped', 'cog-like', 'toothed', etc. The expression used in the Italian text, *corona dentata*, literally means 'toothed crown'.

The Italian text—probably itself a translation—describes the beaters as *spirali frullatrici* (literally = spirals blending) versus *spirali impastatrici* (literally = spirals kneading), but adds glosses to these terms: *impasto di farina ecc* (literally

= mixture of flour etc) versus *impasto tipo panificacione ecc* (literally = mixture type breadmaking etc). The strategy of using glosses rather than single terms, used presumably because the unglossed terms were not felt to be descriptive enough, because the term and its gloss are near equivalents, is itself metonymic; as is the use of 'etc', as this signals that this is an example standing for a class of phenomena. The literal equivalents given above in parentheses, as 'literally = ', are direct translations of the sort an Italian-English dictionary would offer. They are useful in suggesting lexis and adding to the choices available to the translator, but are seldom the best solutions and rarely appear in the final text. In fact, translator trainers often discourage students from using dictionaries, other than technical glossaries, except as a last resort, thereby recognizing that non-literal metonymic translations are to be favoured over literal word-for-word substitutions.

The unusual formulations and typographical errors in the Italian text suggest it has not been written by an Italian native speaker. When the translator is reading the text for the first time and is compensating for the unusual formulations and typographical errors, this is another way in which they are required to process metonymically. The translator has to adjust to what they read, even if it is unexpected, eg replacing *mattere* with 'mettere', *insere* with 'inserire' and *panificacione* with 'panificazione', changes machine translation software is notoriously unable to deal with. This shows that many aspects of a translator's metonymic competence would be drawn upon in carrying out this translation exercise.

Study 2: *Le Figaro* article

This study is based on a translation done in March 2009 by Alexander (anonymized), an MA translation student at a London University. I asked him to let me have an example of a translation he had done for one of his translation classes, and provide me with the source text, his first draft in English and the final version he submitted. The translation he chose was of an article from the French newspaper *Le Figaro* from 2002. Alexander observed that keeping a first draft is not something a translator normally does and that he therefore had to make a conscious effort to provide one. When he gave me the material, I took the opportunity to conduct a retrospective interview with him in which, with the texts in front of us, I asked him to take me through his working practice when doing translations, and explain particularly the process of going from source text to first draft and first draft to final version for this task. Below are extracts from the material he gave me (emphasis added by the author):

> SOURCE TEXT
>
> Ce n'est pas parce que les grandes vacances ont commencé depuis le début du mois que toutes les écoles ont **mis la clef sous le paillasson**. Depuis 11 ans, près de 500 **établissements** s'engagent à accueillir des élèves en dehors du **strict cadre scolaire**, les mercredis et les samedis au cours de l'année mais également durant les vacances, dans le cadre du programme « école ouverte ».
>
> (*Le Figaro*, 20 July 2002:6)

First Draft

It is not that because the long holiday started at the beginning of the month that all the schools **have put the key under the doormat**. For eleven years about 500 **establishments** have started receiving pupils **outside the strict school framework** on Wednesdays and Saturdays during the year, but also during the holidays, in the frame of the 'open school' programme.

Final Version

Although the school holidays began at the beginning of the month, not all schools have **locked their doors**. For eleven years now, about 500 schools have been running **extra classes, outside the regular curriculum**. They run on Wednesdays and Saturdays, both during the school year and during the holidays, as part of the 'open school' programme.

In the sequence source text → first draft → final version we see two 'moves', both involving metonymic shifts in meaning; but whereas the move from the original text to the first draft involves a shift *away* from the meaning of the original text, the move from the first draft to the final version involves a shift *back* to the meaning of the original text. I am calling the first a 'shift away', because a consequence of the transfer from French to English is the generation of a lot of unwanted indeterminacy, or 'fuzziness', while the 'shift back' resolves this, reducing the haze of indeterminacy around the text. The 'shift away' is made up of many individual micro-shifts at word level, caused by many different factors but mainly arising from source language features being retained in the first draft—syntactical features, partial coincidence of categories between languages and effects from cognates (words which look the same). The 'shift back' in the final text is similarly made up of many individual micro-shifts. This is mainly driven by the translator's wish to achieve a final version which is internally coherent rather than faithful to the source text, as Alexander testifies: "I had another look at the text [ie the original], just briefly, to check I hadn't gone off at a tangent somewhere!" (Alexander, interview, 16 March 2009). The expressions in bold in the extract above illustrate these shifts particularly well and are presented again below to show the two 'moves' more clearly. Because the first draft expressions, *put the key under the doormat, establishments, strict school framework*, are more or less literal translations, I have not given any additional explanation of the French, though because they are literal translations, they shift the meaning 'away'; while the final version expressions, *locked their doors, schools, regular curriculum*, are clearly different expressions but shift the meaning 'back'.

mis la clef sous le paillasson	Source text
put the key under the doormat	First draft
locked their doors	Final version

établissements	Source text
establishments	First draft
schools	Final version
strict cadre scolaire	Source text
strict school framework	First draft
regular curriculum	Final version

Study 3: Food Store Promotion Text

Estelle (anonymized), the informant in this study, is an experienced freelance translator working in Germany. As in the previous study, she was asked to make available to me a translation, together with the original text and an early draft. The translation she chose was the text of a publicity website which she had been working on for a fine food store. She delivered this to me via email a few days after submitting it to the client in January 2010. As with Alexander, she was asked to participate in a retrospective post-task interview to discuss the translation, which was conducted on the phone a day after I received her email. In it, both Estelle and I had the texts in front of us and the comments she made were mainly elicited from questions I posed. Below is a page of the original German text, her first draft in English and her final version (emphasis added by the author):

Source Text

In einer Zeit, in der **Marken, Werbebotschaften und Produkte** immer austauschbarer werden, bekommt die Frage nach Authentizität, Individualität und Qualität eine besondere Bedeutung. Die Suche nach dem Echten, dem Wahrhaftigen rückt dabei in den Mittelpunkt. Immer schon ist dies der Anspruch des Familien-unternehmens K——gewesen, Stammhaus veredelten Spitzenkaffees und Treffpunkt von Gourmets aus aller Welt seit Generationen: Es geht bei K——nicht um schnelle Trends oder Moden, sondern immer um die Konsequenz der Qualität. Sie ist die eigentliche Herausforderung, Außergewöhnliches hervorzubringen. Mit **Liebe** zum Detail, **Respekt** vor dem Fachwissen der Mitarbeiter und **Stolz** auf eine lebendige Tradition wird dieses Unternehmen geführt. Denn Qualität und Service erster Klasse sind hier. Berufung und Passion. Jeden Tag.

First Draft

At a time when **brands, advertising slogans and products** are becoming increasingly interchangeable, the demand for authenticity, individuality and quality is assuming great importance. The search for something real, for something genuine, is becoming the focal point. This has however always been the standard pursued by the K—— family-run business; for generations the parent house of the finest coffees and a meeting place for gourmets

> from around the world. At K——, it is not passing trends or fashions that count but persistent quality. This is the real challenge: to create something extraordinary. This company is run with great **attention** to detail, **respect** for the expert knowledge of its employees and **pride** in its living tradition. The company is passionate about first-class quality and service. This is its calling—day in, day out.

Final Version

> At a time when **products, brands and slogans** are becoming increasingly interchangeable, the demand for authenticity, individuality and quality assumes an even greater importance. The contemporary thirst for the real, the genuine, has always been a goal at the family-run Swabian firm of K——. Producing fine coffees for generations and providing a meeting place for gourmets from all round the world, K—— represents enduring quality, not passing trends. A **pride** in a living tradition and the wish to produce something truly extraordinary, a **love** for detail and a **respect** for the expertise of its staff, a **passion** for quality and first-class service are all constantly pursued.

In the first draft, *Marken, Werbebotschaften und Produkte* in the first line of the passage is translated as *brands, advertising slogans and products* (Line 1), a fairly literal substitution, term for term, of the original, but in the final version this becomes *products, brands and slogans*. When asked why she made this choice, Estelle said:

> It just sounds better, more logical. It is like a sequence, first the most general 'product', then 'brand', more specific, and then the actual words they use in their advertising, 'slogan'. I took off 'advertising' because it doesn't really add anything.
>
> (Estelle, telephone interview, 20 January 2010)

And when asked what role the source text played in going from the first draft to the final version, she said she hardly consulted it at all and only went back to the original by way of a "quality check" before sending it off (Estelle, telephone interview, 20 January 2010). The words *Liebe* (love), *Respekt* (respect) and *Stolz* (pride) towards the end of the passage become *attention, respect* and *pride* in the first draft, and *pride, love, respect* and *passion* in the final version. When asked about this, Estelle commented:

> I know. It didn't seem to matter what order they came in, 'pride', 'love', 'passion'. I just moved them around until I could hang the rest of the paragraphs on them in a way which seemed logical [laugh].
>
> (Estelle, telephone interview, 20 January 2010)

This idea of 'moving words around', relying on the recognition of relatedness between concepts in the same unit of text, is a highly metonymic notion.

In the interview, Estelle identified a passage in another section of the translation, which had presented difficulties for her, which she wanted to talk about. The problem revolved around the word *Provenienzen*, literally 'provenances':

> Source text
>
> . . . Über 1,500 **Provenienzen** werden hier präsentiert. Dabei liegt der Schwerpunkt auf den klassischen Weinanbau-gebieten wie Frankreich, Italien, Deutschland und Österreich. . . .
>
> First draft
>
> The wine and spirits department is one of the favourites in the food hall. It stocks wines from over 1,500 different **sources**. The main focus is however on wines **from** the classical wine-growing areas of France, Italy, Germany and Austria.
>
> Final version
>
> The wine and spirits department is one of the favourites in the food hall. It stocks over 1500 different wines, specializing in wines **from** the classic wine-growing **areas** of France, Italy, Germany and Austria.

She says about this:

> I found that particularly difficult. What do I do about the 'provenances'? I can't say "from 1,500 different vineyards" because I don't know if that's true. I don't know they *are* different. First I put "It stocks wines from over 1,500 different sources", but then I changed it to "it stocks over 1500 different wines" without specifying further, and merging it with the next sentence, "specializing in wines from the classic wine-growing areas of France, Italy, Germany and Austria".
>
> (Estelle, telephone interview, 20 January 2010)

What Estelle does is to use metonymic shifts to solve the problem around the word *Provenienzen*. In the first draft, she instinctively distributes the meaning features of the original word to other lexical items, in a way which is reminiscent of Nida's componential-analysis approach (Nida 1964), and modifies this further in the final version to avoid the duplication of the feature FROM, as shown below. These moves all involve metonymic shifts which are operating below the level of whole-word meaning:

> Source text
>
> *Provenienzen* = PLACE; FROM
> (= *provenances*)

FIRST DRAFT

source	= PLACE; ~~FROM~~
from	= FROM

FINAL VERSION

area	= PLACE
from	= FROM

Study 4: Website for a Marketing Company

The informant for this study is the same as for Study 3, Estelle. Here again she was asked to provide an original text, a first draft and a final version, and to discuss the translation in a retrospective post-task interview on the phone. The text is from the promotion website for a German marketing company. The material was sent by email to me a day after being completed in February 2010 and the interview was conducted the same day. This time, instead of supplying the complete texts, Estelle sent me only certain passages she had identified as 'tricky'; and instead of giving just one first draft, she gave me the various options she had considered before writing the first version. She then explained how she came to make the choices she did in an interview which this time was more led by her than in response to my questions. Among the items we discussed was a heading in the text, *Feiner Papierwaren*:

EXTRACT 1

SOURCE TEXT

Feiner Papierwaren

FIRST DRAFT

Fine paperware/ Fine paper goods/ Fine paper products/ Fine stationery/ Quality stationery

A number of possibilities suggested themselves to Estelle (in her 'working memory') for each of the two words in the heading: for *Feiner* she has 'fine' and 'quality'; and for *Papierwaren* she has 'paperware', 'paper goods', 'paper products' and 'stationery'. It is the process of comparing these terms with each other in relation to the German words and as noun-noun constructions which allows her to find a solution. Estelle describes her thought process:

> I think 'paperware' and 'paper goods' sound too ordinary, and 'stationery' suggests just envelopes and business letterheads, that sort of thing, but they do a lot more than that.
>
> (Estelle, telephone interview, 27 February 2010)

The choice she made for the final version was *Fine Paper Products*. To get there, she chose from among two groups of metonymically-related words, making her choices according to connotations she wanted to exclude rather than from any clear sense that one of the choices was the perfect match. The second extract also contains a title with two elements, *Verpackung* and *Marken*:

> **Extract 2**
>
> Source text
>
> **Verpackung** für **Marken**
> N—— macht Verpackungen für Marc O'Polo, Porsche Design, Daimler, Strenesse, Hugo Boss, **Porzellanmanufaktur Meissen**, viele weitere **international tätige Unternehmen** und **gerne auch für Sie**.
>
> First draft
>
> **Packaging the brand/ Packaging brand names/ Packaging proprietary brands/ Brand-name packaging** N—— creates packaging for Marc O'Polo, Porsche Design, Daimler, Strenesse, Hugo Boss, the **Meissen porcelain factory/ Meissen** and many other **companies which operate internationally/ international companies. And for you too?/ We would be happy to produce packaging for you too.**

For *Verpackung*, the only possibility which presented itself was 'packaging'. For *Marken*, she had 'brand', 'proprietary brand' and 'brand name'. The solution she ended up with was 'packaging brand names', for the reasons she gives:

> I felt 'proprietary brand' sounds like washing powder and 'brand' is too general. Actually, I chose 'packaging brand names', rather than looking for anything more fancy, because it is close to the original, and I know the guy who checks these things gets nervous if it is too different, even if there is actually a better translation!
>
> (Estelle, telephone interview, 27 February 2010)

Thus, the checker is using relatedness as one of their criteria for assessing quality. The other choices in this extract—'the Meissen porcelain factory' versus 'Meissen'; 'companies which operate internationally' versus 'international companies' and 'And for you too?' versus 'We would be happy to produce packaging for you too'—again reflect the constant involvement of the translator with closely-related alternatives and the need to choose between them.

CONCLUSION

The Metonymic Theory of Translation presented in this chapter offers a new paradigm, Translation as Metonymy. In it, metonymy, metonymic shifts and metonymic processing play a central role. It explores the explanatory power a general theory of metonymic meaning making can have for the special case of translation. Two areas of translation theory are reframed in the discussion, Metaphor in Translation (MiT) and 'shift theory'. The focus of figurative thought/language in translation is moved from metaphor to metonymy. Figurativeness is reframed as being at the core of translation, not at its margins; the inherent metonymic relations between different languages and varieties of the same language are not only a fact of life but are what makes translation possible at all. The idea of translation 'shift' is also reframed; it is argued that shift theory does not go far enough as it is restricted to instances where differences stand out but should be extended to all of translation. Written translation usually involves two stages: one involves 'transfer' from one language system to another; the other is an editing stage, involving interlingual metonymic processing and intralingual metonymic processing respectively. The four studies considered above show the key role that metonymy plays in the text-to-text transfer of meaning. They show that translation involves metonymy in a number of different senses: in making the original source text, because of the inherent indeterminacy of language and the metonymic nature of meaning making through language; when comparing fragments of the original text with possible solutions in the target language; in solving specific problems through metonymic processing; in making choices which are motivated by metonymic frames in the conceptual system (ie 'conceptual metonymies'); and in the process of revising the first draft formulations to meet text receptor expectations.

In the final chapter, I look at how the metonymic approach laid out in this book might be developed further and how it might lead to the founding of a field of metonymic research with an application to human activities which lie outside linguistics and applied language studies.

9 Metonymics

In this chapter, I give a summary of the achievements of the book as a whole. To do this, I highlight the advantages of exploring a metonymic approach to language and communication and list the insights this offers language professionals. I then outline how a new discipline, based on metonymic principles, might be developed, and how such a programme could serve as a useful tool of investigation and research in different fields. I give examples of the application of metonymy-based research in areas within language studies, not considered in previous chapters, and in further areas of practice outside language studies.

The present book was driven by a desire to explain how such flexibility and subtlety of expression is achieved in language, given the limitations on the linguistic resources available to us, and what it is in the design of the language system which makes it so ideally fit for purpose. I have suggested that the answer to this conundrum is our ability to metonymize, the ability to recognize and manipulate part-whole relatedness between signs and parts of signs. The purpose of this book has been to explore the phenomenon of metonymy in the widest and most inclusive sense, without extending the notion so far that it becomes debased or unworkable, without it becoming a "raggle-taggle collection", a "common dumping ground" (Bredin 1984:47). Metonymy exploits the partial nature of 'the sign' to create new ways of referring, new ways of giving emphasis and new ways of responding to the speaker's need to abbreviate and condense, to skip over familiar avenues of thought which would otherwise be too time-consuming to repeat. It is not only inevitable that language under-refers, but desirable. Exploiting indeterminacy through metonymic processing gives flexibility in language, as Brown recognizes: "the underdetermination of most word-meanings when they are considered in isolation [. . .] contributes a necessary flexibility to human language. Such a flexibility enables the communication of new thoughts" (Brown 1995:16). I have demonstrated in this book that linguistic theory can be reconfigured by using metonymy as an instrument for investigation; that metonymy plays an essential role in communication at different levels within the language hierarchy; and that metonymy seems to occupy a central role in a whole range of social and recreational activities, such that it becomes what the activity is about. I have suggested that engagement in these activities is perhaps an unconscious acknowledgement of the significance of metonymy in our lives. In applied linguistics,

I have shown how discourse analysis, language learning and translation can be recast in terms of metonymy, and how a focus on small changes based on near approximations enables the exploration of notions such as 'metonymic processing', 'metonymic thinking' and 'metonymic competence'. What is the import of this in practical terms? For speakers generally, it means that speech is characterized more as performance than encoding/decoding and that utterances created 'on the fly' are best judged in terms of being 'adequate' rather than being 'correct'. It means that learners who benefit from an awareness of metonymy can be encouraged to abandon the straightjacket of literality and embrace a freer, more fluent approach to language production. The practical benefit for translators is that they can turn what seem at first to be obstacles into solutions; they can be encouraged to abandon the idea that translation is a matter of exact equivalents and embrace the freedom offered by appreciating translation in terms of metonymic relatedness. This metonymic approach offers a new paradigm, and challenges old paradigms, giving a different perspective on the aims of teaching, testing and training in these areas.

I now want to outline how the ideas presented in this book might be taken further by describing how a new discipline based on metonymic principles might be developed. The picture built up in this book has metonymy playing a fundamental role at many levels of meaning making and in many contexts. Metonymy as a guiding principle can be taken beyond the field of language studies to provide a powerful research tool and practical instrument for re-evaluating issues and solving problems in many other areas of human endeavour. I suggest we might call this new field based on metonymic principles, 'Metonymics'. The emergence of Metonymy Studies as a field in its own right reflects the burgeoning interest in metonymy in recent years. This would provide the foundation for the new discipline of Metonymics. Its growth might take a similar trajectory to that of Metaphor Studies, which grew through collaborations across disciplines and interest generated through research groups, conferences, associations, publications and university teaching. Like Metaphor Studies, Metonymics would acknowledge traditional rhetoric and poetics, while drawing on developments in discourse analysis, psycholinguistics, corpus linguistics, computational linguistics and cognitive linguistics.

I now propose to look at a number of areas within language studies, not considered so far in this book, which demonstrate the application of Metonymics. First, Critical Discourse Analysis: in this branch of discourse analysis, which uncovers social inequities by denaturalizing language, competing ideologies are often presented as if they were independent realities and as if words for those separate realities are taken from distinct 'bins'. Metonymics, instead, would view this in a different way: that there is one reality and one code with which to talk about that reality, and that differences in position are expressed by choosing different but metonymically-related words from the shared code. The second area I want to consider here is language analysis in journalism and politics, in particular 'spin'. This can similarly be seen in terms of metonymic choices made from items available to both parties, in order to emphasize certain aspects over others, rather than the journalist or politician mischievously misrepresenting a situation by choosing the 'wrong' term. The 'spun' and 'unspun' versions are related and come about through speakers using metonymically-based choices in their manipulation of codes. A third example is the differences between dialects, language varieties and Creoles. When American English and British English are contrasted using a metonymic approach, the comparison becomes far more interesting than it is usually presented. Differences which seem random and trivial, such as differences of naming, a matter of lists, become differences which reflect the essential nature of things, in all their richness, and reflect the partial nature of meaning making through signs. The two expressions *law enforcement officer* and *policeman* share aspects of reality and are not merely unrelated labels. A further example of the application of Metonymics is in helping us understand how 'identity' is expressed through language, the variation offered by metonymy allowing us to display 'cultural capital' and adopt different 'subject positions', in Block's sense (Block 2007:40).

Metonymics has a particular application to Second Language Acquisition. Vygotsky's concept of 'scaffolding' is suggestive of metonymy, as it characterizes learning as a series of stages rather than a 'one-off' process, where what is new is added to what is known. Vygotsky famously names the locus of its occurrence the 'zone of proximal development', a learning space created by social context, "the distance between the actual development level as determined by independent problem solving and the level of potential development as determined through adult guidance or in collaboration with more capable peers" (Vygotsky in Ellis 2008:983). This zone could be reframed as a zone of "active metonymic processing". Selinker's concept of 'interlanguage' (Selinker 1972) and Schmidt's concept of 'noticing the gap' (Schmidt 1990) are other concepts from Second Language Acquisition studies which can be interpreted in terms of metonymy. 'Interlanguage', "the systematic knowledge of an L2 which is independent of both the learner's L1 and the target language" (Ellis 2008:968), suggests a metonymic relationship between the learner's 'interlanguage' and the target language a learner is striving to learn, the learner's interlanguage being a blend of features of the first and second languages. In this characterization of learning, 'errors' reflect necessary stages in learning rather than accidental lapses, and are the result of "the intermingling of [. . .] core sources of knowledge" (Holme 2004:197). Taking this further, we might say that there is a metonymic relationship between the different stages of the learner's interlanguage as it changes over time, and between innate Universal Grammar-type representations of language and real-language grammars. The metonymic progression through versions of interlanguage and the ability to replace one version with a closely related version permits learning to proceed towards a final 'stable' version of the target language. The concept of 'noticing the gap' is the ability to notice differences between what is known and what is new, allowing learners to identify novel items when they encounter them and add them to what they already know. Observing these associations forms part of Schmidt's 'noticing skills' (Ellis 2008:973). Schmidt observes that "people learn about the things they attend to and do not learn much about the things they do not attend to" (Schmidt in Ellis 2008:973). Noticing 'gaps' means monitoring for metonymy, observing similarities and partial overlaps. These may be differences of phonology, morphology, syntax, lexis, phraseology, markedness, register and voice, or arise through overuse and restricted use. What is learned will overlap to some extent with what is known, certain elements only being repeated: "learning coming from repetition where an element is changed" (Cook 2000:30). Metonymics permits the researcher to overview concepts in SLA and show a commonality across a range of different issues; comparisons are easier to make and issues easier to draw out by the use of this instrument.

'Complexity theory', a holistic approach to understanding change in complex systems, originally developed within the natural sciences, has been applied to Second Language Acquisition, notably by Larsen-Freeman (Saville-Troike 2012:86). Complexity theory (and 'chaos theory') explains how change in complex systems comes about; when applied to Second Language Acquisition, it suggests a common theory of learning in which language acquisition, whether first or second, is little different from other types of learning, and plays down the extent to which language learning relies on innate knowledge. Complexity-theory scholars emphasize the interdependence of the different components of language and propose that the process of learning involves the gradual ordering and organizing of these components with respect to the learner's understanding of the language system as a whole. Metonymics would reframe this approach in terms of metonymic processing. It would suggest that the dynamic ordering and organizing of components in a complex system involves a metonymic process, and that the ability to recognize relatedness between components is at the heart of (language) learning.

Metonymics can be used to reframe and re-evaluate situations, resolve paradoxes and offer solutions to problems in areas beyond linguistics, such as politics, social services, psychotherapy, international development, intercultural communication, arbitration, reconciliation and conflict resolution. Metonymics can help us understand the world by exposing problems which are created by the straightjacket of sharply-defined categories, or what Dawkins describes as "the tyranny of the discontinuous mind" (Dawkins 2011). He lists 'defining poverty', 'deciding where university-degree classification-lines are drawn', 'whether proportional representation voting systems are fair,' 'when an embryo becomes a baby', 'the reliability of weather forecasting' and 'safety testing of new drugs' as examples where 'platonic essentialism', the distinctness of categories, has confused matters (Dawkins 2010). I will now consider areas beyond linguistics, where applying a metonymic perspective to real-world situations could provide a useful framework for research and training. The areas I consider are law, art, mathematics and natural sciences.

In law, the use of precedents in coming to judgements is suggestive of metonymy, judges, barristers and lawyers being involved in the comparison of the particular case they are working on with previous similar cases. Some lawyers claim they merely interpret existing law rather than create new laws, that they give ex post facto rationalizations based on precedent; but their judgements are in effect prescribing new laws. Metonymics would elucidate the processes by which such new laws are made, providing an analysis of the shifts in thought involved and how such shifts are reflected in the language used to codify them. The notion of 'beyond reasonable doubt' also suggests metonymic work is required of those passing judgement, an assessment of where the case in hand lies on a scale between a situation for which there is and is not conclusive evidence. In the philosophy of law, Kelsen's concept of *grundnormen*, fundamental hypothetical rules of law to which all laws can be reduced (Kelsen 1970), is also suggestive of a metonymic approach, whereby a metonymic relationship is sought between an existing law and a prototypical *grundnorm*.

A metonymic approach to art is easy to envisage. The history of art is a story of changes in perception and visualization of images through incremental changes resulting in paradigm shifts in style. The practical reality of making artworks involves the artist in constant manipulations, shifts and substitutions which allow them to achieve their message. Collages are prime examples of metonymic work, such as the parody of the Sgt. Pepper album cover (Figure 5.1). The way people relate to images, thanks to digital photography, is another example of how metonymic processing is part of everyday life. Holidaymakers in documenting their holidays engage in metonymic processing when they periodically look through their photographs, perhaps many hundreds of images, and choose among similar images. Deciding which images to keep and which to delete, or choosing how to crop or reformat an image before printing, involves metonymic processing.

Many concepts in mathematics can be reframed in terms of metonymy. Algorithms and statistics both have at their core functions expressed in terms of partial correspondences and overlaps, though perhaps none more so than calculus. In calculus, continuous functions are understood in terms of a large number of infinitesimal differences, the line of a curve being described in terms of infinitely small but overlapping parts which add up to the whole, a concept suggestive of Metonymics. Fuzzy logic, too, the mimicking by machines of human manipulations, using combinations of basic-level choices, is resonant of Metonymics, such as washing machines programmed to carry out hundreds of possible wash programmes, depending on factors such as weight, absorbency and dirtiness of the washing.

In the natural sciences, the classification of plants and animals is a metonymic processing activity, the relatedness and sharing of features between specimens being used as the basis for deciding to which family, genus or species a plant or animal belongs. Observing the similarity of physical features of plants and animals to draw up taxonomies has been an activity pursued by natural scientists since before Linnaeus; while in more recent times, the similarity in chemical constituents of plants and animals has been used to consolidate and modify existing taxonomies. Metonymics also helps explain why taxonomists often favour traditional illustrations over photographs, as a single illustration can offer a prototypical representation, containing all the distinctive features of a plant species, while a vast number of different photographs would need to be consulted in order to represent the same variation. Botanical and zoological illustrations use metonymy to 'caricature' the features in order to disambiguate species and genera. Darwin's theory of evolution through natural selection looks at how relatedness between organisms can lead over time to dramatic differences, how incremental change results in the 'mutability of species'. It is an example par excellence of a metonymic theory, perhaps the most striking example of a metonymic approach changing our understanding of the world and a single metonymic theory explaining a vast array of data.

It would be fitting at this point to ask where the limits to Metonymics can be drawn. If metonymy is so common and seems to have an application in so many contexts, in which contexts would Metonymics not be useful or appropriate? My response is that I feel Metonymics is best seen as a research tool rather than a body of knowledge. This is a position which metaphor scholars have taken increasingly with regard to metaphor, eg Cameron (2010:7). Thus, there is no reason to set limits on where Metonymics might be applied, as it would soon become apparent when a metonymic approach did not deliver. We might also ask why, given the importance of metonymy, has a discipline such as Metonymics not already been established? I suggest that it is because metonymy, in many of its manifestations, operates 'behind the scenes', that it is part of the mechanics of how communication is enabled and how the fine-tuning of interaction is facilitated. Because of that, it has not been the obvious place to start, it has taken some time to uncover its role and its significance, it has lain undetected for so long because it is such a basic manipulation and therefore one which does not readily reveal itself. It could perhaps be compared to the idea of dedicating decades of research to molecules, only to realize that molecules are made up of atoms, and that it is with atoms that the key lies. A parallel example is the late emergence of interest in restricted collocations. According to Howarth, collocation escaped the notice of linguists for so long as a consequence of our tendency to concentrate on the extreme ends rather than the 'middle ground': "Linguists and teachers have traditionally concentrated their attention on the extreme ends of the spectrum: free combinations and idioms. [. . .] The large and complex middle ground of restricted collocations (not generally recognized as a pedagogically significant category) is often regarded as an unrelated residue of arbitrary co-occurrences and familiar phrases" (Howarth 1998:42). If we apply this image of a spectrum to the present context, metonymy represents the middle ground, literal language and metaphor the extreme ends.

This book has touched on issues around the nature of knowledge. In the discussions of the Metaphor Studies literature in Chapter 3 and Translation Studies literature in Chapter 8, I make the point that theories in these fields are better considered complementary than competing, that each scholar contributes a valid but partial truth to the subject, offering a 'polytheism' of 'multiple theories' (Block 1999:145). The issue of the compatibility of 'rival' theories came to the fore in Metaphor Studies recently, when Lakoff and Fauconnier published a short piece in 2010 in order to disabuse others of the perception that their theories were 'rival' theories, and to make clear that their positions and their work were "entirely compatible" (Fauconnier & Lakoff 2010:3). I revisit the idea of the compatibility of theories here to make a further claim for the scope of Metonymics, that knowledge creation itself can benefit from a metonymic approach. The words used in the discussion above, such as 'complementary' and 'partial truth', the idea that different theories represent different aspects of a phenomenon and that they contribute to the understanding of the phenomenon 'as a whole', are describing knowledge in terms of metonymy. This is a Metonymic Theory of Knowledge and one which informs the book.

Bibliography

Aitchison, J. (1994). *Words in the mind: An introduction to the mental lexicon* (2nd ed.). Oxford: Blackwell.

Aitchison, J. (2008). *The articulate mammal. Introduction to psycholinguistics* (5th ed.). London: Routledge.

Allsop, J., & Woods, L. (1990). *Making sense of idioms*. London: Cassell.

Al-Sharafi, A. (2004). *Textual metonymy: A semiotic approach*. Basingstoke: Palgrave.

Altenberg, B. (1998). On the phraseology of spoken English: The evidence of recurrent word combinations. In A. Cowie (Ed.), *Phraseology: Theory, analysis and applications* (pp. 101–122). Oxford: Clarendon Press.

Anderson, J. (1983). *The architecture of cognition*. Cambridge, MA: Harvard University Press.

Ayto, J. (1986). Fig. leaves: Metaphor in dictionaries. In Mary Snell-Hornby (Ed.), *ZüriLEX '86 proceedings: Papers Read at the EURALEX International Congress, University of Zürich, 9–14 September 1986*, 49–54.

Baker, M. (1992). *In other words: A coursebook on translation*. London: Routledge.

Baker, M., & Saldanha, G. (Eds.). (2009). *The Routledge encyclopedia of translation studies*. London: Routledge.

Barcelona, A. (Ed.). (2000). *Metaphor and metonymy at the crossroads*. Berlin: Mouton de Gruyter.

Barcelona, A. (2002). Clarifying and applying the notions of metaphor and metonymy within cognitive linguistics: An update. In R. Dirven & R. Pörings (Eds.), *Metaphor and metonymy in comparison and contrast* (pp. 207–277). Berlin: Mouton de Gruyter.

Barcelona, A. (2005). The role of metonymy in discourse-pragmatic inferencing. In J. Otal Campo, I. Navarro i Ferrando & B. Bellés Fortuña (Eds.), *Cognitive and discourse approaches to metaphor and metonymy* (pp. 29–44). Castello de la Plana: Universitat Jaume I.

Barcelona, A. (2009). Motivation of construction meaning and form: The role of metonymy and inference. In K. Panther, L. Thornburg & A. Barcelona (Eds.), *Metonymy and metaphor in grammar* (pp. 363–399). Amsterdam: John Benjamins.

Barnden, J. (2006). Metaphor and metonymy: A practical deconstruction. Retrieved on 10 June 2011 from ftp://ftp.cs.bham.ac.uk/pub/tech-reports/2006/CSRP-06–1.ps.gz

Bartsch, R. (2002). Generating polysemy: Metaphor and metonymy. In R. Dirven & R. Pörings (Eds.), *Metaphor and metonymy in comparison and contrast* (pp. 49–74). Berlin: Mouton de Gruyter.

Bassnett, S. (2002). *Translation studies* (3rd ed.). London: Routledge.

Beaugrande, R. de, & Dressler, W. (1981). *Introduction to text linguistics*. Harlow: Longman.

Bell, R. (1991). *Translating and translation: Theory and practice*. Harlow: Longman.

Bell, R. (1998). Psycholinguistic/cognitive approaches. In M. Baker (Ed.), *Routledge encyclopedia of translation studies* (pp. 185–190). London: Routledge.

Bernardini, S. (1999). Using think-aloud protocols to investigate the translation process: Methodological aspects. *Research Centre for English and Applied Linguistics, Working Papers, 6,* 179–199. University of Cambridge. Retrieved on 11 November 2011 from www.rceal.cam.ac.uk/Publications/Working/Vol6/Bernardini.pdf

Bierwiaczonek, B. (2013). *Metonymy in language, thought and brain.* Sheffield: Equinox.

Black, M. (1962). *Models and metaphors.* Ithaca, NY: Cornell University Press.

Black, M. (1993). More about metaphor. In A. Ortony (Ed.), *Metaphor and thought* (2nd ed., pp. 19–41). Cambridge: Cambridge University Press.

Blank, A. (1999). Co-presence and succession: A cognitive typology of metonymy. In K. Panther & G. Radden (Eds.), *Metonymy in language and thought* (pp. 169–191). Amsterdam: John Benjamins.

Block, D. (1999). Who framed SLA research? Problem framing and metaphoric accounts of the SLA research process. In L. Cameron & G. Low (Eds.), *Researching and applying metaphor* (pp. 135–148). Cambridge: Cambridge University Press.

Block, D. (2007). *Second language identities.* London: Continuum.

Blommaert, J. (2005). *Discourse*. Cambridge: Cambridge University Press.

Bowdle, B., & Gentner, D. (2005). The career of metaphor. *Psychological Review, 112,* 193–216.

Bredin, H. (1984). Metonymy. *Poetics Today, 5*(1), 45–58.

Brdar, M. (2009). Metonymies we live without. In K. Panther, L. Thornburg & A. Barcelona (Eds.), *Metonymy and metaphor in grammar* (pp. 259–274). Amsterdam: John Benjamins.

Brdar-Szabó, R., & Brdar, M. (2011). What do metonymic chains reveal about the nature of metonymy? In R. Benczes, A. Barcelona & F. Ruiz de Mendoza (Eds.), *Defining metonymy in cognitive linguistics: Towards a consensus view* (pp. 217–248). Amsterdam: John Benjamins.

Broeck, R. van den. (1981). The limits of translatability exemplified by metaphor translation. *Poetics Today, 2*(4), 73–87.

Brown, G. (1995). *Speakers, listeners and communication: Explorations in discourse analysis.* Cambridge: Cambridge University Press.

Brown, G., & Yule, G. (1983). *Discourse analysis.* Cambridge: Cambridge University Press.

Brugman, C., & Lakoff, G. (2006). Cognitive topology and lexical networks. In D. Geeraerts (Ed.), *Cognitive linguistics: Basic readings* (pp. 109–139). Berlin: Mouton de Gruyter.

Cameron, D. (1992). *Feminism and linguistic theory.* New York: St Martin's Press.

Cameron, D. (2001). *Working with spoken discourse.* London: Sage.

Cameron, L. (1999). Identifying and describing metaphor in spoken discourse data. In L. Cameron & G. Low (Eds.), *Researching and applying metaphor* (pp. 105–132). Cambridge: Cambridge University Press.

Cameron, L. (2003). *Metaphor in educational discourse*. London: Continuum.

Cameron, L. (2008). Metaphor and talk. In R. Gibbs (Ed.), *The Cambridge handbook of metaphor and thought* (pp. 197–211). Cambridge: Cambridge University Press.

Cameron, L. (2010). What is metaphor and why does it matter? In L. Cameron & R. Maslen (Eds.), *Metaphor analysis: Research practice in applied linguistics, social sciences and the humanities* (pp. 3–25). London: Equinox.

Cameron, L. (2011). *Metaphor and reconciliation: The discourse dynamics of empathy in post-conflict conversations.* London: Routledge.

Cameron, L., & Deignan, A. (2006). The emergence of metaphor in discourse. *Applied Linguistics, 27*(4), 671–690.

Cameron, L., & Low, G. (1999a). Metaphor—survey article. *Language Teaching, 32*(2), 77–96.

Cameron, L., & Low, G. (1999b). Preface. In L. Cameron & G. Low (Eds.), *Researching and applying metaphor* (pp. xii–xv). Cambridge: Cambridge University Press.

Cameron, L., & Maslen, R. (2010). Identifying metaphors in discourse data. In L. Cameron & R. Maslen (Eds.), *Metaphor analysis: Research practice in applied linguistics, social sciences and the humanities* (pp. 97–115). London: Equinox.

Carston, R. (2002). *Thoughts and utterances: The pragmatics of explicit communication.* Oxford: Blackwell.
Catford, J. (1965). *A linguistic theory of translation.* Oxford: Oxford University Press.
Chandler, D. (2002). *Semiotics: The basics.* London: Routledge.
Chandler, S. (1991). Metaphor comprehension: A connectionist approach to implications for the mental lexicon. *Metaphor and Symbolic Activity, 6*(4), 227–258.
Chomsky, N. (1965). *Aspects of the theory of syntax.* Cambridge, MA: MIT Press.
Cicero. (46BCE). *De optimo genere oratorum.*
Conklin, K., & Schmitt, N. (2008). Formulaic sequences: Are they processed more quickly than non-formulaic language by native and nonnative speakers? *Applied Linguistics, 29*(1), 72–89.
Cook, G. (1989). *Discourse.* Oxford: Oxford University Press.
Cook, G. (2000). *Language play, language learning.* Oxford: Oxford University Press.
Cook, V. (2002). Background to the L2 user. In V. Cook (Ed.), *Portraits of the L2 user* (pp. 1–28). Clevedon: Multilingual Matters.
Cooper, T. (1999). Processing of idioms by L2 learners of English. *TESOL Quarterly, 33*(2), 233–262.
Cornell, A. (1999). Idioms: An approach to identifying major pitfalls for learners. *IRAL, 37*(1), 1–21.
Cottrell, S. (2007). *The exam skills handbook: Achieving peak performance.* Basingstoke: Palgrave Macmillan.
Coulthard, M. (1985). *An introduction to discourse analysis* (2nd ed.). London: Longman.
Coulthard, M. (Ed.). (1994). *Advances in written text analysis.* London: Routledge.
Croft, W. (1993). The role of domains in the interpretation of metaphors and metonymies. *Cognitive Linguistics, 4*(4), 335–370.
Croft, W., & Cruse, D. (2004). *Cognitive linguistics.* Cambridge: Cambridge University Press.
Cronin, M. (1998). Game theory and translation. In M. Baker (Ed.), *Routledge encyclopedia of translation studies* (pp. 91–93). London: Routledge.
Dagut, M. (1976). Can "metaphor" be translated? *Babel, 22*(1), 21–33.
Davidson, D. (1979). What metaphors mean. In S. Sacks (Ed.), *On metaphor* (pp. 29–46). Chicago: University of Chicago Press.
Davitz, J. (1969). *The language of emotion.* New York: Academic Press.
Dawkins, R. (2010). *The greatest show on earth: The evidence for evolution.* London: Black Swan.
Dawkins, R. (2011). The tyranny of the discontinuous mind. *New Statesman,* 19 December 2011 to 1 January 2012, 54–57.
Deignan, A. (1995). *Collins Cobuild English guide 7: Metaphor.* London: Harper Collins.
Deignan, A. (2005). *Metaphor and corpus linguistics.* Amsterdam: John Benjamins.
Deignan, A. (2006). *Contemporary metaphor theory and applications to analysing language.* Paper presented at the Birkbeck Linguistics Circle, London.
Deignan, A. (2008). Corpus linguistics and metaphor. In R. Gibbs (Ed.), *The Cambridge handbook of metaphor and thought* (pp. 280–294). Cambridge: Cambridge University Press.
Dell, G. (1986). A spreading-activation theory of retrieval in sentence production. *Psychological Review, 93,* 283–321.
Dellar, H., & Walkley, A. (2004). *Innovations upper intermediate—A course in natural English.* Boston, MA: Thomson Heinle.
Dellar, H., & Walkley, A. (2010). *Outcomes pre-intermediate—Real English for the real world.* Boston, MA: Heinle Cengage ELT.
Dirven, R. (2002a). Introduction. In R. Dirven & R. Pörings (Eds.), *Metaphor and metonymy in comparison and contrast* (pp. 1–38). Berlin: Mouton de Gruyter.
Dirven, R. (2002b). Metonymy and metaphor: Different mental strategies of conceptualisation. In R. Dirven & R. Pörings (Eds.), *Metaphor and metonymy in comparison and contrast* (pp. 75–111). Berlin: Mouton de Gruyter.

Dirven, R., & Pörings, R. (Eds.). (2002). *Metaphor and metonymy in comparison and contrast*. Berlin: Mouton de Gruyter.

Drew, P., & Holt, E. (1988). Complainable matters: The use of idiomatic expressions in making complaints. *Social Problems, 35*(4), 398–417.

Drew, P., & Holt, E. (1998). Figures in speech: The role of figurative expressions in topic transition in conversation. *Language in Society, 27*(4), 495–523.

Dryden, J. (1680/2004). From the preface to Ovid's epistles. In L. Venuti (Ed.), *The translation studies reader* (2nd ed., pp. 38–42). London: Routledge. (Original work published 1680.)

Eder, D. (1990). Serious and playful disputes: Variation in conflict talk among female adolescents. In A. Grimshaw (Ed.), *Conflict talk: Sociolinguistic investigations of arguments in conversations* (pp. 67–84). Cambridge: Cambridge University Press.

Ellis, R. (2008). *The study of second language acquisition* (2nd ed.). Oxford: Oxford University Press.

Fairclough, N. (1992). Introduction. In N. Fairclough (Ed.), *Critical language awareness.* London: Longman.

Fauconnier, G., & Lakoff, G. (2010). On metaphor and blending. Retrieved on 4 November 2010 from www.cogsci.ucsd.edu/~coulson/spaces/GG-final-1.pdf

Fauconnier, G., & Turner, M. (2002). *The way we think.* New York: Basic Books.

Field, J. (2003). *Psycholinguistics. A resource book for students*. London: Routledge.

Field, J. (2004). *Psycholinguistics: The key concepts*. London: Routledge.

Fillmore, C. (1982/2006). Frame semantics. In D. Geeraerts (Ed.), *Cognitive linguistics: Basic readings* (pp. 373–400). Berlin: Mouton de Gruyter. (Original work published 1982.)

Flower, J. (1993). *Phrasal verb organiser.* Hove: LTP.

Forceville, C. (2008). Metaphor in pictures and multimodal representations. In R. Gibbs (Ed.), *The Cambridge handbook of metaphor and thought* (pp. 462–482). Cambridge: Cambridge University Press.

Fraser, J. (1996). The translator investigated: Learning from translation process analysis. *The Translator, 2*(1), 65–79.

Frege, G. (1892/1960). On sense and reference. In P. Geach & M. Black (Eds.), *The philosophical writings of Gottlob Frege* (pp. 36–56). Oxford: Blackwell. (Original work published 1892.)

Fromkin, V., & Ratner, N. (1993). Speech production. In J. Gleason & N. Ratner (Eds.), *Psycholinguistics* (2nd ed., pp. 309–346). Fort Worth: Harcourt Brace.

Gardner, H. (1983). *Frames of mind.* New York: Basic Books.

Garrett, M. (1988). Processes in language production. In F. Newmeyer (Ed.), *Linguistics: The Cambridge survey* (Vol. III, pp. 69–96). Cambridge: Cambridge University Press.

Gee, J. (2011). *An introduction to discourse analysis: Theory and method* (3rd ed.). London: Routledge.

Geeraerts, D. (Ed.). (2006). *Cognitive linguistics: Basic readings*. Berlin: Mouton de Gruyter.

Gentner, D., & Bowdle, B. (2008). Metaphor as structure-mapping. In R. Gibbs (Ed.), *The Cambridge handbook of metaphor and thought* (pp. 109–128). Cambridge: Cambridge University Press.

Gibbs, R. (1986). Skating on thin ice: Literal meaning and understanding idioms in conversation. *Discourse Processes, 9,* 17–30.

Gibbs, R. (1993). Process and products in making sense of tropes. In A. Ortony (Ed.), *Metaphor and thought* (2nd ed., pp. 252–276). Cambridge: Cambridge University Press.

Gibbs, R. (1994). *The poetics of mind: Figurative thought, language and understanding.* Cambridge: Cambridge University Press.

Gibbs, R. (1999). Speaking and thinking with metonymy. In K. Panther & G. Radden (Eds.), *Metonymy in language and thought* (pp. 61–76). Amsterdam: John Benjamins.

Gibbs, R. (2008). Metaphor and thought: The state of the art. In R. Gibbs (Ed.), *The Cambridge handbook of metaphor and thought* (pp. 3–13). Cambridge: Cambridge University Press.

Gibbs, R. (2011). Are 'deliberate' metaphors really deliberate? *Metaphor in the Social World, 1*(1), 26–52.

Gibbs, R., & Colston, H. (1995). The cognitive psychological reality of image schemas and their transformations. *Cognitive Linguistics, 6*(4), 347–378.

Gibbs, R., & Matlock, T. (2008). Metaphor, imagination and simulation: Psycholinguistic evidence. In R. Gibbs (Ed.), *The Cambridge handbook of metaphor and thought* (pp. 161–176). Cambridge: Cambridge University Press.

Glucksberg, S. (2001). *Understanding figurative language: From metaphors to idioms.* Oxford: Oxford University Press.

Glucksberg, S., & Keysar, B. (1990). Understanding metaphorical comparisons: Beyond similarity. *Psychological Review, 97*(1), 3–18.

Goatly, A. (1993). Species of metaphor in written and spoken varieties. In M. Ghadessy (Ed.), *Register analysis: Theory and practice* (pp. 110–148). London: Pinter.

Goatly, A. (1997). *The language of metaphors.* London: Routledge.

Goddard, C. (2000). Polysemy: A problem of definition. In Y. Ravin & C. Leacock (Eds.), *Polysemy: Theoretical and computational approaches* (pp. 129–151). Oxford: Oxford University Press.

Goossens, L. (1990). Metaphtonymy: The interaction of metaphor and metonymy in expressions for linguistic action. *Cognitive Linguistics, 1*(3), 323–340.

Gournet, M. (2010). A taste of French creole. *Liaison Magazine, 5,* 47–48.

Grady, J. (1997). *Foundations of meaning: Primary metaphors and primary scenes: A dissertation submitted in partial satisfaction of the requirements for the degree of Doctor of Philosophy in linguistics in the Graduate Division of the University of California, Berkeley.* Retrieved on 12 July 2011 from www.il.proquest.com/uni/dissertations/

Grice, P. (1975). Logic and conversation. In P. Cole & J. Morgan (Eds.), *Syntax and semantics* (Vol. 3, Speech Acts, pp. 41–58). New York: Academic Press.

Halliday, M. (1978). *Language as social semiotic: The social interpretation of language and meaning.* London: Edward Arnold.

Halliday, M. (1994). *An introduction to functional grammar* (2nd ed.). London: Edward Arnold.

Halliday, M., & Hasan, R. (1976). *Cohesion in English.* London: Longman.

Handl, S. (2011). *The conventionality of figurative language: A usage-based study.* Tübingen: Narr Verlag.

Hanks, P. (1979). To what extent does a dictionary definition define? In R. Hartmann (Ed.), *Dictionaries and their uses. Exeter papers in lexicography* (pp. 32–38). Exeter: Exeter University Press.

Hatim, B. (2009). Translating text in context. In J. Munday (Ed.), *The Routledge companion to translation studies* (pp. 36–53). London: Routledge.

Hatim, B., & Mason, I. (1990). *Discourse and the translator*. Harlow: Longman.

Hatim, B., & Munday, J. (2004). *Translation: An advanced resource book.* London: Routledge.

Hawkes, T. (1977). *Structuralism and semiotics.* Berkeley: University of California Press.

Hervey, S., & Higgins, I. (1992). *Thinking French translation* (2nd ed.). London: Routledge.

Hill, J. (2000). Revising priorities: From grammatical failure to collocational success. In M. Lewis (Ed.), *Teaching collocation* (pp. 47–69). Boston, MA: Thomson Heinle.

Hoey, M. (2000). A world beyond collocation: New perspectives on vocabulary teaching. In M. Lewis (Ed.), *Teaching collocation* (pp. 224–243). Boston, MA: Thomson Heinle.

Hoey, M. (2001). *Textual interaction: An introduction to written discourse analysis.* London: Routledge.

Holme, R. (2004). *Mind, metaphor and language teaching.* Basingstoke: Palgrave Macmillan.

Holz-Mänttäri, J. (1984). *Translatorisches Handeln: Theorie und methode*. Helsinki: Suomalainen Tiedeakatemia.

Horace. (20BCE/1989). *Epistles book II and ars poetica.* N. Rudd (Ed.). Cambridge: Cambridge University Press. (Original work published 20BCE.)

Howarth, P. (1998). Phraseology and second language proficiency. *Applied Linguistics, 19*(1), 24–44.

Humboldt, W. von. (1836/1999). *The heterogeneity of language and its influence on the intellectual development of mankind.* New edition, M. Losonsky (Ed.), *"On language": On the diversity of human language construction and its influence on the mental development of the human species* (P. Heath, Trans.) (2nd ed.). New York: Cambridge University Press. (Original work published 1836.)

Hurtado Albir, A., & Alves, F. (2009). Translation as a cognitive activity. In J. Munday (Ed.), *The Routledge companion to translation studies* (pp. 54–73). London: Routledge.

Jääskeläinen, R. (1998). Think-aloud protocols. In M. Baker (Ed.), *Routledge encyclopedia of translation studies* (pp. 265–269). London: Routledge.

Jackendoff, R. (1990). *Semantic structures.* Cambridge, MA: MIT Press.

Jakobsen, A., & Schou, L. (1999). Translog documentation. *Copenhagen Studies in Language, 24,* 149–184.

Jakobson, R. (1956/1971). Two aspects of language and two types of aphasic disturbances. In R. Jakobson & M. Halle, *Fundamentals of language* (2nd ed., pp. 67–96). The Hague: Mouton de Gruyter. (Original work published 1956.)

Jakobson, R. (1959/2004). On linguistic aspects of translation. Extract in L. Venuti (Ed.), *The translation studies reader* (2nd ed., pp. 138–143). London: Routledge. (Original work published 1959.)

Jenkins, J. (2000). *The phonology of English as an international language.* Oxford: Oxford University Press.

Jerome. (395CE/2004). De optime genere interpretandi. Extract in L. Venuti (Ed.), *The translation studies reader* (2nd ed., pp. 21–30). London: Routledge. (Original work published 395.)

Johnson, M. (1987). *The body in the mind.* Chicago: Chicago University Press.

Johnson, M. (2008). Philosophy's debt to metaphor. In R. Gibbs (Ed.), *The Cambridge handbook of metaphor and thought* (pp. 39–52). Cambridge: Cambridge University Press.

Katan, D. (2009). Translation as intercultural communication. In J. Munday (Ed.), *The Routledge companion to translation studies* (pp. 74–92). London: Routledge.

Katz, J., & Fodor, J. (1963). The structure of a semantic theory. *Language, 39,* 170–210.

Kelsen, H. (1970). *Pure theory of law* (M. Knight, Trans.). Berkeley: University of California Press.

Kenstowicz, M. (1994). *Phonology in generative grammar.* Oxford: Blackwell.

Kiraly, D. (1995). *Pathways to translation: Pedagogy and process.* Kent, OH: Kent State University Press.

Kittay, E. (1987). *Metaphor: Its cognitive force and linguistic structure.* Oxford: Clarendon Press.

Knowles, M., & Moon, R. (2006). *Introducing metaphor.* London: Routledge.

Kövecses, Z. (2000). *American English: An introduction.* Peterborough, Ontario: Broadview Press.

Kövecses, Z. (2002). *Metaphor: A practical introduction.* Oxford: Oxford University Press.

Kövecses, Z. (2005). *Metaphor in culture: Universality and variation.* Cambridge: Cambridge University Press.

Kövecses, Z., & Radden, G. (1998). Metonymy: Developing a cognitive linguistic view. *Cognitive Linguistics, 9*(1), 37–77.

Kress, G. (2010). *Multimodality: A social semiotic approach to contemporary communication.* London: Routledge.

Krings, H. (1986). Translation problems and translation strategies of advanced German learners of French (L2). In J. House & S. Blum-Kulka (Eds.), *Interlingual and intercultural communication* (pp. 263–276). Tübigen: Gunter Narr.

Lakoff, G. (1986). The meanings of literal. *Metaphor and Symbolic Activity, 1*(4), 291–296.

Lakoff, G. (1987a). The death of dead metaphor. *Metaphor and Symbolic Activity, 2*(2), 143–147.

Lakoff, G. (1987b). *Women, fire and dangerous things: What categories reveal about the mind.* Chicago: University of Chicago Press.
Lakoff, G. (1993). The contemporary theory of metaphor. In A. Ortony (Ed.), *Metaphor and thought* (2nd ed., pp. 202–251). Cambridge: Cambridge University Press.
Lakoff, G. (2008). The neural theory of metaphor. In R. Gibbs (Ed.), *The Cambridge handbook of metaphor and thought* (pp. 17–38). Cambridge: Cambridge University Press.
Lakoff, G., & Johnson, M. (1980). *Metaphors we live by.* Chicago: University of Chicago Press.
Lakoff, G., & Johnson, M. (1980/2003). Afterword 2003. In G. Lakoff & M. Johnson, *Metaphors we live by* (2003 reprint, pp. 243–276). Chicago: University of Chicago Press. (Original work published 1980.)
Lakoff, G., & Johnson, M. (1999). *Philosophy in the flesh: The embodied mind and its challenge to Western thought.* New York: Basic Books.
Lakoff, G., & Turner, M. (1989). *More than cool reason: A field guide to poetic metaphor.* Chicago: University of Chicago Press.
Langacker, R. (1987). *Foundations of cognitive grammar. Volume 1: Theoretical prerequisites.* Stanford: Stanford University Press.
Langacker, R. (1990). *Concept, image, and symbol: The cognitive basis of grammar.* Berlin: Mouton de Gruyter.
Langacker, R. (1993). Reference-point constructions. *Cognitive Linguistics, 4*(1), 1–38.
Langacker, R. (2009). Metonymic grammar. In K. Panther, L. Thornburg & A. Barcelona (Eds.), *Metonymy and metaphor in grammar* (pp. 45–71). Amsterdam: John Benjamins.
Lazar, G. (1996). Using figurative language to expand students' vocabulary. *ELT Journal, 50*(1), 3–51.
Lederer, M. (1987). La théorie interprétative de la traduction. *Retour À La Traduction,* No. Spécial Août-Septembre, 11–17.
Leech, G. (1969). *A linguistic guide to English.* London: Longman.
Leech, G. (1983). *Principles of pragmatics.* London: Longman.
Leech, G., Deuchar, M., & Hoogenraad, R. (1982). *English grammar for today.* Basingstoke: Macmillan.
Lerman, C. (1984). The functions of metaphors in discourse: Masking metaphor in the Nixon conversations. Expanded version of paper in D. Nilsen (Ed.), *Whimsy 2. Proceedings of the 1983 Whim Conference 'Metaphors be with you: Humour and metaphor'*, 139–141.
Lerman, C. (1985). Media analysis of a Presidential speech: Impersonal identity forms in discourse. In T. van Dijk (Ed.), *Discourse and communication: New approaches to the analysis of mass media discourse and communication* (pp. 185–215). Berlin: Mouton de Gruyter.
Leuven-Zwart, K. van. (1989). Translation and original I. *Target, 1*(2), 151–181.
Leuven-Zwart, K. van. (1990). Translation and original II. *Target, 2*(1), 69–95.
Levelt, W. (1989). *Speaking: From intention to articulation.* Cambridge, MA: MIT Press.
Levinson, S. (1983). Pragmatics. Cambridge: Cambridge University Press.
Levý, J. (1967/2000). Translation as a decision process. In L. Venuti (Ed.), *The translation studies reader* (pp. 148–159). London: Routledge. (Original work published 1967.)
Lewis, M. (1993). *The lexical approach: The state of ELT and a way forward.* Hove: Language Teaching Publications.
Lewis, M. (2000). Language in the lexical approach. In M. Lewis (Ed.), *Teaching collocation* (pp. 126–154). Boston, MA: Thomson Heinle.
Littlemore, J. (2001a). Metaphoric competence: A language learning strength of students with a holistic cognitive style? *TESOL Quarterly, 35*(3), 459–491.
Littlemore, J. (2001b). Metaphoric intelligence and foreign language learning. *Humanizing Language Teaching, 3*(2), 1–7. Retrieved on 10 February 2012 from www.hltmag.co.uk/mar01/mart1.htm
Littlemore, J. (2002). The case for metaphoric intelligence: A reply. *ELT Newsletter, Article 101, June 2010.* Retrieved on 30 May 2011 from www.eltnewsletter.com/back/June2002/art1012002.htm

Littlemore, J. (2010). Metaphoric competence in the first and second language: Similarities and differences. In M. Pütz & L. Sicola (Eds.), *Cognitive processing in second language acquisition: Inside the learner's mind. Converging evidence in language and communication research 13* (pp. 293–316). Amsterdam: John Benjamins.
Littlemore, J., & Low, G. (2006a). *Figurative thinking and foreign language learning.* Basingstoke: Palgrave Macmillan.
Littlemore, J., & Low, G. (2006b). Metaphoric competence, second language learning, and communicative language ability. *Applied Linguistics, 27*(2), 268–294.
Lodge, D. (1977). *The modes of modern writing: Metaphor, metonymy and the typology of modern literature.* London: Arnold.
Low, G. (1988). On teaching metaphor. *Applied Linguistics, 9*(2), 125–147.
Low, G. (2008). Metaphor and education. In R. Gibbs (Ed.), *The Cambridge handbook of metaphor and thought* (pp. 212–231). Cambridge: Cambridge University Press.
Macmillan English Dictionary for Advanced Learners. (2002). Oxford: Macmillan Education.
Malmkjaer, K. (1998). Unit of translation. In M. Baker (Ed.), *Routledge encyclopedia of translation studies* (pp. 286–288). London: Routledge.
McCarthy, M. (1998). *Spoken language and applied linguistics.* Cambridge: Cambridge University Press.
McCreary, D. (2002). British and American English. Language Awareness essay LA18, in *Macmillan English dictionary for advanced learners* (between p938 and p939). Oxford: Macmillan.
Millán, C., & Bartrina, F. (2013). *The Routledge handbook of translation studies*. London: Routledge.
Miller, G. (1993). Images and models, similes and metaphors. In A. Ortony (Ed.), *Metaphor and thought* (pp. 357–400). Cambridge: Cambridge University Press.
Moon, R. (1994). The analysis of fixed expressions in text. In M. Coulthard (Ed.), *Advances in written text analysis* (pp. 117–135). London: Routledge.
Moon, R. (1998). Frequencies and forms of phrasal lexemes in English. In A. Cowie (Ed.), *Phraseology: Theory, analysis and applications* (pp. 79–100). Oxford: Clarendon Press.
Munday, J. (Ed). (2009). *Routledge companion to translation studies*. London: Routledge.
Munday, J. (2012). *Introducing translation studies: Theories and applications* (3rd. ed.). London: Routledge.
Nattinger, J., & DeCarrico, J. (1992). *Lexical phrases and language teaching.* Oxford: Oxford University Press.
Nerlich, B., Clarke, D., & Todd, Z. (1999). "Mummy, I like being a sandwich": Metonymy in language acquisition. In K. Panther & G. Radden (Eds.), *Metonymy in language and thought* (pp. 361–383). Amsterdam: John Benjamins.
Newell, A. (1990). *Unified theories of cognition.* Cambridge, MA: Harvard University Press.
Newmark, P. (1985). The translation of metaphor. In W. Paprotté & R. Dirven (Eds.), *The ubiquity of metaphor* (pp. 295–326). Amsterdam: John Benjamins.
Newmark, P. (1988). *Approaches to translation.* Hemel Hempstead: Prentice-Hall.
Nida, E. (1964). *Towards a science of translating*. Leiden: E. J. Brill.
Nida, E. (1975). *Componential analysis of meaning: An introduction to semantic structures.* The Hague: Mouton de Gruyter.
Nietzsche, F. (1873/1979). On truth and lies in the normal sense. In D. Breazeale (Ed.), *Philosophy and truth: Selection from Nietzsche's notebooks of the early 1870s*. New York: Humanities Press. (Original work published 1873.)
Niranjana, T. (1992). *Siting translation: History, post-structuralism, and the colonial context.* Berkeley: University of California Press.
Nord, C. (1991). *Text analysis in translation: Theory, methodology and didactic application of a model for translation-oriented text analysis*. Amsterdam: Rodopi.
Nunberg, G. (1979). The non-uniqueness of semantic solutions: Polysemy. *Linguistics and Philosophy, 3*(2), 143–184.

O'Regan, J. (2006). This risky order of discourse: The normativity debate in critical discourse studies. *Critical Discourse Studies, 3*(2), 229–235.

Ortony, A. (1975). Why metaphors are necessary and not just nice. *Educational Theory, 25*(1), 45–53.

Ortony, A. (1979). Beyond literal similarity. *Psychological Review, 86*(3), 161–180.

Ortony, A. (1993a). Metaphor, language and thought. In A. Ortony (Ed.), *Metaphor and thought* (2nd ed., pp. 1–16). Cambridge: Cambridge University Press.

Ortony, A. (1993b). Preface to the second edition. In A. Ortony (Ed.), *Metaphor and thought* (2nd ed., pp. xiii–xiv). Cambridge: Cambridge University Press.

Ortony, A. (1993c). The role of similarity in similes and metaphors. In A. Ortony (Ed.), *Metaphor and thought* (2nd ed., pp. 342–356). Cambridge: Cambridge University Press.

PACTE Group. (2005). Investigating translation competence: Conceptual and methodological issues. *Meta, 50*(2), 609–619.

Palumbo, G. (2009). *Key terms in translation studies*. London: Continuum.

Panther, K., & Radden, G. (1999a). Introduction. In K. Panther & G. Radden (Eds.), *Metonymy in language and thought* (pp. 1–14). Amsterdam: John Benjamins.

Panther, K., & Radden, G. (Eds.). (1999b). *Metonymy in language and thought*. Amsterdam: John Benjamins.

Panther, K., & Radden, G. (2005). Metonymy. In J. Östman & J. Verschueren (Eds.), *Handbook of pragmatics 2003–2005*. Amsterdam: John Benjamins.

Panther, K., & Thornburg, L (Eds.). (2003). *Metonymy and pragmatic inferencing*. Amsterdam: John Benjamins.

Panther, K., & Thornburg, L. (2009). Introduction: On figuration in grammar. In K. Panther, L. Thornburg & A. Barcelona (Eds.), *Metonymy and metaphor in grammar* (pp. 1–44). Amsterdam: John Benjamins.

Panther, K., Thornburg, L., & Barcelona, A. (Eds.). (2009). *Metonymy and metaphor in grammar*. Amsterdam: John Benjamins.

Paradis, M. (2004). *A neurolinguistic theory of bilingualism*. Amsterdam: John Benjamins.

Partington, A. (1998). *Patterns and meanings: Using corpora for English language research and teaching*. Amsterdam: John Benjamins.

Pawley, A., & Syder, F. (1983). Two puzzles for linguistic theory: Nativelike selection and nativelike fluency. In J. Richards & R. Schmidt (Eds.), *Language and communication* (pp. 191–226). London: Longman.

Petrie, H., & Oshlag, R. (1993). Metaphor and learning. In A. Ortony (Ed.), *Metaphor and thought* (2nd ed., pp. 579–609). Cambridge: Cambridge University Press.

Pinker, S. (2007). *The stuff of thought*. London: Allen Lane.

Pollio, H., Barlow, J., Fine, H., & Pollio, M. (1977). *Psychology and the poetics of growth: Figurative language in psychology, psychotherapy and education*. Hillsdale, NJ: Erlbaum Associates.

Pragglejaz Group. (2007). MIP: A method for identifying metaphorically used words in discourse. *Metaphor and Symbol, 22*(1), 1–39.

Pustejovsky, J. (1995). *The generative lexicon*. Cambridge, MA: MIT Press.

Pym, A. (2010). *Exploring translation theories*. London: Routledge.

Quine, W. (1960). *Word and object*. New York: John Wiley.

Rabassa, G. (2005). *If this be treason: Translation and its dyscontents*. New York: New Directions.

Radden, G. (2000). How metonymic are metaphors? In A. Barcelona (Ed.), *Metaphor and metonymy at the crossroads* (pp. 93–108). Berlin: Mouton de Gruyter.

Radden, G. (2005). The ubiquity of metonymy. In J. Otal Campo, I. Navarro i Ferrando & B. Bellés Fortuña (Eds.), *Cognitive and discourse approaches to metaphor and metonymy* (pp. 11–28). Castello de la Plana: Universitat Jaume I.

Radden, G. (2008a). The cognitive approach to language. In J. Andor, B. Hollósy, T. Laczkó & P. Pelyvás (Eds.), *When grammar minds language and literature: Festschrift for Prof.*

Béla Korponay on the occasion of his 80th birthday (pp. 387–412). Debrecen: Institute of English and American Studies.

Radden, G. (2008b). Generic reference: An instance of the INSTANCE FOR TYPE metonymy. Paper given at the *Third International Conference of the German Cognitive Linguistics Association*. Leipzig, Germany. 25–27 September.

Radden, G. (2009). Generic reference in English: A metonymic and conceptual blending analysis. In K. Panther, L. Thornburg & A. Barcelona (Eds.), *Metonymy and metaphor in grammar* (pp. 199–228). Amsterdam: John Benjamins.

Radden, G., & Kövecses, Z. (1999). Towards a theory of metonymy. In K. Panther & G. Radden (Eds.), *Metonymy in language and thought* (pp. 17–59). Amsterdam: John Benjamins.

Radford, A. (1997). *Syntax: A minimalist introduction*. Cambridge: Cambridge University Press.

Reddy, M. (1993). The conduit metaphor: A case of frame conflict in our language about language. In A. Ortony (Ed.), *Metaphor and Thought* (2nd ed., pp. 164–201). Cambridge: Cambridge University Press.

Reeve, R. (2002). *The book of urban legends*. London: Michael O'Mara Humour.

Reiss, K., & Vermeer, H. (1984). *Grundlegung einer allgemeinen Translationstheorie*. Tübingen: Niemeyer.

Richards, I. (1936). *The philosophy of rhetoric*. Oxford: Oxford University Press.

Riemer, N. (2002a). Remetonymizing metaphor: Hypercategories in semantic extension. *Cognitive Linguistics, 12*(4), 379–401.

Riemer, N. (2002b). When is a metonymy no longer a metonymy? In R. Dirven & R. Pörings (Eds.), *Metaphor and metonymy in comparison and contrast* (pp. 379–406). Berlin: Mouton de Gruyter.

Robinson, D. (2003). *Becoming a translator*. London: Routledge.

Ruiz de Mendoza, F. (2000). The role of mappings and domains in understanding metonymy. In A. Barcelona (Ed.), *Metaphor and metonymy at the crossroads* (pp. 109–132). Berlin: Mouton de Gruyter.

Rumelhart, D., & McClelland, J. (1987). *Parallel distributed processing* (Vol. 1). Cambridge, MA: MIT Press.

Salkie, R. (1995). *Text and discourse analysis*. London: Routledge.

Saussure, F. de. (1916/1983). *Course in general linguistics* (R. Harris, Trans.). London: Duckworth. (Original work published 1916.)

Saville-Troike, M. (2012). *Introducing second language acquisition*. Cambridge: Cambridge University Press.

Schäffner, C. (2004). Metaphor and translation: Some implications of a cognitive approach. *Journal of Pragmatics, 36*, 1253–1269.

Schäffner, C., & Shuttleworth, M. (2013). Metaphor in translation. Possibilities for process research. *Target, 25*(1), 93–106.

Schleiermacher, F. (1813/2004). On the different methods of translating. Extract in L. Venuti (Ed.), *The translation studies reader* (2nd ed., pp. 43–63). London: Routledge. (Original work published 1813.)

Schmidt, R. (1990). The role of consciousness in second language learning. *Applied Linguistics, 11*, 129–158.

Scovel, T. (1998). *Psycholinguistics*. Oxford: Oxford University Press.

Searle, J. (1993). Metaphor. In A. Ortony (Ed.), *Metaphor and thought* (2nd ed., pp. 83–111). Cambridge: Cambridge University Press.

Selinker, L. (1972). Interlanguage. *International Review of Applied Linguistics, 10*, 209–231.

Semino, E. (2008). *Metaphor in discourse*. Cambridge: Cambridge University Press.

Semino, E., Deignan, A., & Littlemore, J. (2013). Metaphor, genre and recontextualization. *Metaphor and Symbol, 28*(1), 41–59.

Seto, K. (1999). Distinguishing metonymy from synecdoche. In K. Panther & G. Radden (Eds.), *Metonymy in language and thought* (pp. 91–120). Amsterdam: John Benjamins.

Shuttleworth, M., & Cowie, M. (1997). *Dictionary of translation studies*. Manchester: St Jerome.

Simon, S. (1996). *Gender in translation: Cultural identity and the politics of transmission*. London: Routledge.

Sinclair, J. (1991). *Corpus, concordance, collocation*. Oxford: Oxford University Press.

Snell-Hornby, M. (2006). *The turns of translation studies*. Amsterdam: John Benjamins.

Sperber, D., & Wilson, D. (1986). *Relevance: Communication and cognition*. Oxford: Blackwell.

Sperber, D., & Wilson, D. (2008). A deflationary account of metaphors. In R. Gibbs (Ed.), *The Cambridge handbook of metaphor and thought* (pp. 84–105). Cambridge: Cambridge University Press.

Steen, G. (1999). Metaphor and discourse: Towards a linguistic checklist for metaphor analysis. In L. Cameron & G. Low (Eds.), *Researching and applying metaphor* (pp. 81–104). Cambridge: Cambridge University Press.

Steen, G. (2007). *Finding metaphor in grammar and usage*. Amsterdam: John Benjamins.

Steen, G. (2008). The paradox of metaphor: Why we need a three-dimensional model of metaphor. *Metaphor and Symbol, 23*(4), 213–241.

Steen, G., Dorst, A., Berenike Herrmann, J., Kaal, A., Krennmayr, T., & Pasma, T. (2010). *A method for linguistic metaphor identification: From MIP to MIPVU*. Amsterdam: John Benjamins.

Stern, J. (2008). Metaphor, semantics and context. In R. Gibbs (Ed.), *The Cambridge handbook of metaphor and thought* (pp. 262–279). Cambridge: Cambridge University Press.

Sternberg, R. (1990). *Metaphors of mind: Conceptions of the nature of intelligence*. New York: Cambridge University Press.

Sticht, T. (1993). Educational uses of metaphor. In A. Ortony (Ed.), *Metaphor and thought* (pp. 621–632). Cambridge: Cambridge University Press.

Stillar, G. (1998). *Analyzing everyday texts: Discourse, rhetoric, and social perspectives*. London: Sage.

Talmy, L. (1985). Lexicalization patterns: Semantic structure in lexical forms. In T. Shopen (Ed.), *Language typology and syntactic description* (Vol. 3, pp. 57–149). Cambridge: Cambridge University Press.

Taylor, J. (2002). Category extension by metonymy and metaphor. In R. Dirven & R. Pörings (Eds.), *Metaphor and metonymy in comparison and contrast* (pp. 323–347). Berlin: Mouton de Gruyter.

Thomas, B. (1996). *Advanced vocabulary and idiom*. London: Nelson.

Tversky, A. (1977). Features of similarity. *Psychological Review, 84*(4), 327–352.

Venuti, L. (1995). *The translator's invisibility: A history of translation*. London: Routledge.

Venuti, L. (Ed.). (2012). *The translation studies reader* (3rd ed.). London: Routledge.

Vinay, J., & Darbelnet, J. (1958/1995). *Comparative stylistics of French and English: A methodology of translation*. Amsterdam: John Benjamins. (Original work published 1958.)

Warren, B. (1999). Aspects of referential metonymy. In K. Panther & G. Radden (Eds.), *Metonymy in language and thought* (pp. 121–135). Amsterdam: John Benjamins.

Warren, B. (2002). An alternative account of the interpretation of referential metonymy and metaphor. In R. Dirven & R. Pörings (Eds.), *Metaphor and metonymy in comparison and contrast* (pp. 113–130). Berlin: Mouton de Gruyter.

Watcyn-Jones, P. (2002). *Test your idioms*. Harlow: Longman.

Whitney, P. (1998). *The psychology of language*. Boston, MA: Houghton Mifflin.

Widdowson, H. (1983). *Learning purpose and language use*. Oxford: Oxford University Press.

Widdowson, H. (1990). *Aspects of language teaching*. Oxford: Oxford University Press.

Wilss, W. (1998). Decision making in translation. In M. Baker (Ed.), *Routledge encyclopedia of translation studies* (pp. 57–60). London: Routledge.

Wray, A. (1999). Formulaic language in learners and native speakers—survey article. *Language Teaching, 32*(4), 213–231.

Wray, A. (2000). Formulaic sequences in second language teaching: Principle and practice. *Applied Linguistics, 21*(4), 463–489.

Wray, A. (2002). *Formulaic language and the lexicon.* Cambridge: Cambridge University Press.

Wright, J. (1999). *Idioms organiser*. Hove: LTP.

Yu, N. (2008). Metaphor from body and culture. In R. Gibbs (Ed.), *The Cambridge handbook of metaphor and thought* (pp. 247–261). Cambridge: Cambridge University Press.

Index of Scholars

Subject Index

For Product Safety Concerns and Information please contact our EU
representative GPSR@taylorandfrancis.com
Taylor & Francis Verlag GmbH, Kaufingerstraße 24, 80331 München, Germany

www.ingramcontent.com/pod-product-compliance
Ingram Content Group UK Ltd.
Pitfield, Milton Keynes, MK11 3LW, UK
UKHW022119190926
475702UK00013B/1526
9781138245310